A HANDBOOK FOR
COLLEGE TEACHERS

A HANDBOOK FOR COLLEGE TEACHERS

an informal guide

EDITED BY
BERNICE BROWN CRONKHITE
DEAN, RADCLIFFE GRADUATE SCHOOL

GREENWOOD PRESS, PUBLISHERS
NEW YORK

First Greenwood Reprinting 1969

Library of Congress Catalogue Card Number 71-94581

SBN 8371-2549-9

PRINTED IN UNITED STATES OF AMERICA

FOREWORD

From what sources are our college teachers to come? With what backgrounds and training should they be endowed? Inevitably the tendency is to look to our graduate schools for the large majority of college teaching recruits. The pace of expanding knowledge is so swift, and the areas to be covered are so vast, that nothing less than an orderly, lengthy, and sometimes grueling disciplining of the mind suffices as preparation. College presidents and department chairmen, in seeking candidates for appointment to college faculties, are in practice almost forced to look for men or women with doctor's degrees.

The graduate student has had in most cases, however, little opportunity to think about teaching. During his post-graduate years emphasis has been placed quite properly on mastery of a subject in a given field of knowledge. A small percentage of students in a graduate school may be able to gain apprentice experience in teaching by serving as assistants, section instructors, or teaching fellows, but the majority face a class for the first time after they have left the graduate school, degree in hand. Now and then a young scholar will be found so well versed in his subject and so filled with enthusiasm for it that he is able readily to convey what he knows and inspire his students to surpass themselves. Others, less fortunate, succeed as teachers only after long and wasteful floundering, if at all.

In a sense, teaching cannot be taught, since essentially it must be a flaming and an outgoing of the spirit. It is possible, however, that men and women who have succeeded as teachers can offer some guidance which will be helpful to the novice who has a latent capacity for teaching.

With this in mind, an extracurricular course of evening lectures was arranged by the Radcliffe Graduate School for graduate students of Harvard and Radcliffe who looked forward to college teaching. It represented a middle way between the two extremes of a formal required course in college teaching methods added to the heavy Ph.D. program on the one hand, and the leaving of both the spirit and mechanics of good teaching entirely to chance on the other.

This book, based on the lectures, is directed to the beginner. Even the scholar-teacher, however, who has a live and developing interest in knowledge and in human beings, may find here experiences and ideas which will renew the sense of freshness and awareness indispensable to good teaching. There is such a thing as a "mental golden rule" which devolves on scholars who enter the teaching profession; the rule is to say not only what one thinks one says but also to say what the listener thinks one says. The more fully the rule is observed, the greater and more inspiring the teaching will become. For in addition to sound scholarship, there are always those two human factors to be considered in the teaching process—the teacher and the one to be taught.

There is an organic and significant pattern in the lectures and discussions on which this book is based. The arrangement follows the clear intention of proceeding logically through the many relationships to be entered into by the beginning teacher. Four lectures or chapters deal with the relationship between teacher and student; four with varieties of teaching method in the humanities, the natural sciences, and the social sciences; one with some of the visual and other instruments of teaching; one with the "mechanics" of speech, since a teaching genius unheard is a teaching genius lost; four discuss the young teacher as a person on a faculty, joining professional societies, traveling abroad, or undertaking research and publication; two face the question of how to obtain a teaching position; and three concluding chapters present the main developments and trends of the educational process in relation to our American society.

In substance the discussions remain as they were orally presented, though by permission modified—we hope without loss of the original spontaneity—to the written form for book publication.

It is a pleasure to be able to express in print the appreciation of the graduate schools and the graduate students of the very great kindness and generosity shown by those who gave the lectures represented here. Everyone invited to participate accepted, and all the speakers stayed on for question periods and for the informal discussions which followed during a coffee hour. I wish also to acknowledge indebtedness to my husband, Leonard W. Cronkhite, for suggestions and constructive criticism at each step in the organization and preparation of the manuscript. To the Carnegie Foundation for the Advancement of Teaching are due special thanks for financial assistance in developing the course and in publishing the handbook.

At a time when there is much controversy over educational practices at all levels of instruction, and where wise as well as scholarly teachers are sorely needed, a book of this scope may well prove to be provocative and helpful to our teachers-to-be.

Bernice Brown Cronkhite

Cambridge, Massachusetts
October 1, 1949

CONTENTS

THE RELATION BETWEEN TEACHER AND STUDENT

IVOR A. RICHARDS

Chapter I

THE TEACHING PROCESS

The "lecture" critically examined. The spoken as contrasted with the written word. Relation between teacher and student skeptically analyzed. Degrees of depth of ignorance. Teacher and student as persons. Growth as a professional obligation. What is good teaching?

How unhappy the word "lecture" is! It suggests something designed to be read and read aloud, when most often any merit the thing might have would turn on its seeming to be given without notes and to be an exhibition of thinking or, at least, of composition in progress. There are few matters concerning his craft which the teacher should study more than these differences. They are its very elements. Speech and reading come to the ear and to the attention with different gaits. They are apt for different ends. They are vehicles which should have different cargoes. In spite of the many styles of each, what rides well in one commonly goes to bits in the other. It is odd therefore that so many teachers—and some eminent people are among them—will without compunction read out to their classes papers *written for print*—as though they had never been in an audience themselves. Odder still, how many, when they speak off the cuff, do their level best to sound like a slowed-down book. Talk of "The Teacher's Relation to the Student!" Nothing wrecks it more than these careful mismanagements.

This is a talk made over for printing, an impromptu oral performance recast to be read, and I am doubtful whether it makes its points or keeps its tone when its rhythming is left to the reader. However, let me leave it as near the stenotype version as is tolerable. As usual, I discovered from this version that most of the sentences started in a promising fashion but didn't end. I don't think that makes an enormous difference to the value of what is communicated. Often what people will supply towards the end of your sentence is better than anything you would have thought up. What you meant to say is of no importance anyhow, whoever you are and whatever, almost, the occasion on which you are speaking. It belongs to the past; but what people think they understand from you is a part of the dream-supply of the future. So in general don't, as teachers, mind too much whether you said exactly what you meant to say. Say something which will make people think, and you've fulfilled your function. Very little thinking on the whole goes on. We contrive the most extraordinary formal occasions for it, which most often turn out to be blank cartridge affairs. And then it happens like a miracle at some odd moment when nobody was intending to do any thinking at all, just by chance. But it's the quantity of thinking, deservedly so describable, that matters.

I am a little uneasy always at calling the people we teachers talk to "students." That is their official title, I know. How current, I wonder, is the word "fishy" for things that are suspect? The best derivation of the word "fishy" that I have found, for something you may have your doubts about, is that it is short for "official." I rather prefer the word "pupil"; it is a little less grandiose, and not so risky, for it would be rash, wouldn't it, for any teacher ever to assume that any of the people he was talking to were students?

My topic is the relation of the teacher to the pupil—or shall I say student?—the person addressed, the audience, the recipient.

And I've only one solid piece of advice to give on that, which is: "Don't have a relation. Don't have one; don't." It is a heavy handicap on any person professing to teach if he assumes any fixed relationship to the person he is teaching; there cannot be a fixed relation; and there cannot be any real utility in discussing what should be *the* relation of a teacher at this level—we are talking about *higher* education. The situation is much too complicated and shifting.

Let's look at the actual parts of the situation. It will vary first and very importantly with the capacity of the teacher. What should come out the whole time, if anything worth-while is to be said to an audience gathered together in the cause of higher education—what should come out clearly and be operative throughout all the discourse—is the teacher's consciousness of his or her own ignorance. You will not often find yourself really talking, in the cause of higher education, about anything you know much about.

Higher education—I'm not talking about anything else—should begin pretty high. There are all sorts of things, of course, in the routine of higher education which are just making up for the lack of preparation for it. But I am not talking about that; that belongs to another world, about which I think one should think rather differently. I am talking about people who aspire to take a part in the very queer thing that we like to label "higher education," which is the attempt to release some possibilities of the latest experimental phase in the biologic development. And almost nobody who takes this part and acts seriously as "The Teacher" can ever dream that he or she knows enough about what he or she is teaching to *dare* say anything very positive about it.

I have just committed myself with great severity to a very positive proposition. I suppose hoisting all these doubts into liberation must need some sort of security and positiveness as its basis. We don't, I think, praise our sense of ignorance enough here. All higher education must be founded on a collective consciousness of ignorance. But ignorance is a relative matter. I remember a great teacher of mathematics who, looking back at his pupils through fifty years, remarked, "The depths of their ignorances varied."

That is a great thing for a teacher to remember from the beginning: not only does the depth of one's own ignorance vary, but the depths of ignorance of the audience vary also. These are the first of the innumerable variables that come into the formula for the relation between the teacher and his audience: the teacher's own degree of consciousness, moment by moment, of the depth of his own ignorance of his subject, and what he expects to be the various depths of the ignorances of his audience. It is all a very complicated calculation, which becomes more puzzling with every year of teaching. I was not expecting, until quite recently, to give a lecture on the Old Testament and to discover that most of the audience had no more than heard of Genesis.

And for you, if you do go into higher education, probably the number of shocks of this sort will increase, decade by decade, through your professional life. Higher education is going, in all probability, to be able less and less to expect adequate preparation for those who are, somehow or other, mixed up in it, as students or as teachers. There is so much more, you see, decade by decade, which comes into the preparation. That isn't a gloomy thought. The last thing one would wish to see in higher education would be any *confidence* on the part of those who are professing in it, or on the part of persons who are participating in it from the other, the more exacting end.

Will you now consider once again, for the millionth time, the nature of a person. You, as teachers, will be speaking as persons; you will be addressing people you regard, fundamentally, as persons, not things. There is much to contrast between a person and a thing, and much to apply in teaching. We know a great deal about the political aspects of the freedom and dignity of the person and should regard with a great deal of seriousness all those sorts of liberal concepts of individuality. But there is another side to being a person that is worth looking into, and I think almost as important for every teacher, as a teacher, to remember. If you want to survey at some length the history of the word "person," perhaps the most convenient place, after the dictionaries, would be Gordon Allport's book *Personality.* Many of you no doubt know the chapter there, Chapter II, "Defining Personality." It gives a kind of historic analysis of the ingredient senses of the word. Much of this stems essentially, I think, from Michel Bréal, the Frenchman who first separated off the history of the shifts of meanings of words and christened that special study "semantics" —after which, of course, people shifted the word to mean anything they pleased. Well, this analysis can readily be found. I'm not going to try to reproduce it here but it is a fascinating story and really instructive—above all for any person who has to sit or stand up somewhere and address other persons. The fundamental fact, very early in the history of the word, is the stress on its meaning as a mask, something that you put over your face, and thenceforward what you say is quite different. We all know very deeply indeed what putting on a mask does, and the effect of listening to someone who is speaking through a mask. This goes right back to the very heart of authority and to the whole business of enacting, representing, being *something not one's self,* which is perhaps a main origin of religion. It is a deep subject indeed. I want only to point out that anybody who comes before an audience as a teacher is inevitably and necessarily wearing a mask and is, by profession, a representative, as any mask-wearer must be, of something other than himself. In this case it is something much more important than himself—a *subject,* a permanent concern of the intellect—and you will be acting the part of a person competent to represent a subject, that is, to profess it.

Now we come to the terrific topics: "The Nature of Your Profession" and "The Import of the Word 'Professor.' " You see, a professor professes; he cannot possibly possess. He has got to profess in the profound knowledge that he cannot possess. Every higher level teacher has to expound a subject which he or she does not begin to understand. That is the nature of this quite unholy calling that some of you (I hope to be suitably discouraging) are in mind to pursue. Down below, in all your judgments as a teacher, there is a court of appeal: Higher Education. But up here you have no such shelter. Up here you will not know the more important parts of what you are teaching, or what you are really talking about, or why you should say what you say about it. You can't hope to. That is in the nature of an intellectual, a growing, subject. The things that are the growing points really live. And not only the tender little new green twigs. The roots, the foundations of the subject, grow and wander about too. In between there is plenty of dead wood which you will find yourself developing a taste for. It stays put. And then there is the solid trunk on which all the branches depend, and that too sometimes looks very like dead wood.

Higher education has, or should have, to do with the shifting, the experimental—with the laws of the shifts, the conjecturing about them. All the parts of the field that are not radically experimental should be handed down, and again down, to the earlier phases of the educational process. Although, right down to the infant's first day, the little core of established practice—the solid trunk—is surrounded, as we know, by vast cocoons of trial and error. It is worth noting that this phrase "trial and error" is almost as good an association pair as "knife and fork." If you say "knife" to people, a thousand to one they say "fork." If you say "trial," "error" comes along—not quite as certainly but fairly well. It would be a rare individual who, if you said "trial," would reply "triumph." "Trial and error" records, as it were, the human experience in the matter of experiment.

I am trying to say something about the obligations of a professor. It's a daunting business being a professor; you will *not* know—either about your subject or your practice—nearly enough to justify you. You will not know what to expect *in* your teaching or *from* your teaching, not to the end. You will go on being more and more surprised unless you cease to carry on the practice of higher education and flunk into a kind of simulacrum of the activity which approximates it to what's proper in the lower, more settled areas of the subject. You see, in higher education, you are conducting a series of experiments in human growth. You are not handing on a tradition unless by tradition we mean here a general art of keeping sane. Any concept which grew up traditionally is itself a piece of interpretation which will change decade by decade in these times. A little while ago, it changed generation by generation, but the rate of change in fundamental interpretation of the tradition is increasing. We continue for a shorter time to be at all certain as to what the proper view should be about any part of the picture, almost any part. I have to exaggerate and summarize, but that's true of the field. So, you're going to feel, when you teach on a higher level, that you're not handing out anything that you've securely received. And you should not feel any security. And, maybe in the measure of the importance, the variability increases. It's the things that are neither roots nor twigs, that are somewhere down in the trunk, it's those that stay put. But within inquiries into the philosophic bases and sources and the fundamental determinants of the growth of the subjects—these are the roots—there is change and change and change again. Constancy is not part of the Idea of Man. And up again when you get to the leaves and twigs and buds and flowers, up at the top of the imaginative tree, there again you find variation from season to season, pliant to the passing wind of discussion which itself changes more suddenly than ever. Anyhow, I'm insisting, through these elaborate images, that higher education is concerned with the biologic growth of this most unpredictable organism, the collective intelligence of Man, or collective sensibility of Man, if you like. You are experimentally preparing for future experiments.

Now, if you are going to join this profession (which I would very earnestly dissuade you from, and I hope such talk as this has that effect) I call your attention yet again to this word "professor." It's a grim title. In earlier times the typical professor turned up with a beard and a wand and a bowl of goldfish, and did tricks which everybody knew were fraudulent, yet they couldn't quite see how. In my youth the word "professor" seemed to belong, and naturally, to the circulating conjurer who, if he was really first class, wasn't seen through. Shaw, in one of his great moments, in *The Doctor's Dilemma,* makes one of his characters cry out, "Every profession is a conspiracy against the laity"—one of Shaw's best lines, not likely to be forgotten. It's indecently true. Any old hand at the trade should give credit to that view to any person proposing to become an initiate in the profession.

Now with various indirect suggestions, I have tried to raise in your mind the conjecture whether possibly scholarship is a fraud. I'm not going to say it is. I'm going to offer you, if I can, a kind of balancing-pole, by which you will have, if you join this curious trade, to walk in public an endless slack wire over incredible abysses. It's a quivering wire, which seems to be constantly and maliciously shaken, but you will have to walk it right through to the day (which won't be very cheerful when it comes) when you are retired Emeritus. All your lives, you will be teetering on that wire. You will never be quite sure whether you are uttering words of inspired, really quite unprecedented and extraordinary aptness for the development of your pupils' intelligence, or whether you are being completely inept. Often you will find yourself incompetent enough to be fired at once if anybody was intelligent enough to see you as you are. You will find yourself, during your lectures, in your private conferences, quite constantly starting sentences without the faintest idea of where they are going to end. There is no teacher who does a lot of live lecturing who doesn't find himself or herself on momentous occasions saying, "Now this is one of the most . . ." and just folding up there. That is not an abnormal experience. But don't give this away to the people you are going to teach. You have got to keep your prestige with your students. How that is done is another mystery of the profession, about which you may know more after you have had years of experience. But, I think this is good advice: "Never doubt *yourself* publicly." The right thing to do is doubt particular points publicly. Confess your ignorance. Oh yes, that is all right. That creates a great deal of academic atmosphere all around. But don't ever begin to mumble and hum and haw about your own judgment. You ought to know quite clearly what you know and don't know in public. In private, it is a different matter.

All this is concerned with a question I want to answer for you and which you must then answer for yourselves: "Am I, or am I not, a fraud?" That is a question which is going to mean more and more to you year by year. At first, it seems agonizing, after that it becomes familiar and habitual. Much later, it becomes harder to describe, almost hopeful. Well, here's this invisible and intangible mental balancing-pole. Remember, now, you have to get a good hold on it and be ready to lean on it. You have to keep on tranquil good terms with this question, not forget it, not let it get into the unconscious. You have to admit you don't know nearly enough to do the job you are patently trying to do. Does it show impudence on your part to be trying to do it at all? You've got to get quite used to feeling like that. The job can't be done. The more experience you have with people you're trying to teach, the more evident it will be that it's impossible to teach them. This at the high levels of course. At the very homely level, right down at the beginning of a subject, it is different. It's all very optimistic there. The gaiety of infant schools is something that all people concerned with higher education ought to enjoy from a distance from time to time.

High up, making a good job of turning people's interests to the things you believe they should care about is a concern which has to fight for its life. There are so many "professional" distractions, the greatest of which, of course, are frequently entailed in fulfilling the requirements for a degree. The possession of a degree, with whatever glories and excellencies go with it, is no guarantee whatever that the aim we are concerned with, if we are genuinely concerned with higher education, has been advanced one whit. No, that can't help but be recognized all the time. And yet, with that recognition, one can't help but admit, too, because of the balancing-pole, that the institutions which really deserve honor and which are able, through their degree system, to award honor are an indispensable fulcrum, without which nothing could be done. There is a characteristic magical intervention of a pseudo-Platonic Idea here. I call on Plato, partly because Plato founded the institution of the university, and his own academy lasted so well that even Oxford or Paris has not yet carried on so long. But Plato is more to the point because of the notion that the degree really enters into a person and guarantees competence. That is the crudescence of the Platonic Idea, the religious Idea; the mythologizing of something we must know how to doubt and not doubt. All this is part of the mysterious balancing-pole. I suppose all your lives, as teachers on the level of higher education, you will be torturing yourselves with this invisible call, wondering whether you can be adequately inspired.

I take the notion of inspiration here very seriously indeed. The best things that any elderly teacher can ever claim to have said as a teacher will be things, I think, that he had no intention of saying and no idea afterwards of what led him to say them. The things that he will most wisely regret, if he is wise at all, will be spending hours saying things he knew so well and everyone else knew so well that there was no occasion to say them. I think the notion of making contact between mind and mind should be discarded at this level. It is the allurement of thought by thought, something quite different from any contact as such that builds the world. In my experience I have rarely known what the best teachers, the people who did most for me, were talking about, and I couldn't bear to go away without seeing whether *they* knew. They were good at keeping me there without satisfying my expectations either way. They didn't know they were doing that. They were just behaving like human beings.

I began by saying, "Don't have a relation with the audience, with the pupil." There is a good deal of educational nonsense, I think, talked on this point. People will tell you that a good teacher must do this and that, have a deep interest in every one of his students, must know them intimately and be really concerned with their intellectual, moral, and other kinds of development. I think this is no more than the reflection of the student's favorite myth that knowing the professor socially would be helpful. I have known superb teachers who to the end of their days couldn't tell one student from another, orally, optically, or even intellectually. That is very disturbing, but I think such teachers are speaking to the "all in each in all men," to use a phrase of Coleridge. I have often suspected that Coleridge himself was talking most of his life to this "all in each." And there have not been many more influential teachers.

Coleridge, of course, wasn't as a rule widely understood. But how intelligible ought a lecturer in higher education to be? Some people think that a talk should be entirely comprehensible so that the audience becomes one. This I take to be a booby trap that has haunted and frustrated much intellectual endeavor. You have no stimulation for a person whatsoever if he thinks he understands what you are saying and why you say it, completely. But how wide should the gap be between what the student is offered and what he gets? There is, as it were, a piece of elastic between you and your audience. You must not snap the elastic or you have lost them. On the other hand, you must have the biggest possible tension on the elastic and this must be pulling at them most of the time. That is the whole point of teaching. Otherwise why do it?

Why, anyway, do we teach at the university level? That is good final question—one of those we ought to start with and keep alive all the time. It is hard to know at what level one is working when he says it is at the university level. The university level isn't defined. We are apt to say that university-level teaching is an art and, therefore, there are no fixed rules as to how we should pursue it, as to what should be taught before what, or anything else. That might be right enough if the university level were really solid, but it isn't solid. It has patches and drops in it. You never know what you may not have to deal with at the university level. So the simpler, earlier modes of instruction are often needed as well. Most university teachers would be the better for having had to teach for a while in a good school. But it must be a good school and a short while.

There is a general suspicion that really good teaching is everywhere getting scarcer and scarcer. If so, perhaps it is because this final question, "Why do we teach?" is less active than it was. On the whole it is only people with fairly clear and firm convictions who can bear to keep that question stirring. A way to quiet it is to say, "Why, people teach for all sorts of reasons." But that is to mistake the question, which was not about the motives but about the end of this universal human activity. And on that—after all this skepticism—I owe you a confession of a conviction: I think that genuine teaching at all levels, but more clearly as it mounts, knows and works through knowledge of its end—which can be put in many ways. But as I have mentioned Coleridge, I will use his sentences though their substance is Plato's. They come from Appendix B of *The Statesman's Manual.* "All things that surround us, and all things that happen to us, have but one common final cause; namely the increase of consciousness in such wise that whatever part of the *terra incognita* of our nature the increased consciousness discovers, our will may conquer and bring into subjection to itself under the sovereignty of reason."

WILLIAM G. PERRY, JR.

Chapter II

CONFLICTS IN THE LEARNING PROCESS THE STUDENT'S RESPONSE TO TEACHING

The teacher's hopes and bewilderments. The student's view of teachers and education. Passive and active resistance in the young. The biological-psychological Me-They cycle. The development of the Self in maturity.

One of the practical hints which others have given you on the art of lecturing is that you should always have the beginnings of your lectures "down cold." This is a very valuable idea. If you have your opening words nearly automatic, then when you get up in front of your audience and suffer the inevitable stage fright, you can let the lower nerve centers take over. You can get started even though your upper nerve centers are, for the moment, paralyzed with adrenalin. Altogether it is a lovely picture. It works too. That is, it works when you really know what you are going to say—when you really know what you want to talk about. We might hope that this will be most of the time.

But there will come other times, toward the middle or the end of a course, perhaps, when you begin to feel that your audience is somehow going dead on you, and for good reason. You watch them at the lectures in which they take down the answers that you give them, these positive things that you know, and as they write them down, you begin to wonder if that might not be the end of it after all. You knew your stuff, you said it; and they wrote it down. And then as you think things over, you suddenly come to a point when it seems most important to you to talk about the things that you are not so sure of, the things that you wonder about, the edge of the thoughts that you have been working with, the fringes of that boundless ignorance that Professor Richards spoke of. And you decide that now you want to talk about that. Then what are you going to do? You can spend your ten hours of preparation making up your speech, but you will not find a beginning that is worth a hoot. All your pat beginnings will sound more businesslike than you mean to be. And you cannot stand up in front of people and say: "Today we are going to talk about my uncertainties under three headings"—and so there you are. And that is always the time when the stage fright is worse. If you are going to talk about your uncertainties, your lecture is either going to work or it isn't. And if it doesn't, what disaster! To find yourself isolated from your audience, all alone with thoughts like that! It is hard to begin and you don't know what to say. It is a very painful feeling indeed. And that is the kind of lecture this is.

I suppose we might begin in such a way as this. It may be, after all, that some of these doubts I have in mind, these wonderings and so on, are in your mind too, and we might explore them a little and see in what direction they take us. You have noticed, I know, that there is something a little paradoxical in all this business of teaching. There is so much that seems so wonderful about it, and so much that seems so puzzling and terrifying. We cannot be too sure of what it is going to be like. Are we going to be as good at it as we hope?

There are lots of different motives that take us into teaching. Some of them we will talk about, some of them we will hide from others, and some of them we will hide from ourselves. Possibly one of the strongest motives is one of those marginal ones that we will tell to ourselves but perhaps not to others. We know that we are going into teaching at least in part because teaching is surely one thing that we can do much better than we have seen it done to ourselves. We may except our one "great" teacher, but on the whole that is one thing that we are sure of. So we feel a confidence about the matter, and we think that we will be pretty good at it. And then sometimes we wonder. If it is really as easy as all that, why isn't it done better? And this question makes us very uneasy.

So we come to these lectures and we get a lot of reassurance. There is a kind of theme running through these lectures: that even though there is *this* you should keep in mind and *that* that you should keep in mind, just the same, if you really love your subject enough and are enthusiastic about the teaching, everything will be all right. But then, just when we are feeling better, the same old paradox reappears. One lecturer will make a little remark about "those moments of black despair that all teachers have," and this echoes once or twice. Just when we are ready to forget about it, the next man says, "There are these moments, but you will live through them." We begin to wonder secretly about these moments. What are they: just something that happens to everybody? Or are they an occupational disease of teachers? One's confidence has to be pretty good to stand up against this sort of thing.

I think that it might be good to get some of these moments of black despair up where we can look at them and see what they are made of. I should warn you in advance that you should take everything that I have to say about the difficulties of teaching with a grain of salt. I am an educational garage man. That is what a counselor is; he deals in other people's trouble. So perhaps I take a dim view, or get too close a view, of some of the difficulties in education. In any case, I hope that you will find your faith in teaching strong enough to stand up against anything that I may say. In fact, you may even glean a little encouragement for yourself from the notion that when things go wrong it may not be entirely your fault.

It might be a good idea to review some of our fundamental

faiths to begin with. Some of these things have been said so often that they sound a little corny when we put them into words, but nonetheless we do believe in them. We believe, don't we, that the education of the young is fundamentally the hope of the world? And we believe that through breadth and liberality of education we can get and give the kind of understanding of humanity that will prevent world-wide disasters—we believe this, or why else are we going into teaching? They don't pay you anything. And we have heard—we have gotten a little tired of the words perhaps—but we have heard from commencement speakers for years about the fountain of knowledge, and we have been going on in our education to drink more and more at the fountain of knowledge, and they tell us this will bring us more understanding and breadth, and that we will be more interested and more interesting people, and better citizens. And we have been told that knowledge is power, and furthermore that it brings with it responsibilities. We have been told that, and we believe it. So here we are as teachers, and prospective teachers, on the edge of acquitting our responsibilities. We have drunk deep of this fountain of knowledge, we have it near us in our libraries, and we are now going to graduate and become dispensers of the waters of the fountain of knowledge. Corny, but true.

Our responsibility is to dispense knowledge, first of all in a way that is clear, and second in assimilable quantities. You have heard about being clear: "Write it on the blackboard so somebody can see it, for goodness' sake, see it from the back row," and you have been told not to stand in the way of what you have written, and not to mumble in your beards—if you have them. You have been told these things, and it is obviously your responsibility to be clear and not to muddy up the waters of knowledge by being slovenly in your organization or in your speech. After you are clear and love your subject and have an enthusiasm for teaching, everything will be all right. There will not be any conflict, even, between love of subject and love of teaching. In fact, I suppose, you have all been told that there is really no conflict whatever between scholarship and teaching and that they really go together.

Well, if all this is so, why these moments of black despair?

Why these moments of futility and of frustration that we hear about? What about them? Let us not suppose that they don't happen or that they aren't real.

What about the day when you look at your students and realize that except for the two or three bright, eager people, whom you have allowed to fool you all along into thinking that everything was going fine, no one is doing any thinking at all? How about it when you look at your group and see not eager souls thirsty for the fountain of knowledge, but a bunch of lunk-heads who are just sitting there, their mouths wide open and their pencils poised: "Say it, sir (or madam), say it, and we will write it down." What about the day when you discover among these people a conspiracy to parrot none of the things that you mean, and all of the trivialities that you say? And they will point out that it was what you said, even when you know that it is jargon, just words that do not mean a thing.

How about the day when you discover among these people another conspiracy to protect themselves from getting any knowledge whatever, no matter how good for them? How about it when you find that an informal organization exists among your students, an agreement to spend less time on their work than both you and they know is for their own good? And you have set out supplementary reading and offered grades as rewards for writing extra papers, and nobody does them. I think we have all heard ourselves, to our own shame sometimes, saying to other students after we got a good grade, "Well, that was pretty good luck I had there; you know I didn't crack a book."

What about the day, too, when you discover that whatever you do and say in class is consistently misinterpreted, and that your students look upon you as a person who seems to have nothing realistically to do with you at all. That is, you will start your class and find that some people in it think you are just wonderful and yet you haven't done a thing to earn it; they don't know you yet, you have just started, but they feel that you are the good father or the good mother that they have always looked for. And if you look carefully you will find a less vociferous group, but one that makes itself felt, that thinks that you are all that is evil that they have ever seen in their lives; probably because you remind them of Uncle Abner or Aunt Matilda, or perhaps they have just come from a class where they got rather mistreated for some error of their own, and since they could not take it out on that teacher, they take it out on you. After this sort of beginning, anything that you do doesn't seem to have much to do with the case, except that the people who thought that you were wonderful at the beginning will become so disappointed in you in the end that they will hate you violently; and the people who hated you in the beginning may discover—some of them—that you are not so bad as they thought you were, and so they will think that you are equally and absurdly wonderful, and you will stand in the middle of all this with a sense of futility and nonentity.

So in the end, after you have tried persuading and being reasonable and exerting the strong arm and being stimulating, and after you have tried those deep and penetrating silences—after you have tried everything, there will come a day when you will sit down with a student toward the end of your course, and the student won't have done anything, not a stroke of work. So you sit down over a beer or a cup of coffee, and you take your insignia off, and you say, "Now what goes on here?" The student will say to you: "Well, I wish I knew really. I know what I *should* do, and I really would have liked to have done it, and I want to do well, and I loved your course, and yet I kept putting all the work off, or something. I just didn't get it done, I don't know why; I guess I just lack will power or something." And then both of you will look at each other across Mark Hopkins' glorious log and wonder about the educational system.

When these moments of futility come, what are you going to do? You are going to look at these people and say to yourself, "Shall I give up my dream? Shall I give up this hope that I have started with, or not?" And then an idea will come to you: "Maybe there is something wrong here, maybe—I've got it—they weren't taught right in high school." So you take your responsibility with you and go into high school teaching, and there you meet the same thing. You wonder again and say, "Oh no, the trouble is in elementary school." So then you go to elementary school and you say, "These parents!" So you quit elementary school and you go and have children of your own—then you will really be in trouble.

Where then, may I ask you, is your love of your subject? Where then will be your scholarship? Surely you will have given up scholarship for education, won't you? For where will your precious subject be then? What has history to do with child training? Or have you given up? Maybe you haven't after all. You see, there will come a day when, if you are really honest, you may catch an echo. You may find yourself saying, "Now, Sally, two more spoonfuls of beans or no dessert; it's not fair to keep everybody waiting, two more spoonfuls of beans or no dessert." Just as you get through saying that you think, "Wait a minute, where have I heard that before; where have I said that?" And in your mind you will hear yourself saying way back there in your college classes, "And now for next week you will hand in a paper of no less than 2,000 words on the subject of the Elizabethan Concept of the Tragic Hero, and in view of the fact that papers have been coming in quite late and out of fairness to those who get their papers in on time, I will have to mark down half a grade for every day a paper is late." Two more spoonfuls of beans or no dessert. When you hear that echo, you are just about ready to begin to think about education. And by the way, if you have two children and you hear Sally's older brother across the table saying, "Don't eat 'em, Sally, don't eat 'em, we don't want any dessert, let's both be excused," then you will be ready to think about the conspiracy.

It begins to look, in fact, as if education did not consist solely of this fountain of knowledge. Education has been defined, and quite helpfully, as the transmission of the culture from one generation to another. Of course this gets us into a definition of culture and so forth, and things get a little complicated. But nonetheless we can suppose that culture is a term which must be applied not only to those things which are the rewards and benefits of the society and those things that we can all get from knowledge—understanding and the richness of life—but it must also refer to the "do's" and the "don'ts," the "this-way's" and the "not-that-way's" of the society. Now since the teacher is someone who has been hired by the community to engage full-time in this transmission of the culture, you will find that you are not just a Ganymede or a Hebe standing at the fountain of knowledge with a little cup, but rather you will find that your students are quite properly responding to you as if your other hand, the one you have behind your back, had brass knuckles on it. They will be responding to you as if you were saying, as you must say—as you cannot escape saying whether you put it into words or not—not only, "Come and drink from the fountain of knowledge," but also, "And while you are at it, bud, you do it our way *on time;* if you don't, you will not only not get these lovely things, but you will be sent shamefully home, a *failure.*"

Now what do people do under stresses and threats like that? They resist, just as Sally resists eating those beans, not because she doesn't like beans, but because she is afraid that by liking them, now that you have told her to eat them, she will somehow be losing something. She doesn't know quite what, but she feels that something dreadfully important will be lost. So what students do in their resistance is to conform to the letter of what you say. They will eat two spoonfuls of beans, with one bean on each. They will say the letter of what you require them to repeat, but they will reject the spirit, even if they think it will be good for them. I remember saying to my boy the other day, "You forgot to pick up your shoes." He replied, "Well, you didn't tell me to pick up my shoes, you told me to pick up my clothes." So when you make an assignment from page such-and-such to page such-and-such, and when you ask some questions about it, you may say, "Look at these papers; no one has thought about this." And the response will be, verbalized or not, "You didn't tell us to think about it, you just told us to read it."

What I should like to do, therefore, is to abandon for a while all thoughts of the teaching process, of the giving end of education, and to examine the receiving end. What I am going to do is to try to explore how the educational world looks to the student—perhaps, indeed, how the world itself looks. By this I don't mean what he will or can tell you about it; I mean, rather, what his assumptions are and what his frame of reference is, the more or less unconscious basis of his behavior. Here I am launching those tentative suppositions in which one must explore the sea of one's ignorance. I am going to draw a kind of chart in the hope that it may keep us from becoming utterly lost.

When we as children first come into the world and look around to see what the world is made of, we see soon enough that the world is made of They. And what are They like? They tell us, do they not, what we *ought* to do? They tell us our *duty*. They tell us what is *necessary*. And it is necessary to do a lot of things that we don't like in the world, so They say. It is necessary to do a lot of things that are unpleasant. So that this business that They tell us about is by their own account *unpleasant*. So this is the world and its demands.

But now, as I look at this world, I begin to think of my own individuality and separateness, and I say to myself, "Who's Me?" Well, I am little and I am helpless, but I obviously have to be something quite different from all this if I am going to have any differentness, any individuality, which seems so precious to me. And what is the opposite to all that They stand for? Why, it is obviously what I *want*. So it follows that my individuality and my integrity, for which I will fight to the death, consists of what I want—that is, of my *wishes*—all of which I associate with the *pleasant:*

ME	THEY
integrity conceived as residing in:	*perceived as representing:*
wants	oughts
wishes	duties
the unrestricted	the necessary
the pleasant	the unpleasant

Clearly, now, I am faced at once with a number of serious difficulties. In the first place my integrity demands that I get what I want. If I do not, I am not only frustrated, I am much worse than that: I am somehow less Me. On the other hand, a lot of things that I want can be attained only through They, and They disapprove of other things that I want. If I do not give up these tabooed wants and do a certain amount of the unpleasant, then They will not love me any more, and that would be fatal to all my wishes. Furthermore, I may feel in part genuinely fond of They in that They do give me some things I want. Another difficulty is still more confusing. I soon discover, let us say at the age of three or four, or five, that They got me so young, when I was unable to defend myself, that They went and put a little bit of They in Me and I can't get away from it; it keeps nagging me all the time.

The dilemma is very serious indeed, and is made worse by the conflicting nature of my wishes. I wish to be dominant and independent; I wish also to be dependent and loved. However, I blind myself to this internal source of difficulty and concentrate on what seems the external problem of getting what I want and placating They. There are all sorts of attempted solutions to this almost insoluble problem. The most obvious one is the Social Contract of Rousseau—that is, the compromise. In this solution I simply do a number of the things that They say I ought to do, and then I hope that They will leave me alone to go forth and do some of the things that I want. The trouble with this solution is that the compromise never really seems to be accepted by either side; both sides seem to be trying to beat the game and to ask for more. It is a very uneasy situation. I do some of the things that I want to do for a while; then I get a guilty conscience and do some of the things that I ought to do for a while; then I feel frustrated and so I go and do what I want to do, and then I get conscience-stricken again, and back and forth, back and forth, I go. And all this time the sensation keeps piling up that somebody is wasting time.

We might digress for a moment here and look at a curious application of this Social Contract in the educational world. It is perfectly clear to Me, in the educational world, that what They want is for me to be good; what They want is for me to do my duty, which is to sit down and do this studying that I have been given to do. If I do that, their part of the bargain is that They will give me the good grade that I want, so we get the curious formula which you find running throughout education, namely: work through time equals grades. This is a kind of basic moral law. It does not matter what I say on an examination; if I have done the work I should get the grade, and if my roommate, who has done none of the work, reads my notes before the examination and goes in and gets a higher grade than I do, that shows that They are unfair.

We might digress a little further. My integrity, my sense of Me-ness is bound up with my wishes, and since They invade my integrity with all these "don'ts" and "ought's," and since the Social Contract is not working very well and I am getting a little resentful, it is very natural for me to decide that I really could have everything that I wanted if it were not for They; given half a chance I would prove as omnipotent as I secretly believe myself to be. This feeling, which we have all shared, is exemplified by a student who once said: "I really could cut loose from everything; I could cut loose from my parents and my wife and from everything, just as a friend of mine has done who is now down in Ceylon. I could do that, only I don't think I ought to. I could be really perfectly independent and get everything that I wanted. I just don't do it because I don't think I *should.* Besides that, of course, I gain such satisfactions from my family." I said, "You mean that if you went to Ceylon you wouldn't have those satisfactions that you want?" He replied, "No." He was still blind to his contradiction. Then suddenly it struck him, and he said, "This is the first time I've ever realized that I couldn't really have everything I wanted if it wasn't for them."

If it is natural and easy for us to engage in this kind of thinking about our omnipotence, we can carry it one step further. I shall bethink me of the future; I shall conjure up an ideal picture of what I shall become. I shall be a doctor, a really great doctor; I shall be so clever that everyone will admire me, and I shall know so much that I can do anything I want. Now it is a highly commendable thing to be a good doctor and to make discoveries that will ease the lot of the human race, and here, you see, is where I satisfy They, especially the They of my own conscience. So here I have an ideal which seems to satisfy both my need for independence or power and my conscience. There is only one trouble with it—the minute that I try to put it into action, They get in my way again; They require that I study German and various aspects of physics and literature which will be really of no use to me. Naturally, it is an invasion of my integrity to study these requirements and somehow I have a terrible time with them. "I won't eat those beans if They tell me to; no matter how good they may be, no matter how fine the dessert, it is not worth the price of my integrity, and I won't do it." Or if my revolt is not as conscious as this, I will simply relegate doing them until "tomorrow."

We had better not digress any more, for we could probably digress forever and still have an over-simple picture of the matter. It is my opinion, anyway, that from the particular point of view of which we have been speaking—that is, the child's point of view—the problems of life are actually insoluble. It has always been my suspicion that Rousseau never quite grew up. Let us go back to the point where we felt that in the midst of all these attempted solutions somebody was wasting time.

It is this very notion of time that is crucial. Until now we have made no mention of time. Time is an aspect of reality, and we have made no mention whatever of reality. To the child there is no such thing as reality directly; there is only what They say is necessary, and even when what They say is necessary or real actually happens, even that appears to be just an "I-told-you-so" of grown-ups. Time, as one aspect of reality, does not apply to Me. In fact Me is at its most omnipotent in the timelessness of tomorrow. One of the most obvious solutions to the dilemma of the Me is to do what I want to do today and do what I ought to do tomorrow. Perhaps it is in large part through this sensation of wasting time that reality first comes into awareness—that I get my first glimpse of just plain fact. It is this stunning revelation of the factual, the notion that I cannot go to Ceylon and have everything that I want, that breaks down utterly the dichotomy of the They and the Me. And here we are on the brink of maturity. For now that this dichotomy is broken down, we can have a look at the frame of reference from which the sensation that I have been wasting time arises. The whole sensation implies a new value system, some wholly different frame of reference in which defending the integrity of my wishes is not what I really want to be doing. Here it is that I discover that the person who has been wasting time is my Self.

It is upon the difference between the Me and the Self that everything that I have to say hinges. The difference is one of essential personal identity; it is a felt difference that concerns who I am—that concerns what makes up, for me, my personal individuality. We have already seen that for the child identity is conceived as consisting of wishes, especially those wishes which the child holds in contradistinction to They. No internal conflict or contradiction is accepted among these wishes; all conflict is projected and seems to be externally imposed. But for the Self wishes suddenly lose their distinctive and individual character. I suddenly perceive that everyone has much the same wishes, and furthermore I see these wishes as an aspect of fact and reality. They then lose their glorious simplicity and can be seen in all the conflict and complexity which is really theirs. For the first time, therefore, I am confronted with the real issue of *choice*. The individuality and integrity of the Self is therefore conceived to reside not in my wishes, but in the act of choosing in the midst of the complexity of reality. This reality consists not only of my wishes, but also of society and of physical limitations, including that of time. Up until now I had confused freedom with independence, now I realize that freedom is not the independence to follow one's wishes, but the act of choice among personal values. And personal values for my Self include not only wishes in the narrow sense of impulses, but also objective purposes in a real world *and* many of those responsibilities and obligations and duties which I have previously seen only as the demands of They. In this new frame of reference it is no longer either a loss of integrity, or an act of masochism, to do something unpleasant; it may be simply useful or productive. And though I still have both my wishes and my "ought's," my integrity is not at issue between them; it is, in fact, expressed in my act of choice whichever way I choose in relation to a particular set of circumstances in reality.

reality—SELF—others
integrity conceived
as residing in:
|
choices
|
purposes
|
facts—action—facts

As an illustration we might consider the matter of the language requirement. Almost all colleges and graduate schools have a language requirement, and as students we buck it. It is a great symbol, the language requirement; it is the last great apotheosis of Their incredible and unreasonable demands. When it comes time to sit down and do that German, we read the newspaper, we read *Life,* we sharpen our pencils, we do anything to delay the awful moment. When finally we do get to work, we do just what we feel we are "required" to do: we turn the word-cards over, we translate word by word from this or that, and if nothing comes from all our labors, it is not our fault, it is Theirs; and the fact that nothing ever seems to come out of it just goes to show how right we are. The language requirement appears as a price we are forced to pay for a degree which They withhold. It obviously is not the business of a Me, it is just a requirement of They, and I spend a great deal of time expanding upon its archaism and injustice. From the point of view of the Self, however, the matter looks very different indeed. You have come to this store of your own choice, to buy a certain article, an A.B. or a Ph.D. And how in this store does this article come packaged; in what form does it appear on the counter? It always includes the language requirement. It is not, if you please, a price that you pay, but rather part of the product that you buy. You may not want this accessory, you understand, you may not consider it reasonable, and you may wish that the product came packaged without it; but if the management is not disposed to change the package, you have, in fact, a choice of taking the article or leaving it. If you choose to take it, it is not an invasion of your integrity to fulfill the language requirement, it is, in fact, an expression of your own choice in regard to reality; and because the Self is primarily the chooser, it is an act of Self-expression. Certainly it may be unpleasant or dull, and even frustrating of other purposes that you would like to substitute for it; but for the Self, frustration is not purely an imposition from the outside and a threat to integrity, rather it is one of the conditions of life, because even my own wishes are often incompatible. Hence, dull or not, it can be done with a will.

In the event that you have been subscribing at all to this, you have probably been looking at yourself, if not with alarm, at least with some concern, with the question, "Am I a Me or am I a Self? Am I a child or am I an adult?" I doubt that you will find a ready answer. The question would have been prompted by the way I have been presenting this. I have seemed to imply that a person is either a child or an adult, but this is because such things as authority, necessity, and the unpleasant are so sharply different in quality when looked at from the two points of view that there are really no in-betweens; it is an all-or-none proposition. The two frames of reference are separate, distinct, and self-contained, but what makes growth into maturity look like a gradual thing is, I think, first that we take the point of view of Self in one area of life at a time and, second, that even in those areas in which we have attained it, it is notoriously unstable. A student, for instance, may attain a mature frame of reference in his social relationships and remain a child in his school work. He may feel and act as an adult in his summer job and in the fall drag his feet, as a pupil, reluctantly to school. He may feel and act as an adult away from home, but when he returns to the family that treats him as a child, he will feel like one. It is this jumping back and forth from one frame of reference to another that is the basis, I believe, of the instability of adolescence. Of course it stays with us, to a degree, all our lives.

So far I have painted the frame of reference of the Self as so much more comfortable and desirable that this critical instability may seem strange. Let us have a look at a few of its discomforts. Being a Self is a very risky and frightening business. As a Me I still have claims on that day when things go wrong in life. When

I fail, when I am disappointed, when I am hurt, I can call on Them for comfort, for love, for reassurance, for protection. If I am a Self, I no longer have these claims in anything like the same degree. In fact I am alone, and I have not yet learned that to be alone, as all human beings are, is not necessarily to be lonely. Hardest of all, I must, to be a Self, allow my wishes, my omnipotence, and my fantasies to suffer real defeats in the face of reality. I may never be a really great doctor, and to be even a mediocre one, or even a failure, I must sweat. Even if I turn out to have ability and have worked hard, just plain circumstances may defeat me. Can I stand this without the compensation of Their sympathy and support, without being able to demand that They play fair? And deeper down than any of this, can I really trust my Self? If I try to rely on choice instead of upon the compulsions of "ought's" and "must's," will I ever get anything done?

We might take this last question and see how the fear operates to tip us out of the mature frame of reference. Suppose that I am approaching my academic work, and the language requirement too, with all kinds of maturity. I have kept in mind my own choice; I have come to this institution because I chose to; I accept the language requirement as an aspect of reality; I accept the notion that time applies to me; and I choose, therefore, to do the language requirement now rather than tomorrow. I am doing my German, and my roommate comes in and asks me to make a fourth at bridge. Now I enjoy bridge; furthermore I haven't played for quite some time; furthermore I have been working very hard. I deserve (what frame of reference does that word come from?) a bit of a change, a little relaxation. I am sorely tempted. Suddenly I am afraid. I am afraid that I will go and play bridge and not get that language requirement done. I suddenly lose confidence in the Self to choose wisely. I cannot say to my roommate or to myself, "That sounds nice, but I want to get this German done." I cannot voice a simple preference. Instead, I say, "No, I really *ought* to do my German, I really *must* get it done." Now understand me, it looks as if I have not capitulated. I have not said to myself that I can do the German "tomorrow" and I have not gone off to play bridge. But I have capitulated. I have lost confidence in my own capacity to choose, and I have called upon the "ought's" and the "should's" and the "must's" to compel me, to do the deciding for me; and in the next hour, how I will resent it! I have set They up again as my masters, and how I will buck them! I will feel frustrated, I will think about the bridge, and somehow I will defeat my efforts to learn anything. Of course I may be able to get something done for a while by glorying in a kind of masochistic righteousness, but I won't keep it up for long. My spell of self-righteousness will only give me the excuse for taking the whole week end off. From the mature point of view it would have been better had my Self actually chosen to play bridge and to deal with the consequences. I am not arguing against the value of a conscience; I am saying that if we set up the conscience as our compulsive authority instead of as our guide, then we may react as children toward it. To rely entirely upon its compulsion is to surrender the integrity of the Self, to abnegate the function of choice. Until one has had a little experience with the Self, it is hard to believe that we, as people, could really *prefer* to do our work. We say, "I have to drive myself to work." Who is driving whom here? Self-expression is the act of doing what we as *whole* people prefer.

Perhaps we can turn now to the subject of education. I was talking with a student the other day who relied so heavily upon his conscience and upon his parents that though he had the intentions of doing college work, he could not see them as his own. Whenever he told himself that he ought to get to work, he sounded to himself so much like his parents that he resisted his own statements. There was a constant strife between the parent in him, who was trying to make him do things, and the child in him, who was in revolt. Things had gotten a little pressing just before examinations, and he had begun to do a little work. He had decided, he said, that the only trouble with him was that he had no incentive. "But recently," he said, "I've had a lot of incentive; in fact I can't remember being so incensed in all my life."

What I am trying to say is that being incensed may be the normal and appropriate state of mind of the young while being educated. Education is the way that we get at them. We force the culture upon them, the "do's" and the "don'ts" and the "ought's" and the "must's," and when they start doing these, can they eagerly espouse them and keep their integrity, or must they resist to live? Watch them. They go on slow-down strikes and become slow readers. They bewilder themselves by their "laziness." They appeal to you, in conscience-stricken despair. And when they do their work, is their main purpose to learn something or to placate you? It is very profitable and enlightening to look at the act of studying as the process of placating authority in the educational world.

Does this sound extreme? I remember when I first went into the business of helping students to study better, more efficiently and all that. I assumed, of course, that everybody wants to be efficient—that is to get the same results with the least effort—and for all I know this still may be a perfectly reasonable assumption. When a student came to me, I would try to show him how to be efficient. He would say, "Here are my notes. I take lots of notes. I don't really know what is the matter, I'm not getting anywhere, that's all. I've been working and working and working, but I don't get the grades." Well, he would have plenty of notes, all right, stacks of them, all very neatly arranged, and most of them copied right out of the book; so I would show him, as kindly as possible, how inefficient all this was, how he had written and written but hadn't learned a thing. And I would show him how to learn much more and to do about one-fourth of all that copy work, and then he would say, "I don't know why I didn't think of that before; why that's marvelous! Thank you so much, sir." And he would run off. In a few weeks I'd see him again and say, "How are you getting on these days?" And there would be that same mass of verbatim notes. And while I sat there, feeling that wave of the teacher's despair, the student would say, "I tried your method, sir, really I did [whose method?], but I don't know, really, sir, it just seems *better* this way."

Now the student was right. I had been trying to give him an efficient way of learning something, whereas he already had a very efficient way of satisfying his conscience, which was what he was mainly trying to do. You cannot imagine a more efficient way to satisfy your conscience than sitting for hours and writing out those notes. The note goes from the book up one finger and one arm, and across the shoulders, and down the other arm onto the paper, and your mind and heart and soul can be off on something else more pleasant. No extra effort at all. Such a method for such a student is admirably designed to fit his purposes. Do you suppose, as a teacher, that your main problem will be your students' stupidity? Or does it begin to seem as if your main problem might be the extraordinary wisdom of their resistance?

No wonder, then, that you will suffer moments of dark despair.

At this point I hesitate to remind you that this is an excursion into my ignorance and that I have no more idea of what to do about these things than you have. I may have offered you the sorry consolation that when you fail to educate a student it may not be wholly your own fault. But surely I am not going to leave you with this, and surely there must be something that you can do about the situation, in addition to the big job of accepting it. Nobody knows the answer to this one, but it may help a little if we look back over the implications of what we have been saying.

From what we have said, it seems to follow that the good teacher's greatest responsibilities and greatest skills lie not in his love for the subject or in the clarity of his exposition, or in his enthusiasm, but in his handling of the problems of resistance. That is to say he will accept the fact that his students will react to him not in terms of who he is, but as a They, and he will, in the face of this, attempt to create a situation in which his students may more readily become Selves in the educational world.

We might expand on the first of these a little. You will be told by another lecturer, "Naturally you never will pull your rank on your students." Now I don't think you will either, not if you have acknowledged that you have a rank and are willing to accept the consequences. The only teacher who pulls his rank is the person who refuses to accept either the rank itself or the adolescents' reaction to it. If you refuse to accept your disciplinary function as an educator, either in kindergarten or in graduate school, and pose, in your own mind, simply as the students' guide and friend, you will be very vulnerable indeed. For when a student turns the hostility which he has accumulated for those who do not let him have what he wants (and he could have it if it were not for Them), when he turns that full blast on you, with an accuracy which he has learned from long experience, and hurts right on the sore spot, what will you do then? If you take it personally, you will pull your rank on him out of your own self-preservation. But if you see it in its context, it will not look like a personal affront, and you will deal with it educationally in its own terms. But more important, if you acknowledge to yourself what your role is and how your students view you, then you will be able to handle your authority productively instead of denying it. That is, you will be able to use it in ways in which it will do the least harm by exciting resistance. Denying it does not do away with it; it simply leaves it out of control. We have all been taught by the teacher who stands between his subject and his students, so that he seems to represent his subject in such a way that the subject matter is inextricable from our reaction to his authority. The admonition which you received earlier not to stand between your students and what you had written on the blackboard referred to something much deeper than the interference caused by your bodily opacity. The good teacher stands to one side of the direct line between his students and his subject. Then his authority can be perceived as a separate matter, and his teaching can be interpreted as assistance rather than imposition.

The job of helping students to discover their Selves in the educational world follows directly from this sort of thing, but it is so complex, so subtle, and so obscure, that I dare not venture far upon it. Certainly it must have something to do with the complicated job of acknowledging one's authoritative position and still treating one's students as persons with integrity and freedom of choice. It would be easy to say that if we want our students to act and think of themselves as mature, we must treat them as mature. It is correspondingly easy to suppose that any teacher who fails to do so fails because of the limitations of his own character. But this is a very harsh judgment indeed, because once more it leaves the students' response out of the picture. The adolescent's desire to be treated as an adult is a highly ambivalent desire. With being an adult come all the difficulties and handicaps which we mentioned. For most of his life, too, the student has developed his skills and his sense of security in dealing with an authoritarian They. He has learned that the way to deal with teachers is to get them to commit themselves, to find out what they think and hand it back to them on examinations. Suppose, then, that you start encouraging your students to think for themselves, and you withhold your own convictions as stultifying to this process. The anxiety and the panic and the hostility will be indescribable. How much of it can you stand? Can you permit the organized conspiracy to promote a whispering campaign on the campus to the effect that your course is vague and indeterminant? Can you let your students complain to the dean that you do not tell them what to expect? Can you allow the head of your department to learn that the students "aren't getting anything" out of your section meetings? Experience with this sort of thing has shown that the students will eventually reverse themselves, but it takes a full academic year for them to do it. Do not judge your colleagues too harshly should they fail to carry through the experiment.

I should like to venture one idea from the counseling process itself, even though I am not very sure how generally it may apply. It sometimes seems to me that the greatest source of anxiety among college students is their sense of personal isolation from their teachers. By personal isolation I do not refer to the lack of teas and social gatherings and bull sessions, or to any specific item of academic paraphernalia. What I mean is the sense that the only connection one has with the professor and the institution at large resides in one's academic record. As one student said, "I feel like a B-minus walking around on two legs." The anxiety of this personal isolation is the breeding ground of infantile defensiveness and resistance. A large part of it is doubtless inevitable and only an indirect expression of homesickness, but much more of it seems to be a vicious by-product of the fixity of student-teacher roles in our education. When a student comes to you after class with a question about a mathematical problem, what he may really want to say is, "I'm scared to death, I don't think anybody knows I'm here, and nobody cares. Please, teacher, acknowledge that I count, that I am a person, and that you are paying attention." But he cannot say this. He cannot say that in mathematics he is lonely; so he asks a question about a problem, and what are you to do? Can you do anything but answer the question? I do not know. I only know that in the counseling clinic where such things are, after all, infinitely easier to do, more difficulties with mathematics are resolved by accepting and acknowledging how the student feels than by demonstrating some difficult point in a proof.

Now one cannot engage in a Rogerian non-directive interview while erasing the blackboard at the end of a lecture, but in the briefest of these student contacts there can be an enormous difference in quality. The difference resides in the implied topic of the conversation. It can be perfectly clear that the topic of conversation is the subject matter and nothing more, or it can be equally clear that the topic of conversation is the student in his emotional relation to his work. If this is important in the brief moments after class, it should be infinitely more so in the longer office hours. It is extraordinary how simple a matter it really is to give a student a sense of personal relatedness to the community of scholars. All one really has to do is to try to see how he himself at this particular moment sees things and feels things and to show him that one somehow understands. It is in the student's sense of the warmth of being understood, of being therefore personally related, that he is set free from his anxiety so that he can do his academic work productively.

And it is not impossible that it is through the warmth that you may convey this way that the student may come to feel that it may be worth while to grow up. If grown-ups are impersonal, authoritative, and intellectual, then it is perfectly clear that being mature means to give up having fun. It means to the student that to grow up and be a Self must carry with it an absolutely intolerable loss, the discard of *all* his impulses and desires, and that to be a Self will not only mean to be alone, but to be lonely indeed But if you are warm and attentive to your students' feelings, then they will realize that you, too, put some value on feelings, and that maybe it would be possible to grow up and still have feelings and still have fun. In that case, since you eat beans, maybe they will try them, too.

GORDON W. ALLPORT

Chapter III

HOW SHALL WE EVALUATE TEACHING?

Can we measure the difference between good and bad teaching? A pilot study experiment. Conditions of the experiment. The criteria used by expert observers to evaluate teaching and the criteria obtained from students. The summary of findings must be considered in the light of many factors such as the appropriate teaching method. How far is "drill," for example, suited to elementary and "permissive" to advanced courses, and is a varying combination of the two desirable in all teaching? Teaching as an art is observable, is capable of some analysis, and is improvable.

For those who are charged with the conduct of our social institutions the postwar period has turned into a period of self-examination. Evaluation is in the air. No longer do we assume complacently that our schools, churches, courts, social services, industries, communications, government—as now run—are equal to the tasks assigned to them.

In this self-critical trend the social scientist finds himself deeply involved. One organization asks him, for example, to help determine whether the accomplishments of a certain social agency justify the effort and money spent on its program. Another asks just what the educational (or propaganda) effects of a certain film, radio series, or comic strip may be. Still another wants to know what gains accrue to the student who spends a summer at a volunteer work camp in this country or abroad. Someone else asks whether programs for the improvement of race relations in America are reaping tangible results. Almost unheard of ten years ago, such requests for help in evaluation are now pouring in.

Education has not escaped the knife of self-scrutiny. Commissions to search the pedagogical soul have recently published their findings—a well-known example being the Harvard report on *General Education in a Free Society*. Prior to the troubled postwar period the impact of higher education was automatically assumed to be wholly favorable. Now, however, even this benign assumption is being submitted to empirical testing.

While taking for granted the value of higher education as a whole, we have at the same time taken for granted the methods of teaching employed in our college classrooms. Young teachers, commencing their careers, naturally began to teach in the manner in which they themselves had been taught, and thus perpetuated the merits and errors of academic practice. In many institutions the Ph.D. degree carries with it the comfortable assurance that the recipient is "qualified to give instruction to other candidates for higher degrees in his own subject." Where this optimistic phraseology originated I do not know. Universities are not usually given to such bland overstatement. At any rate, once launched upon a career of college teaching the instructor has enjoyed prerogatives of a semi-mystical nature. In former years these privileges were symbolized and enforced by the wearing of robes in the classroom. Who would dare to "evaluate" the performance of the old-time *Gelehrter*? Even to suggest such a possibility would be a lese majesty. What goes on in the classroom is sacred ritual. It may not be pinioned for observation or assessment.

This traditional immunity is now disappearing. We dare to ask, "What makes good teaching good? what makes poor teaching poor?" It is our right, we now think, to ask instructors to submit themselves to scientific observation so that their virtues and defects may alike be impartially viewed. Perhaps we shall find out that a good teacher is born and not made. If so, this will be a discovery of considerable importance. More likely we shall find that a good teacher is both born *and* made—and, if so, it follows that we can improve some portion of his performance. It seems very likely that college teaching can be much better than it is. But before we can make it so we shall have to develop methods for discovering what goes on in the classroom, and what its effects really are.

A PILOT STUDY

In order to exemplify this thesis I shall describe a pilot study that I have recently carried out in collaboration with Mr. Gardner Lindzey. It is limited in scope and confined to the problem of teaching weekly section meetings in a large elementary course in social science. The subject matter of this course, entitled "The Social and Psychological Foundations of Behavior," is not, I think, a distinctive factor, for the considerations we encounter undoubtedly hold for any section work in large elementary courses in social science. What must be kept in mind is the fact that we are concerned only with the evaluation of *section meetings,* not of the course as a whole. In addition to the weekly sections, composed of approximately twenty students each, the course required attendance at three lectures and a considerable amount of uniform reading.

The weekly discussion group is commonly employed as an educational device in American colleges, especially in large elementary courses. No one seems to know whether the practice is justified or how it may be utilized to secure maximum educational benefit. Whether our procedures and findings have applicability to other types of instruction I cannot say. Teaching methods appropriate to small elementary discussion groups would seem in many respects inappropriate to large plenary lecture sessions, to laboratory instruction, to tutoring, or to advanced seminars. Separate studies should be made of each of these teaching situations.

Since our study is of a limited and pioneer nature I regard the few findings we have to offer as of less importance at this stage than our report on the experimental procedure. This procedure is undoubtedly subject to improvement, and yet I place it on the record at this time for the convenience of those who may wish to build upon it.

THE ONE-WAY SCREEN: AN INDISPENSABLE AID

A small class, at least after its initial meetings, is a closed society. It develops a routine of its own, a set of interpersonal adjustments and expectations, its own peculiar teacher-pupil relationships. Though less closely knit than a family group, it bears nevertheless a certain resemblance to one. For example, a stranger entering a family circle upsets drastically its normal routine. Similarly, an outsider who is neither teacher nor pupil "unstructures" the situation that normally prevails in a classroom. This is especially true if he is a person with prestige or a note-taking observer. His presence is a distraction and tends to destroy the very situation he wishes to study. Roles that are automatically carried through when he is absent become self-conscious and are but awkwardly maintained when he is present. For this reason it is not too much, I think, to say that the objective study of the behavior of students and teachers in small classes was virtually impossible before the invention of the one-way screen.

Our pilot study was conducted with this modern aid. A comfortable and brightly lighted classroom with an informal arrangement of tables and chairs was entirely visible from an observation chamber through a chromium-painted plate glass. From the classroom the screen appeared as a large shiny mirror. Several observers could sit comfortably in the observation chamber with unobstructed view, able to hear every word that was spoken by virtue of an amplification of the voices picked up by concealed microphones in the classroom. At no time during the class hour could the teacher or students see or hear the observers.

A question of ethics arises. Is it honorable to eavesdrop? No—not unless one has the permission of those who are "spied upon." In our pilot study the teachers involved were of course informed and willing. If students asked questions concerning the "mirror" they were told frankly what it was and that sometimes the class would be under observation. Oddly enough, the question did not arise in most of the classes, and it so happened that a large number of students sat the whole semester through without knowing what was going on. At the last meeting of the section, however, the story was told—at the time the students were asked for their evaluations of the section meetings—and all were given an opportunity to visit the observation chamber. The students were so delighted with the "deception" that they readily forgave the slight ethical lapse.

One asks, "But does not knowledge that the observation room is being used upset a classroom situation as badly as if the observer himself were visibly present?" Not so. Experience with one-way screens shows that after a short period of amused self-consciousness adaptation rapidly sets in. With adult subjects—and even more with children—one can say that for all practical purposes if the observer is out of sight he is out of mind. It is sometimes true that the teacher himself remains keenly aware that his conduct of the class is under scrutiny. This fact, of course, motivates him to do his best, but so firmly imbedded are his habits of teaching that he does not basically alter his style. In spite of himself his virtues and defects as a teacher are plainly visible.

For a completely satisfactory experiment in the evaluation of teaching other conditions are indispensable. One is that the sections to be studied should be well matched. Otherwise a teacher's success or failure may be due to the caliber and condition of his class and not to his own pedagogical skill. Needless to say, the subject matter and assignments for all of the experimental groups should be the same. Further, the sections should be of the same size, with the same proportion of freshmen and upperclassmen; they should meet at comparable hours of the day; they should be matched for sex—all male sections, or all female, or all coeducational; they should be equated in terms of initial ability and previous background in the subject. This last, and most important, condition is hard to fulfill, especially in the case of freshmen. There are, however, prognostic scores usually available for first-year students based upon high school records, scholastic aptitude tests, and like documents. In the pilot study reported here the matching unfortunately was not adequately carried out. For this reason final course grades, the most obvious evaluative test that can be used, are not reported.

WHAT VARIABLES SHALL WE OBSERVE?

We come now to the most difficult question of all. Given a one-way screen, competent observers, and willing pedagogical guinea pigs, how are we to measure educational accomplishment and its causes, or impediments? Obviously we must select certain variables for the observers to fix their attention upon. As in any scientific experiment two sets of variables are needed: the dependent, whose change we wish to measure, and the independent, whose impact we wish to know. In our design, these requirements become the evidences of educational progress in the student and the style of teaching employed.

Briefly stated our goal is to correlate one set of variables with the other, that is, to discover to what degree the response—the "educational progress"—of the student is a function of the behavior of the instructor.

The first step—the selection of measures dealing with the educational progress of the student—raises a basic issue. We are confronted immediately by the momentous question, "What is the goal of college education?" Unless we know our goal we cannot measure progress toward its attainment. Our job is to measure favorable change. What change is favorable?

One answers such a question, of course, on the basis of his own philosophy of education. A certain authority may tell us that college education "aims to liberate the individual mind so that it may function creatively, and to develop a firm and democratic character structure." Would anyone seriously disagree with this proposition—*or* be able to translate it into concrete terms? It is not possible, at least with our present knowledge, to measure gains in "liberation of the mind," in "creative functioning," or in the "firmness" or "democratic" bent of a "character structure."

I am not saying that it is futile to search for an inclusive statement of the goals of higher education. To be adequately comprehensive such a statement will of necessity be formulated in abstract and untestable terms. But while the philosophical search continues we may be permitted, I assume, to start experimenting with a limited and operational set of criteria for measuring educational gain.

We might, for example, agree for a start on some of the proximate goals of classroom work. If we may assume, for instance, that on the whole it is better for students to attain high grades in their work than low grades, we can proceed to find out whether one style of teaching achieves more of this educational good than another. If we may assume, further, that on the whole it is better for students to take part in a class discussion than to sit silently, we can find out the conditions under which they are most likely to participate. If we can agree, to give one more example, that it is a sign of good teaching for a student to report at the conclusion of a course that he has had a valuable educational experience, then we can determine the conditions of teaching under which he makes this judgment rather than its reverse.

Keeping at this level of proximate objectives, let me list certain testable criteria of good teaching. If some of them seem debatable, they can at least be included provisionally and the debate postponed until we come to the interpretation of our findings.

For a very good reason, which will shortly appear, I am arranging these testable criteria in two provisional lists—one that rests upon the analysis of the classroom behavior by "expert observers," the other upon the subjective report of the students themselves concerning the value of the section meetings. The proximate criteria used by the observers to assess the educational value of teaching in small classes are as follows:

1. *Students' grades.* Although this traditional measure of success is ordinarily interpreted as an achievement score earned by the student, it is also conceivably a function of the excellence of teaching. It may be used as a measure of the teacher's achievement provided that subject matter is identical in various classes and that these classes are matched for initial ability and attainment and for other factors, so that the only independent variable operating is teaching style.

2. *Attendance records.* In so far as attendance at section meetings is voluntary, as is usual with students in good standing, it may safely be assumed that the average attendance will be determined in part by the educational value the student himself places upon the class work. This measure is unsafe to employ, however, unless the classes studied meet at comparable hours of the day, and are not menaced by competing football schedules or adjacent holidays.

3. *Student participation.* In the American college system it is generally assumed that good teaching will evoke some form of overt participation from

the student. It is true that some shy and quiet students may never "spill over" into participant activity even though they benefit from class instruction. Still, on the average, each of the following measures may be assumed to give an indication of the effectiveness of classroom instruction:

(a). Number of different students who recite, ask questions, or otherwise participate during the hour.

(b). Number of students whose hands are raised during the hour, or who give visible signs of wishing to participate, whether or not time and circumstance permit them to do so.

(c). Number of students who discuss intellectual issues with the instructor after class, or during his office hours—if this fact can be determined.

(d). Ratio of participation during the first and second halves of the class period. A poor teacher may often dampen the ardor of his class so that participation deteriorates during a badly managed hour. In interpreting this measure, however, care must be used, since a decline in participation may be due to other and desirable factors: for example, the instructor may justifiably use more time during the last half-hour to explain the lesson, thus deliberately reducing student participation.

4. *Manifestations of students' interest.* Since there is no learning without interest, it may be assumed that all measurable indicators of interest in the classroom are valid criteria to employ. The following items are accessible to observation and report.

(a). Occasions of inattentiveness. An observer can without difficulty count instances where individual students "go out of the field," that is, fall asleep, read newspapers, yawn prodigiously, or are caught napping when asked a question.

(b). Over-all ratings on interest. Experience shows that at the conclusion of an hour's class observers can give a reliable judgment on the general level of interest or boredom that prevailed during the session.

(c). Indications of hostility. On the negative side it seems well to record evidences of disapproval on the part of the class. Most groups, of course, refrain from openly expressing dissatisfaction with the teacher. Yet on occasion one finds signs of open rebellion, such as sharply phrased objections or complaints, derisive laughter at the teacher's expense, or mumbled mutinous comments.

5. *Observers' summary judgment.* On the basis of these various criteria, interpreted by his long watching, an experienced observer may give a summary judgment of the proximate educational value of the section teaching as a whole. This summary judgment enables him to weight the various criteria as he thinks proper and to include considerations too subtle to be ensnared in the analytical measures listed above.

In addition to these judgments by didactically minded observers, we must take into account also the students' own opinions. Granted that the student, like the observer, does not know the ultimate value of the instruction he has received for his later life, still he has an important opinion regarding the merits of the course he has just completed. If only one judgment is obtained from the students at the end of the course it may well take some such form as follows:

1. On the whole do you regard the section meetings you have attended in this course as very much worth while——; moderately worth while——; of doubtful value——; a waste of time——?

(If more specific judgments are desired, some or all of the following items may be employed. If used, they should precede the above over-all evaluation.)

2. How would you judge the value of the section meetings in supplying information or ideas supplementary to the main requirements of the course, that is, not pointed directly to preparation for examinations? Considerable value in this respect——; some value——; little value——; no value——.

3. How about preparation for examinations? Considerable value——; some value——; little value——; no value——.

4. How would you judge the instructor's distribution of section time between the following methods? Too much "lecturing" by instructor——; too little "lecturing" by instructor——; neither too much nor too little——. Too much "drill" (recitation)——; too little "drill"——; neither too much nor too little——. Too much general discussion allowed——; too little general discussion——; neither too much nor too little——.

5. Did the instructor seem well informed on all matters pertaining to the course? Yes, fully——; adequately——; not well enough informed——; very inadequately informed——.

6. Did the section meetings seem well planned and organized? Very——; moderately——; rather poorly planned——; very poorly planned——.

7. On the whole did you find the section meetings interesting? (This is not a judgment of their value but only of their interest.) Very interesting ——; moderately interesting——; rather uninteresting——; very dull——.

8. On the whole would you say that the section meetings have increased your curiosity concerning the subject matter of the course? That is to say, because of the section meetings, are you more likely to take additional courses or to read "on your own" material dealing with this branch of social science? Yes——; no——; doubtful——.

In addition to the use of some such evaluational rating sheet the student should be asked to add free comments to explain or amplify his judgments.

We now have in hand our "dependent" variable—a set of presumably valid, if proximate, measures for good teaching. With their aid we shall try to establish the educational value of section meetings. The reader will note that some of the criteria call for quite objective measurements, such as grades, number of hands raised, attendance; some call for detailed ratings by observers or students; some call for over-all "synthetic" ratings. Though varied in type all these criteria are accessible and practicable to use.

ANALYSIS OF STYLES OF TEACHING

Next we need to define our "independent" variable—the style of teaching whose effectiveness we seek to determine. This task is more difficult; for any analysis of personal style—and teaching is a very personal style—is a baffling undertaking. Some would regard it as audacious and presumptuous. I suggest that we not be deterred by the charge of presumption. For even our critics, who may temperamentally dislike social and psychological analysis, frequently take the liberty of pronouncing on the attributes of a good teacher. They may, for example, tell us about Mark Hopkins and the log. When they do so they are making an intuitive and unproved judgment. Our empirical approach, if less graceful, attempts to put the diagnosis on a verifiable and teachable footing.

As in the case of our dependent variable—effectiveness of teaching—we need to break down our independent variable—the manner of teaching—into concrete and measurable items. Let us list some of them, realizing that future experience will undoubtedly improve the list. The reader should bear in mind that the following items are not yet *proved* to be associated with good, or with poor, teaching. They are merely accessible and measurable differences in style. Some of them, we suspect, will turn out to be true characteristics of the effective, or ineffective, teacher; some will not. The correlation remains to be established. These measurable aspects of teaching style are:

1. *Stating the agenda.* Some teachers make clear at the start of an hour, perhaps verbally, perhaps with a blackboard outline, what will be covered during the period. Occasionally, of course, the agenda for the hour are so clearly defined by the assignment that a restatement would not be helpful. Still it is possible to estimate whether or not a teacher characteristically sees to it that the agenda for the day are clear.

2. *Proportion of time spent in lecturing or expounding.* Some teach-

ers do all or most of the talking; others say relatively little during the hour, assigning most of the time to student discussion.

3. *Teacher-member centering* vs. *student-student centering.* Usually the teacher is a necessary focus, a relay point, in class discussion. Sometimes, however, one notes that a class for a time appears to run itself. Students talk directly to students, perhaps arguing in a lively fashion, without the teacher's intermediation. It is possible, and potentially profitable, to count such episodes, for they would not occur unless it was part of the teacher's style to encourage and permit them.

4. *Directive* vs. *non-directive questioning.* Some teachers use a straight drill or recitation method of conducting a class. The teacher asks a question and the student gives the *right* answer if he can. We may call this "directive questioning." At the other extreme a teacher may open the class and keep it going by "non-directive questions," such as, "What aspect of the assignment would you prefer to discuss?" "Any comments on Mr. X's observation?" "Do you feel satisfied with the text's treatment of this point?" Most teachers, of course, employ both types of questions; but the proportion characteristically differs from instructor to instructor.

5. *Commendation and acceptance.* Some teachers give occasional praise for a student's contribution to the discussion; some do not. Some have other ways of "tying in" the student who has spoken with the on-going stream of the discussion so that he may feel "accepted." Experience shows that it is relatively easy to count instances of this practice in teaching.

6. *Rejection of student.* Conversely, one may count instances where the teacher, by word or manner, implies that the student is "off the beam," or that his contribution is not welcome. Rejection of a student's response is not the same as correcting a wrong answer. It is possible to tie in a wrong answer so that the student himself does not feel rejected.

7. *Disregard of student.* One may count the number of times a teacher fails to see upraised hands, or if he sees them, fails sooner or later to acknowledge them. There are times, of course, when nearly all the hands in the class are waving in the air. No teacher could acknowledge them all. But habitual oversight, included in an over-all rating on the teacher's tendency to disregard students' efforts to participate, can provide a useful measure.

8. *Use of blackboard.* Some teachers often use the blackboard; others, teaching the same subject matter, seldom or never do so. Some are remarkably explicit in their outlines or diagrams; some draw an ambiguous sort of illustration and "doodle" on the board as a nervous accompaniment to their stream of speech. Observers are in a position to rate the instructor's use of the blackboard. Does he use it often? Is his meaning clear?

9. *Use of illustrations from everyday life.* In elementary courses, to which our discussion is confined, it may be that an important teaching variable is the tendency of the instructor to fortify the lesson with fresh illustrative materials drawn from common experience. The number of such instances during an hour's teaching can be recorded.

10. *Digressive material.* An observer thoroughly familiar with the course being taught can judge to what extent the instructor has permitted wide digression and irrelevancy to creep into the discussion. It is not expected that occasional digression will correlate with bad teaching; indeed it may be essential to good teaching. But over a period of time it is well to know whether an instructor's teaching style is or is not marked by persistent wandering from the subject.

11. *Note taking.* In most section meetings it is "up to the student" whether or not he wishes to take notes. The observer, of course, cannot count every occasion on which any student writes in his notebook. He can, however, estimate whether there was much or little note taking during the hour. Presumably this variable reflects the style of teaching—for some teachers give little summaries, or otherwise *stimulate* note taking; others do not. Which is the better style we do not yet know. Of course, if the teacher commands or suggests that notes be taken the variable should not be employed.

12. *Humor.* The observer can note down occasions when there were scattered smiles, also outbursts of laughter. In the long run these records are bound to reflect the instructor's own humor and his tendency to introduce a light touch into the conduct of his class.

All of these twelve variables are based on objective measures. The observer counts the number of happenings of a given type during a class period. Three additional variables are recommended, of a more subjective nature, calling for the use of a rating scale. A four-point scale has been found useful for this type of recording.

13. *Self-confidence.* Many teachers are manifestly ill at ease; others, whatever they may feel inside, give the appearance of poise and self-confidence. Ratings on this variable are relatively reliable.

14. *Vocal assertiveness.* An over-all rating on this variable seems potentially useful. Some voices are definitely outgoing, some withdrawn. There are, to be sure, subtler variables pertaining to voice quality that might be studied; but for our initial list we shall include only this broad characteristic of vocal habit.

15. *General organization of the teaching hour.* Over and above the particular features of style included in this list, it seems worth while to obtain an over-all rating on the extent to which the instructor carried through a plan of organization in his work for the day. Was the hour well-structured or was it haphazard?

DO STUDENTS AND OBSERVERS AGREE ON "GOOD" TEACHING?

We are now ready to report the results of our small pilot study, remembering that it has dealt with five sections only.

The first discovery we make is that on the basis of their over-all evaluations observers and students do not entirely agree on the merits of their teachers. The following table indicates the degree of agreement (the rank order coefficient of correlation is about .50).

Over-all Evaluation of Instructors A, B, C, D, E

Rank Order	By Student	By Observers
1 (best)	A	C
2	B	B
3	C	A
4	D	E
5 (poorest)	E	D

There is agreement that A, B, and C are good and that D and E are poor. The reversal of positions for D and E will not concern us. The reversal of positions for A and C is more serious. We can best obtain light on the discrepancy by presenting abbreviated case studies of these two instructors, the one rated best by the students and the one rated best by the observers.

Instructor A (observers' view): This instructor is both lively and relaxed in manner. He often speaks while pacing up and down with both hands in his pockets, pipe dangling from his mouth, or he straddles the back of a chair or puts his feet on an adjacent support. He talks rapidly, his voice sometimes sinking so low as to be almost inaudible. His manner is modest, and his remarks often apologetic. While class discussion is in progress he sometimes looks up a point in the textbook, a habit that usually gives the impression of insecurity and withdrawing.

Yet in spite of his apparent lack of poise—or possibly because of it—he seems to be in excellent rapport with his class—to be "one of the boys." He looks young; a stranger entering the classroom would have difficulty distinguishing teacher from pupil. His manner is totally "permissive." A student feels free to say anything—and does so. The class is animated at all times, and sometimes nearly every hand is simultaneously waving in the air. The result is a confused crosscurrent of ideas, not well controlled by Mr. A. Characteristically he will allow the class to ramble in all directions, and then engage in a rather long stretch of "lecturing" in order to expound some concept that has eluded the free-for-all discussion. Sometimes he introduces the names of authors or expounds ideas at too advanced a level to be grasped by the class. On the whole he does not seem to be entirely familiar with the subject matter and promises to "look up" points that he cannot handle in class.

All the while a markedly friendly atmosphere pervades his teaching. He uses first names of the students, an unusual custom in the college, and issues a sincere invitation to the students to consult him during his office hours—which they take advantage of. Further, he employs undergraduate humor in a wholly authentic manner—again seeming to be "one of the boys" in this important respect. Social distance between himself and the class is zero.

Instructor A (students' view): Nearly every member of the class, when asked to comment on A's style of teaching, wrote favorably of the "permissiveness" of his manner. It was said to be *friendly, helpful, informal, democratic, stressing student participation.* Favorably mentioned also were his use of office hours, his humor, his modesty, his willingness "to find out what he doesn't know." A few commented on his seeming ill at ease, his halting manner of speaking, and his too low voice.

Since the students definitely like A, they readily excused the faults that seemed to the observers more serious. For example, the lack of planning, organization, and control of class discussions, noted by the observers, were "perceived" by many students to result from "lack of time to cover the ground." This extenuating perception is especially interesting in view of the criticism made of less popular teachers who were often accused of "using the time badly." Approximately half of A's students spoke of "lack of time," whereas this protective statement seldom appeared in the protocols from other sections. Thus is a popular teacher readily excused for his shortcomings.

Instructor C (observers' view): Unlike Instructor A, this teacher establishes considerable social distance between himself and the class. Of the five teachers he is the only one who places a table or desk between himself and the class while conducting sections. His manner is brisk and businesslike. The agenda for the day are well outlined on the board and in his own mind. He is explicit concerning every detail: in calling the roll, in advising students whether or not to take notes during the hour, in directing students with unsatisfactory grades to call on him during his office hours. Much of the time he reminds one of an army drill sergeant. (Mr. C had previously taught gymnasium classes.)

Yet unlike the proverbial drill sergeant, C is courteous. He tells students not to trouble to raise hands, but to speak up freely: "Break in any time you want to ask a question." "Excuse me for interrupting you." He also uses students' first names but not as often or as consistently as does Instructor A.

Mr. C is a master of the subject matter of the course, and keeps closely to the material presented in lectures and textbooks. He summarizes pertinently and frequently. Occasionally he "lectures," in a more assured manner than A, indicating explicitly what he plans to discuss, how he proposes to approach the topic, and where his material comes from.

On the whole, he shows a strong style of leadership, oddly mixed with moments of apology, with colloquial and slang expressions inconsistent with his usual dignity and distance of manner. His voice is forceful and his speech fluent, although he tends to talk too rapidly and too loudly.

Instructor C (students' view): More than half the students commented favorably upon the organized approach characteristic of C's teaching: they praised his good agenda, good planning, good control of section meetings. Others remarked upon the freedom in discussion, on the lively, energetic, personable manner of C. One or two saw virtue in his "varied style of approach."

But it is clear that this "varied style" troubled many students. They could not interpret what to them were inconsistencies in his manner. Why was he both formal and informal, slangy and pedantic? Some suggested that he was "not sure of himself," some that he was "too sure of himself." One thought he was "trying hard —perhaps too hard." He was criticized for being too explicit concerning points already clear to the student.

Contradicting the observers' judgment, some students criticized C for his failure to coördinate the lectures, reading, and section work. Yet to the observers "coördination" was one of C's strong points. We may be dealing here with the tendency of students to cast about for some "respectable" reason for their vague dissatisfaction. Or perhaps the observers are at fault in overestimating the didactic success of C's efforts at coördination.

The most striking fact that emerges from a comparison of these cases is that students and "experts" judge over-all value of teaching on different bases. The students seem to favor the section conducted in an informal, friendly, permissive, equalitarian manner by a teacher who is authentically one of the boys—modest and humorous. They sense A's keen interest in *individual* members of the class and his eagerness to help them in any way he can. The "experts" see greater value in sections conducted more after the fashion of a drill, marked by good organization, with adequate coverage of ground. Students were obviously disturbed by the inconsistency in C's style. They did not know just where they stood with him. It may well turn out that *consistency* is an essential attribute of really good teaching. It may not matter whether the instructor is formal or informal in manner, so long as he maintains the role he has once established—that is, so long as he appears to the student to be *himself*.

Readers of these sketches may detect in both instructors evidence of personal insecurity. It would not be surprising, for both are virtual beginners at the game of teaching. But note the different ways in which A and C handled their subjective insecurity. Instructor A is ill at ease in a "winning" manner. The students sympathize with him; he is just like themselves in his discomfort (they seem to think). Instructor C perhaps tends to overcompensate, to protect himself, to overexert. Although from the observers' point of view C's effort leads to effective teaching, students are in some cases alienated by his manner, even while they appreciate his ability.

THE INTERLOCKING AND PATTERNING OF TRAITS IN THE TEACHER

This comparison of cases leads us to a consideration of prime importance.

When a scientist analyzes his datum—it has often been pointed out—he destroys, or at least disregards, the pattern that he dissects. In advocating the use of fifteen measurable items pertaining to style of teaching, have we not done irreparable damage to the personal configuration of the teacher? It is, after all, the *patterned impact* of the instructor's personality as a whole that affects the students. The cases of Instructors A and C demonstrate the point. Even granted that our fifteen variables are well chosen for correlational purposes, may they not be weighted variously, offset, or reinforced, by other non-measurable features of the instructor's style? A certain mannerism in teaching, for example, might negate or confer a special meaning upon all the variables we have chosen to study. Since this mannerism might never occur in another teacher, and could not therefore appear in our list of traits, its influence cannot be ascertained by our method of procedure.

All this is very true. Indeed we have a particularly impressive instance in the case of A. By both observers and students he was judged to lack self-confidence. Now it turns out, as the next section will show, that in general teachers appearing to lack self-confidence are rated lower than those who appear to be high in this trait. But A is an exception. So congenial to the students is A's total manner that his lack of ease is perceived as something charming, as making him more human. It does not detract from his effectiveness.

Therefore I concede that serious danger lies in the analysis of teaching style into an arbitrary set of variables. And yet I maintain that the nomothetic mode of analysis employed in our pilot study is entirely justified as *one* method of approaching the problem of evaluation. Of course we must use case studies, "clinical portraits," of individual teachers in order to interpret and modify our statistical findings. But let us not conclude that because we have to employ these case studies there is therefore no merit in the method of quantitative empiricism. Although our teacher A is certainly an exception, it still remains true—as a statistical generalization—that good teachers usually appear to the students to be self-confident individuals.

QUANTITATIVE FINDINGS

I now report the quantitative findings, that is, the statistical generalizations of this pilot study. They must be accepted with caution, for they are based on the observation of only five sections.

Because we have so few cases I shall not attempt to state the correlation of all the teaching variables we have listed with every one of the criteria of good teaching in our first two lists. Rather I shall report only those features of teaching style that seem *provisionally* to distinguish between the more effective teachers and the less effective.

The observers rated Instructors C and B quite close together at the top of the series, also D and E quite close together at the bottom. The following variables seem to distinguish, with statistical significance or else fairly high probability, better teachers from the poorer teachers (observers' criteria): teacher-member centering, well-organized hour (not haphazard), little digressive material, self-confidence (not ill at ease), note taking, commendation and acceptance.

Turning to the students' judgment we list the variables that distinguish the two most effective teachers, A and B, who were rated quite close together, from E who stood alone at the bottom of the list: directive questioning, self-confidence (not ill at ease), commendation and acceptance, humor (recorded laughs and smiles), student-student interaction, less rejecting behavior.

Both observers and students agree that effective teachers commend and accept the student and that apparent self-confidence is an asset, in spite of the ill-at-ease manner of Mr. A. Beyond these agreements we find a basic difference in emphasis. Observers tend to find "drill" methods more prominent in good sections; whereas students claim greater educational value in sections marked by an informal manner and humor.

One feature of the students' list calls for special comment, "directive questioning." In keeping with their general preference for informal, permissive sections we might expect students to favor non-directive questions from the instructor. In the long run, I suspect, such a finding will emerge. But in our particular cluster of five cases we are dealing with another "exceptional" circumstance. It so happens that Mr. A employed questions of a directive type, but in a very *permissive* manner: the students merely used these questions as springboards for their own free discussion. Also it happens that Mr. E (the least popular teacher) *phrased* his questions in a non-directive fashion, but his manner negated the effect. His style of teaching had the unfortunate air of rejecting the student's contribution: after the student had lighted his candle, E had an unhappy way of extinguishing the flame.

From this instance, as from the case of A's lack of self-confidence, we learn again that quantitative generalizations should never stand alone. In the case of any given teacher they must be freely modified whenever a consideration of the total patterned style indicates the need to do so.

A SUGGESTED DICHOTOMY FOR FUTURE EXPERIMENTS

As I have already implied, many of the teaching variables we have listed can be ordered into two groups—those indicating a DRILL type of teaching, and those indicating a PERMISSIVE type. Characteristic of the drill type would be high scores in stating agenda, time spent in lecturing or expounding, teacher-student centering, directive questions, use of blackboard, little digressive material, note taking, and high general organization. Characteristic of the permissive type would be not stating agenda, little time spent on lecturing, high student-student interaction, non-directive questions, less use of blackboard, more digression, little note taking, and less organization of hour.

The remaining variables in our list are not reproduced here, for they do not bear exclusively on either style of approach and yet are well worth retaining for use in some experimental evaluations.

Now this dichotomy, if I mistake not, reflects at the present time the most discussed issue in the whole realm of college teaching. The drill method is on the defensive. It leads, we are told, to memorization, to parroting, to apathy—even to an authoritarian and reactionary bent of mind. Only under the influence of a radically permissive style of teaching does the student learn to think for himself, to find meanings suitable to his own world of experience and adapted to his own "growing edge." In our pilot study, so far as it goes, students tended to report more educational gain from sections conducted, broadly speaking, in the permissive manner.

I think we need to ask certain questions that only further experimentation and evaluation can answer: (1) Shall we take only the students' criteria of educational value, which by present indications favor the permissive and informal approach or shall we give weight also to the observers' criteria which at present seem to favor the drill approach? Or, may we not in the future work out a combined and improved test of educational progress giving both sets of judgments due consideration? (2) May it be that one method results in more gains in an elementary course, and the other method in more gains in an advanced course? (3) May it not be that a combination of permissive and drill methods may be the most effective of all styles of teaching—and that this combination remains to be discovered through further empirical study? Those who have used the permissive method extensively report that although the terminal gains are very great, the early weeks often seem aimless and boring to the student and frequently arouse hostility and resentment. Whether this stage is inevitable in the process of liberating the mind is something we do not yet know. Perhaps it could be by-passed with a judicious inmixture of drill methods to provide the student with more content to nourish his growing process.

All in all, it seems to me that the next stages in our research may most profitably be directed toward exploring further the effectiveness of these two styles and their combinations.

OTHER EVALUATIONAL METHODS

The reader may feel that the experimental design I have described in this chapter is narrow and brittle. The perspective, it may be said, is foreshortened and will not give us the vision we desire. Are we not in danger, the critic will ask, of confusing measurement with evaluation? Evaluation is a subtle process and can only be applied in education by ascertaining the gains of the individual student in an individual way.

I am sympathetic with this view. At the same time I maintain that my proposals, if carried through, would give us safer and more enlightening generalizations than those we customarily lean upon. No avenues should remain unexplored. If we are to learn how to teach more effectively we shall have to study the teaching process and its results from *all* possible angles.

We should, I agree, seek to broaden our indices of success-in-teaching as we have listed them. Especially we need usable criteria that will tell the long-range effects of a course of instruction. Perhaps we should ask for student evaluations, say, ten years after the completion of the course. Even in the shorter haul it should be possible to devise additional and perhaps better criteria for measuring educational gain. Evaluative essays written by the student at the end of the term would be enlightening. Furthermore, achievement tests, especially tests for *ability to think for oneself,* if they can be devised, might be administered before and after a course is taken, and the results interpreted as a measure of the effectiveness of the teaching. These and other developments are sorely needed. So lively is current interest in improving instruction that I am confident they will soon take place.

Teaching, we all agree, is an art. It represents the impact of a personality possessing specialized knowledge upon other personalities whose knowledge in the same field is less specialized. Art, of course, is a matter of personal expression. The secret of its creative utterance is hidden deep in the recesses of personality. But every art—teaching included—makes use of skills, and these skills are learned during the period that the artist is in training. In part, then, it seems likely that teaching ability is made, not entirely inborn. Hence teachers can presumably be taught to teach, or at least to teach more effectively. But first we need to advance our knowledge of the conditions of good teaching. In this chapter I have sketched one method by which this may be done.

WILLIAM H. WESTON

Chapter IV

VALUES, METHODS, AND CRITERIA IN TEACHING

The nature of teaching. The teacher's responsibilities and objectives. How can he best fulfill them? The parts to be played by subject matter, teaching methods, students, and teacher. How weakness in one may be overcome by strength in the others. Consideration of the student as a person. The exact use of words. Discussion of the advantages and disadvantages of the lecture and group discussion. Two schools of thought regarding examinations. Their function and value.

You, the graduate students of today, are the instructors and assistant professors of tomorrow and the associate and full professors of the day after. The emphasis, hitherto centered on receiving instruction, is for you now changing increasingly to giving it, and increasingly through your own experience you will test the possible applicability here of the adage that it is better to give than to receive.

Evaluation of you as a teacher may well center around four questions of attitude. What do you regard as the nature of teaching and of the essential factors involved therein? What do you regard as the responsibilities and obligations you must meet as teachers? What are the objectives you intend to attain, and by what means may you most effectively attain them?

First, let us consider your point of view, your attitude toward teaching and toward the components involved in it. It is my conviction that your effectiveness as teachers will be materially aided if you regard teaching and learning, which is the obverse thereof, as natural and fundamental processes despite the embellishments and elaborations with which they are bedecked in some of the literature on education. For mankind, teaching and learning have been going on since the beginning; for the individual, learning and teaching go on from the drawing of the first breath until the last. On these two processes survival, development, and progress are dependent. They are as natural a part of you as anything you do.

To attain eminence as a teacher is not to be especially chosen and set apart but to develop your teaching effectiveness by sound hard work, by intelligent effort and understanding. You will, I hope, steadfastly retain your faith in the honesty and naturalness of teaching, despite the interference of academic politics which set up a School of This and an Institute of That, despite frustrating harassment from zealous and well-meaning administrators who formulate teaching into credits, semester hours, and student-contact hours; apportion it into majors and minors, into areas and fields of concentration or distribution; regiment it by committees, boards, departments and divisions; record it on pink, green and blue slips, on specially punched cards and business machine forms; evaluate it by the research papers you have failed to publish during the preceding year and the honorary degrees you have failed to receive from renowned universities or alma maters in the less favored fringe.

The essential components which teaching involves, as I see them are four: the subject matter, the teaching methods, the student, and the teacher.

Of these components the subject matter is the least important. Certainly each field by its nature contributes to knowledge and to progress, each field by its effect on the diverse personality patterns of men secures its representatives and adherents. The teaching methods are somewhat more important because they influence more strongly the response of the student, and it is taken for granted that with resourcefulness, ingenuity, and tenacity you will build your knowledge, experience, and understanding into the increasing effectiveness of your teaching methods. Essentially, however, it is the teacher's intense interest in the subject and his stimulating enthusiasm in teaching, combined with the responsive interest and enthusiasm of the student, that are the most important factors. Consideration, therefore, centers chiefly on the student and the teacher.

The student, as an individual, is a highly complicated creature. Since the student you will teach tomorrow is yourself as you were yesterday, you are aware of his complexity and you recognize his major components. You realize that he has a fundamental pattern which inheritance and early background have established and that he has certain innate ability, intelligence, and aptitude, and you understand that at the college level of his development, in the one or two courses under your guidance, you will have no effect whatever on these. You may, however, as you come to know the student, gain enough understanding of his background to enable you, if he seeks your guidance, to enable him to analyze his needs and avoid drifting into a life work that is completely at variance with his whole pattern. You will realize that there are certain components of the student's make-up to which you can contribute greatly. Especially you can add to his effective knowledge, increase his skill, stimulate his interest and enthusiastic drive, broaden his understanding, and strengthen the maturity of his attitude.

The students as a student body will be of the highest educational level, but they will not be all of one set pattern, and in your classes whether large or small you will find many different types represented. Some will be intensely interested in the subject and eager to work with you, others will be taking your course because it seems the least repulsive of the possibilities available for fulfilling the requirements for distribution, or because it neatly fills an hour otherwise left vacant. Some will have the possibilities and potentialities of a Madame Curie or a Louis Pasteur of the future. You will find on the other hand that the problem child is disconcertingly present in your classes. Since no lecture concerned with any aspect of education is complete without using the word "challenge," I would be derelict to my duty if I failed to point out that this very diversity in your students is a challenge to your capacity as teachers. Certainly, from my own experience I can assure you that it contributes to the enduring fascination of teaching.

The fourth component, the teacher, is also a highly complicated creature, for he is, after all, a human being. Like the student, the teacher has fundamental patterns which inheritance and early background have determined, and certain intellectual capacities, inherent abilities, and qualities of aptitude. When you start teaching, or even before, it will be helpful to you to subject your own patterns and capacities to careful objective study, for you realize that by understanding yourselves and making the most of what you have, you can accomplish more in your teaching than those who are more gifted than you but unable or unwilling to analyze themselves and to organize and direct their abilities. Your other assets—your knowledge, skill, and understanding, your interest and enthusiasm—are under your control, capable of being developed and coördinated to the highest possible effectiveness.

It is the interaction between these four components—the subject, the methods, the student and the teacher—that achieves the results. The inadequacies of one or the other may be counteracted. Subject matter which is of especial interest, in combination with brilliant and enthusiastic students, will compensate for shortcomings on the part of the teacher and inadequacies in the teaching methods. Similarly, all of us as students can remember courses in which the subject was not in itself absorbing, the teaching methods were decidedly casual, and we, as students, were certainly not brilliant; but the teacher, through qualities we appreciated at the time without specific analysis, made that course a memorable and enlightening chapter in our development. Occasionally there occurs the rare and perfect combination, with all of the components especially favorable, and their interaction consummately effective. That is magnificent and I hope in your teaching you will experience it many times. Of these components —at least at college level with the selected students you will be teaching—the teacher, in my opinion, is the most important, and that is what you, in your teaching, should remember.

THE TEACHER'S OBLIGATIONS

Next, after your view of the nature of teaching, there is the matter of your obligations and responsibilities as teachers. We need not here consider your obligations to the college, the administration, the department, for those will be impressed upon you with forceful frequency by directives from deans of the faculty, chairmen of departments, and directors of laboratories, as well as by rulings from numerous and zealous committees and boards. Since, however, there will be little if any emphasis on your obligations to the student, some consideration here of that aspect of your responsibility as a teacher may prove helpful. Inevitably you have at least made conscious or unconscious resolutions that when you become a teacher there will be certain things you will *not* do. You will not, I feel sure, take harmful advantage of the authority over the student which your position confers upon you. You will, when necessary for the salvation of the student or the morale of the class, quietly administer the salutary squelch to excessive bumptiousness and pomposity, or judiciously acquaint the persistent apple-polisher with your awareness of his tactics. Yet you will never hold up the student to ridicule or belittlement or subject him to any of the other sadistic cruelties that you may possibly have seen practiced by teachers. Some of you still remember, from service in the war, instances of the abuse of power by those whose rank was inherent in the symbolic emblems on their uniforms rather than in their qualities and abilities. You still recall your feeling of frustration and irritation over the arbitrary regulation that the one with the higher ranking emblem was thereby right, while he of the lesser symbol was necessarily wrong. For the students, your natural rank is determined by your qualities and ability as a teacher far more than by your academic titles and degrees.

You will, I am sure, never regard a student as a competitor who threatens your preëminence, or feel an envious resentment toward him if, in his rapid development, he shows promise of surpassing you. On the contrary you will rejoice in his progress and take pleasure in the realization that you have contributed to it. Your function is that of a teacher. You are not a professional tennis star, but a track coach whose skillful guidance and enthusiastic persistence develop the student's ability to surpass your own previous records in the half mile or the high hurdles. Human progress moves forward through the contributive activities of many individuals, and if your teaching advances the development of your students and helps them to contribute more than you yourself have contributed, then let that be your contribution.

You will never forget that the student is a person with the same essential rights and dignities as you yourself. You are his superior, certainly, in knowledge and experience in your field, otherwise you should not be teaching him, but do not let this mislead you into assuming thereby that he is your inferior. There is the stage of development, the discrepancy in ages to be considered, and you will be wise to remember that there was a time when Noah Webster was taught how to spell w-o-r-d and when Einstein was guided through the steps of addition and subtraction. Even if the student's personality irritates you extremely, your responsibility demands that he shall receive from you the same impartial fairness, the same helpful instruction as the congenial and likable lad who is such a pleasure to teach. One of the richest rewards of teaching is to foster the astonishing development of unexpected capabilities from seemingly unpromising material. I have known the fascination of working out the circulatory system of the cat in Comparative Anatomy to start a student on the road that led to his becoming a famous surgeon. I have seen a student, hitherto comfortably drifting, become so fascinated by watching a microscopic mold start from a single spore and run through its cycle of development to the final production of hundreds of spores that his aroused interest extended to course after course up to the achievement of high honors in biology. Colleagues in other fields could give you many other instances; perhaps your own experience offers them also.

In addition to your obligations to the student there are other obligations that you will bear in mind. You will, of course, be ever mindful of your need to keep up with the rapid developments which mark the progress of your subject, yet to increase your familiarity with the classical work of the great pioneers of the past. Being aware of human frailty, of the tendency to become stale, you will try to maintain your balance and your freshness and to keep up the vitalizing interest of your own research.

OBJECTIVES

What are your objectives in teaching? You probably have encountered two points of view in most critiques of teaching. One of these is the interpretation which regards teaching as the stuffing or translocation of factual matter from the stuffer or teacher to the stuffee or student. This school of thought emphasizes a large number of solid facts, compounded according to a time-tested curricular recipe, with suitable seasoning, and regards the examination as an expressing, or squeezing out, of enough representative, compacted content to satisfy the test requirement that no matter how thin you slice it, it is still biology. The other theory is the "make 'em think" or voltaic pile interpretation, which regards teaching as applying suitable chemicals to the inactive zinc and copper constituents of the student so that he may become a producer of current, and regards the examination as a test of the intensity of discharge, and of the brilliance of the sparks given forth.

You will realize that your teaching will profit by both these points of view, for the young traveler whom you are preparing for his journey through difficult territory will need both an ample supply of facts and an adequate understanding of how to meet emergencies. Considered from the biological point of view, your objective as a teacher is not only to provide the student with material, but also to catalyze his processes of assimilation, synthesis, and elaboration. The material he takes in will not merely be stored, but will change to meet his needs, with the result that the raw material loses its identity as stuff you furnished him in your course and becomes an integral part of the make-up and activities of his own being. It is to be hoped that your contribution to his development will help him to be a more knowledgeable, productive, understanding, and contributive creature. If so, you will have attained your highest objective as a teacher.

A next and last consideration concerns the essential means by which you attain some of the objectives of your teaching—the lectures, discussions, quizzes, term papers, reports, and examinations.

In your teaching give serious thought to words, for they are the most important tool you use, the essential medium of your lectures, conferences, and discussions, of your interpretations and explanations, of your entire advisory counsel and guidance. Consider your predicament, the predicament common to all mankind but especially serious in the case of the teacher: how are you going to engender in the minds of others the knowledge, comprehension, and understanding which is in your own? That this can be done at all is an awe-inspiring achievement; the degree and exactness with which it is done will measure your effectiveness as a teacher. In this process, words are the essence. They can result in understanding or in misunderstanding, they can arouse antagonism or coöperation, discouragement or enthusiasm, apathy or activity; they can lead to retrogression or to progress. You therefore will not be content to take words for granted or to take refuge in the heedless Humpty-Dumptyism that "words mean just what I intend them to mean, neither more nor less," but will give earnest thought to the power of words. In this endeavor there are books which will prove helpful to you. Already, perhaps, you know *Language in Action* by Samuel Ichiyé Hayakawa, a book I like very much because the attitude is that of a true teacher and the viewpoint has the unusual advantage of derivation from Japanese ancestry, education in Canada, and years of teaching in Illinois. Perhaps you are familiar with the contributions to the analysis and understanding of the meaning of language made by Professor Richards.

LECTURES

Lectures will play an important part in your teaching. Their advantages are obvious. In no other way can you, at one time, transmit so much to so many with such effectiveness, as through speech. There is no instrument or medium with the affective power of the voice. Hence the vast difference between the printed textbook or the mimeographed correspondence school course and the lecture given by one who is keenly interested, as well as expert, in the subject. The factual matter gains vividness, the interpretations command responsive attention. Yet the lecture has certain disadvantages which are all too obvious to you. It is a flowing continuity moving on in such an interdependent sequence that any interruption, such as a fit of coughing, a dropped notebook, or the slamming of a door, will mean for some students the loss of essential ideas. Also, because it is a continuous stream of communication, the pressure on the student of keeping up with adequate notes may prevent his keeping pace adequately in understanding. In spite of its disadvantages the lecture remains the most effective means by which you may transmit to your whole class of students the subject matter of your teaching.

The notes from which you lecture will be your indispensable major aid. They may be of several different types and may follow various systems, but they must meet the requirements of furnishing you adequate guidance and material in readily accessible form. They must provide you with the continuity, the emphasis, transitions, and relations, and the essential points you will need, yet be so readily available and so easily comprehended that you follow them successfully with only an occasional glance. Obviously, for this purpose the original complete notes which you prepared so carefully and fully will seldom serve because they will comprise a total fifteen to even forty or more closely written pages. If they were prepared with the purpose I have stated in mind, with suitable indications of underscoring, spacing, indenting, and numbering, and with bold easily read type, and if you have an appropriate lectern or table, of suitable location, lighting, and size, and if you can remain close by and do not have to move around to blackboard, screen, models, and charts, you may be able to use such notes successfully. Usually, however, you will need to prepare a condensed outline, a brief table of contents, in compact form on one or two pages of heavy, not flimsy, paper, or on large cards, in bold type, skillfully designed for comprehension at a glance. Always, of course, you need to know your lecture so thoroughly—not only from the point of view of content, but also from the point of view of delivery—that your effective presentation will require a minimum of reference to your notes whatever their form may be. You will, of course, work out your own system and contrive the type of notes that best suits your individual needs, but these suggestions may be helpful.

In your direct and spontaneously spoken lectures you will make use of what you have learned in the years you have been at the receiving end of lecturing. You will pay attention to your rate of delivery, for you know the effects of dragging slowness or of extreme rapidity; you will heed the tone of your voice because you have experienced the effects of excessive loudness or softness. These important qualities are influenced by such factors as the pressure of time and the acoustics of the room, but chiefly by the shock effect of the strain of lecturing. This shock effect, familiar to the biologist from W. B. Cannon's investigations of the part played by adrenalin in fear or rage, is more generally familiar under such names as stage fright or "mike" fright. Take comfort in the fact that all lecturers, however experienced, feel this effect to some extent, and in the realization that you will learn to control it. As you have been told, you will find it helpful to know the first part of your lecture so thoroughly that, in the first grim moments when you are getting underway, you can automatically speak effectively, until you steady down and are fully in control. It will help you, if instead of starting right off with the lecture as soon as you step onto the platform, you pause a moment and take a couple of slow deep breaths before you begin.

Some lecturers, however, quite apart from initial shock effect, have a tendency to speak too rapidly or too slowly. The machine-gun technique certainly captures the attention of the student but it wears him down with its battering barrage. On the other hand, the student's attention will wander if you go too slowly, or he will be straining to get you over the next few words as he would to get a pole vaulter over the bar. You will find it helpful to watch the students' reactions as you lecture, for thereby you can set the steady pace that is suitable for the class as a whole. You will find also that occasional changes of pace and changes in sentence length are helpful. If, for example, after an evenly flowing description of, let us say, the embryological development that culminates in the first beating of the heart, you pause and then say: "This activity never ceases as long as the animal lives," the point thus emphasized is vividly impressed on the student's mind. The volume, the loudness or softness of the voice, is important.

Since your own experience in receiving lectures has given you awareness of such shortcomings, you will strive to avoid them. You will gauge the increasing effectiveness of your lecturing by the response of the students and their behavior during your lectures. You can do this because of the separate currents of thought that go on in your mind while you are lecturing. While your primary mental activity is concentrating on the content and presentation of your lecture, a secondary current will be concerned with the students' reaction. By observing the attentiveness of the class you can tell which method of delivery is indicated, whether the "fire-hose focus" or the "park-spray spread." The former is the technique of a fireman coping with a conflagration by directing the stream at the point which needs it most and steadily boring in. The latter is the technique of the Park Department spraying trees on the common with a spacious spread which generously spatters sidewalks, fences, parked cars, and everything else in the general vicinity. If you observe a local lack of attention in five or six students sitting together in the right rear of the room, you will do well to concentrate there, or if a student in the seventh row left is drifting into an uneasy slumber you might beneficially focus on him, unless, of course, your sympathy prevents. If there is general attention throughout the class and all is going well, you will probably direct your communication with a more general coverage.

By observing the students you can sense when something goes wrong and act to remedy the situation. If a general air of depressed restlessness pervades the class, perhaps the room is getting stuffy and a brief pause while windows are opened will be helpful. If, when all is progressing smoothly, you see students who have been attentively taking notes suddenly look up with expressions of bewilderment, probably you have made some obvious slip, reversed the meaning by using a negative instead of a positive, or telescoped your words, or pulled one of the boners which occasionally enliven a lecture inadvertently. If, after some noise or interruption, you see some of the students frantically consulting their neighbors' notebooks you will realize that they have missed a point and you will repeat it. Since your genuine interest in the students extends beyond their response to your lecturing, you will see that Glotz, A. Z., '51, who has just returned from the infirmary, still looks ill and you will make a mental note to see that he has help in making up what he has lost; you will observe that Yates, J. B., '52, is having difficulty seeing the board from the rear row and will make a mental note to have him shifted to the front.

There are other aspects of your presentation, of the delivery of your lectures to which you will give heed. Your objective is to transmit to the students certain knowledge and understanding quickened into vitality by your own sincere interest and contagious enthusiasm. You are striving for effective presentation rather than for impassioned oratory. To be natural and sincere in this effectiveness is the important requisite. The criteria by which to decide whether to use this or that technique in your lecturing are chiefly whether this or that helps or hinders the effectiveness thereof from the standpoint of teaching. Therefore, if you have the accent and peculiarities of speech of the Deep South, or of Down East, or of the Middle West, and begin your teaching in New York or even Boston, do not be concerned and do not let even the jibes of critics make you self-conscious. Differences in accent and pronunciation are minor; they do not hinder your lecturing and they will gradually change. Concentrate instead on correcting the errors or habits of speech which do hinder the effectiveness of your presentation.

The clumsy constructions, the grammatical faults, the faulty references, you will, of course, endeavor earnestly to avoid. Yet remember that although your carefully considered and painstakingly revised writing, if thus marred, is judged severely, there is, quite rightly, great leniency toward similar errors in a spontaneous and vigorous lecture. Despite your care, you will be astonished occasionally by errors you hear yourself commit in the heat of lecturing when your thoughts outdistance your words. These are not so detrimental as you might fear and certainly not so injurious as are errors of fact or misleading statements which firmly establish misunderstanding.

Of all the factors which contribute to effective lecturing, your attitude—indeed, your spirit—is outstandingly important. Your interest and enthusiasm are the essential ingredients without which a lecture is lifeless. If you yourself are not interested in the material which you are presenting, and not enthusiastic over the qualities, significances, implications, and potentialities you are interpreting, how can you expect four hundred or even four students to find much of interest in the subject or see much of significance in its implications? But, if you have this interest and this enthusiasm, the student is quickened and stimulated and gains more from your teaching. If, moreover, you are interested not only in the subject but in teaching the subject, and interested in the students not only as the audience of your lecture but as individuals to whose development you gladly contribute, then the students, and the effectiveness of your teaching, benefit. Your naturalness and poise, and the inner spiritual qualities of which these are the expression, are of prime importance.

Do not try to play a part or put on an act in your lecturing; do not strive to impress the students with knowledge or understanding or other qualities you do not possess—be more concerned with developing those qualities. From various subtle and unconscious sources the student is analyzing, appraising, and evaluating you. The extent and penetration of this evaluation differ among individuals, but the total of it, in even a small class of twenty or thirty at the selected level of college and university, is highly effective. It is enlightening to realize that while you are lecturing the student is not only gaining an understanding of the subject but is also gaining an understanding of you and is deciding that you will be strict but fair in your grading, that you are honorable in your dealing with students, that you would give him sound counsel to help him decide whether to go into medicine or teaching. How students do this, when your lecture has had no reference whatever to such matters but has dealt, for example, strictly with photosynthesis, is of interest, but need not be discussed here.

You will realize, therefore, that your concern is not only to make your lecture ready for comprehension and evaluation but to make yourself ready as well. If your attitude toward lecturing to your class is that of enthusiastically doing your best to present material you sincerely believe is interesting and worth while, rest assured that you need feel no concern over the student's appraisal of you. You need not be austerely formal. If you would naturally present some point in a humorous or colorful way, go ahead and do so, for the students will sense that this is genuine and unaffected, and the point will be vivid and memorable to them. Here, as in other aspects of lecturing, the criterion of acceptability is whether this procedure helps or hinders the effectiveness of your teaching, not whether some bearded bellwether prowling the corridor resents this appreciative response from students who endure his own lectures in unresponsive silence.

Immediately after lecturing you will probably feel worn and weary from the reaction, for you have been under strain and have expended a tremendous amount of energy. If, however, you take even a few moments to sit quietly alone and think back over the lecture, you will find it is still fresh in your mind for objective scrutiny. You will see that in general it was successful in coverage and content, in clarity and emphasis, but you will remember that you slighted this point by overemphasizing one of less importance, that you took too long in your description of a process and hence hurried too rapidly through the necessary explanation of it, that you failed to bring out the significance of an aspect in its relation to something covered in a previous lecture. Even though the pressure of your schedule permits you only a brief interval for such retrospective reviews, you will find them enlightening and advantageous, for they will enable you in your next lecture to correct these inadequacies and will contribute steadily to improving the effectiveness of your lecturing as week after week goes by. If your schedule permits, and if appropriate facilities are available, you will gain humbling enlightenment and invaluable assistance from playing back and carefully studying the unprejudiced verbatim recordings of inexorable wire recorders or phonograph transcriptions.

Also, if you are staunch souls who can take it as well as dish it out, you will profit by giving a large class an opportunity to evaluate the content and presentation of the lectures as well as the effectiveness of other aspects of your course by filling in anonymous questionnaires. While these will lack the critical maturity of an older and more experienced audience, their uninhibited directness and blunt frankness will be revealing and informative. Taken as a whole they will be helpful to you in your efforts to improve your lecturing, especially in the illuminating spotlight they turn on the mannerisms or habits of which you, under the strain of lecturing, have been unaware. Students are sure to note, for example, such habits as pacing back and forth, rocking from heel to toe, breaking up pieces of chalk, aimlessly moving books around on the table, or jingling keys and coins in the pockets. The quantity and intensity of their reactions will give you adequate basis for applying your own essential criterion and judging whether such mannerisms are of negligible importance or whether they detract from your lecturing. Also their reactions will give you the comforting reassurance that your interest and enthusiasm outweigh minor inadequacies, thus encouraging you in your continued efforts to improve.

You will find it helpful, in your periodic quizzes or tests, to direct an occasional question specifically at some point which you have covered carefully in a recent lecture, and then to study the answers as an index to the effectiveness of your presentation of that point. Guided by the answers of the class as a whole, compared with those of your students who are especially keen in comprehension and effective in expression, you can estimate to what extent you were successful and can plan such improving modifications as may be indicated.

Steadily, as you continue developing the effectiveness of your lecturing, your confidence, poise, and maturity will strengthen; your mastery of the subject as well as of its presentation will increase; your lectures will be worth hearing.

GROUP DISCUSSION

When you come to consider the advisability of using group discussions in your teaching, you will naturally weigh their advantages and disadvantages, consider the general requirements which must be met if they are to serve effectively, and think over the ways in which you can best fulfill your functions and obligations.

For the student, the method of group discussion has certain

very definite advantages. Chiefly it induces him to participate and contribute to a far greater extent than is possible in other procedures. In formal lectures he is at the receiving end, prevented from contributing and usually so busy absorbing and recording that his participation in the development of concepts or ideas is much restricted. In a laboratory, his direct study of the material and his experimentation gives him stimulating participation and, to the extent that the attitude of the teacher, or the aptitude of the laboratory assistant and the congeniality of his associates permit informal discussion, he also has opportunity to contribute. But group discussion requires his taking part and contributing his own ideas and interpretations. Moreover, it helps to clarify his comprehension and understanding of the points under discussion. Perhaps from the lectures or the text he gained an inadequate impression, or indeed, even an erroneous conception, of the matter. If so, as he and his fellows contribute their points of view, misconceptions are straightened out, additional aspects are added, and the point is fully developed, clarified, and understood. Also there is for the student the advantageous effect of the impact of interpretations and points of view other than his own. One student will have a certain point of view which seems to him the only one possible, yet in group discussions he becomes aware that others, who heard the same lectures, read the same text, and reviewed the same literature, regard the matter very differently. Furthermore, discussion fosters the engendering of additional ideas because the student's concentration on the topic under the stimulus of the interchange of ideas and the catalytic effect of the development of an interesting train of thought, leads to new ideas; suddenly the student sees—since this and that are so, then something else must follow. Finally, discussion gives the student practice in expressing himself effectively, for on this his contributive participation will depend. Although students differ greatly in this capacity, in general most of them are helped by this practice and all of them will profit by the opportunity to strengthen their articulateness, their ability to express ideas clearly and effectively in informal discussion.

From the viewpoint of the teacher, the group discussion has the strong advantage of never requiring the many long hours of painstaking preparation which are necessary for effective lecturing. Yet it places considerable responsibility on the teacher, for while discussion occasionally will progress effectively even though he merely looks on approvingly, usually his leadership, stimulus, and guidance will be required.

The disadvantages of group discussion should also be weighed against the advantages. One serious disadvantage, of course, lies in the limitation of numbers; it is impracticable to carry on such a discussion with general participation by most of the students in a group of more than ten or twelve. Hence, even a moderate-sized class of thirty or forty must be divided into three or four groups for discussion, with proportionate demands for adequate time and teaching staff. Also, in the natural sciences at least, group discussion usually involves getting away from the fundamental source of information, the material itself, and necessarily deals with concepts, theories, and ideas to such a level of abstraction as to lose force; or else, if it is purposively centered on the material, the ground could be covered more effectively by observation or experiment in the laboratory. Moreover, group discussion is open to the danger of fostering a certain superficial glibness and putting a premium on ability to talk volubly *about* a subject without demanding much direct knowledge or understanding of the thing itself. This, of course, is disadvantageous only if the topic is concerned with things which have extensional reality. Perhaps one of the most valuable by-products of group discussions under your guidance will be that the students may learn to distinguish between true effectiveness in developing a topic (as maps explain an actual territory) and mere facility in tossing back and forth words about words, about feelings about words about ideas, or in pouring forth the jargon, the cant, the gobbledygook, the clichés, the slanted emphases, the presymbolic utterances that arouse only reactions and feelings rather than thought.

If group discussion is to serve effectively as a means of teaching, certain requirements must be met, and the part you as teachers play in this—the guidance, stimulus, and control you contribute—will be highly important. Perhaps the most obvious requirement is that the topic be favorable for group discussion.

It is useful, therefore, to have your topic somewhat controversial in nature, and profitable to have it follow after a lecture in which you presented a theory or concept that permits different interpretations, or to have it originate from reviews of scientific articles which are not in agreement. Yet it should be one that does not doom the discussion to pinwheel pyrotechnics which, however brilliant and scintillating, merely go round and round in circles. On the contrary, it should permit progressive development of a line of reasoning or a train of thought which broadens understanding and clarifies comprehension even if it does not settle the matter for all time. Another obvious requirement, since participation by the students is essential, is that the students should have something to contribute, some knowledge, background, or experience that is pertinent.

Still another requirement is that the contributive participation of the students in the group should be as general as possible. This places heavy responsibility on you, since students differ greatly in initiative, confidence, articulate expression, and other qualities which contribute to their readiness of speech, as well as in the receptivity, quickness of comprehension, and fertility of thought which enables them to profit by the give and take of discussion. Indeed in your first discussional sessions, you will be reminded more than once of Omar's observation: "Some loquacious vessels were, and some listened perhaps, but never spoke at all." The ebullient extrovert whose self-confident loquacity has been fostered by the progressive school will be eagerly ready to express himself immediately and at length on every point which comes up. Perhaps nevertheless this will prove helpful in starting the discussion. Perhaps he will activate others, usually less ready, by arousing their opposition. Perhaps he thinks quickly and clearly, expresses himself effectively, enjoys taking part in developing ideas, and in general is a strong asset in group discussion. Perhaps his urge is more for self-expression than for expression of constructive ideas so that he overwhelms the train of thought. In any case it is your responsibility to ensure that his participation helps rather than hinders the effectiveness and value of the discussion for the group as a whole.

In contrast there is at the other extreme the silent student sitting inconspicuously in the corner, interested in the subject and mentally responding to the discussion with his own contributive ideas, but handicapped by a diffidence which hinders his open participation so that he becomes discouragingly frustrated as he sees others present the very ideas he was developing before he can bring himself to speak. Obviously the discussion procedure will not yield much of value for such a student, nor will his potentialities be useful unless you tactfully and unobtrusively draw him into the discussion. Not only for those representing these two extremes, but also for the diverse and less extreme types of students who make up the bulk of the class, your guidance and control of the discussion are highly important. Clearly, then, the most essential requirement is that you as the teacher, in addition to your knowledge of the subject, have the qualities of enthusiastic leadership and of understanding on which the effectiveness of a group discussion will depend. It is your responsibility not only to make certain that the topic is favorable in nature and adapted to the knowledge and experience of the students, but also to ensure that the atmosphere is unforced and informal and that your guidance fosters the exchange of ideas, the constructive interaction of different points of view, the productive participation of the whole group. If you are reasonably successful in achieving these things you will find group discussions can serve as a useful supplement to other teaching procedures.

EXAMINATIONS

From your own experience as students you undoubtedly have some very definite opinions of examinations from the viewpoint of the examinee—call him the victim, patient, subject, recipient, or what you will. As teachers your point of view now changes to that of the examiner and you will have the opportunity to see for yourselves whether this newly assumed position is better or worse. In considering examinations from the viewpoint of teachers, your first need is to determine what their purpose is to be. You, of course, are trying to secure a dependable evaluation, both quantitative and qualitative, of the knowledge and understanding the student has gained from the course. The reason for this evaluation is twofold, first, it is one of the acceptable bases on which you can appropriately establish the final grade required by the educational system of which you are a part; second, it aids you toward appraising the effectiveness of your teaching.

Since examinations have these definite objectives, we are concerned with the means by which they may be attained and should consider such pertinent matters as the nature and utility of different types of tests, the suitability of various types of questions, and the requirements to be met in preparing the examination paper and grading the students' answers. With the various types of tests you are familiar from your own experience. Aside from the intelligence tests and aptitude tests which have more general or more basic purpose, the types chiefly used in college courses are two: the practical or laboratory tests and the more widely applicable, formal written examinations. The practical tests confront the student with specimens or other suitable material and require him to give certain information derived from his study. If carefully devised and skillfully managed, such tests effectively reveal the student's ability to observe, interpret, and comprehend, and show his skill in employing techniques of manipulation and experimentation. Such tests usually have the disadvantage of being so limited in scope that they do not disclose the student's grasp of larger concepts and broader generalities, but they can be extended to accomplish this. They have, however, the very grave disadvantage that their heavy demands on time and staff render them impracticable for large classes. You will find them very helpful in teaching the natural sciences when the size of the class and the nature of the material are favorable.

The formal examination, which includes the hour, mid-semester, and final examinations customary in most college teaching, are of very wide applicability and hence all too familiar to you. It will be helpful, therefore, for you to consider the requirements involved in the preparation of such examinations; the importance of coverage and emphasis, and the applicability of the various types of questions to your needs. The emphasis and proportionate representation demand your consideration, for your examination cannot possibly encompass all the material covered in the course.

There were inevitably certain facts, processes, and concepts more significant and important than others, hence you will stress these, trying to proportion the emphasis and scope so that it is justly representative. If one aspect of major importance occupied one quarter of the course and another, far less important, was covered with suitable brevity in part of one lecture, you will not allot to the former only a small part of one question, with a value of two points, and devote to the less important aspect a whole question, with a value of fifteen points. To do this would be unjust to the student who has every right to assume that the proportionate emphasis you gave the subject matter in the course was indicative of the actual importance of the various aspects covered.

You will endeavor, also, to have the length and the difficulty of the examination proportionate to the time available, to limit your requirements so that the average student will be able to complete the examination in the three hours or so allotted him. In the first final examination you prepare you will be guided by your experience with the shorter hour examinations throughout the course, but if in doubt you will find it far better, from the viewpoint of satisfactory grading, to have your final examination too short rather than too long; for, in an overlong examination, evaluating how much of the incompleteness is due to the inadequacy of the students and how much to your excessive demands is distressingly difficult. As you learn to gauge the time required so that it fits the allotted three hours do not be disturbed unduly by the debonair disparagement of those who say, "That was a pushover; I breezed through it in an hour and forty minutes!" or by the laments of others who complain, "That was brutal, I didn't have a chance!" Go over their respective books with care, for you will probably be able to help the speed boy to realize that his answers should have been more extensive and to guide the plodder toward closer adherence to the essential points required.

You will give serious thought to the types of questions you use and to their exact form and wording as well as their clarity and freedom from misinterpretation. The two main categories of questions, the objective and the essay, are familiar to you and you have very definite opinions as to their applicability. The objective questions, whether they be of the multiple choice, or the true or false, appropriate or inappropriate type, are all in a sense modifications of the multiple choice principle: the student, with various possibilities presented to him, must mentally achieve brief judgments as the basis of his selection. These questions have the advantage that their brevity permits covering such a large area of subject matter with such large numbers of pin-point choices that the total is favorable for percentage evaluation, and also that they can be graded rapidly and accurately by machines. The essay question has the advantage of being highly versatile, suitable for any type of question from brief definitions to long explanations, interpretations, or descriptions. It is especially adapted to covering broad concepts with which the objective type cannot successfully cope and it gives advantageous evidence of the student's ability to express his knowledge effectively. Which type of question you use will depend somewhat on the tradition and custom of the department in which you teach, somewhat on the size and nature of your course, but chiefly on which you consider most effectively contributes to the purposes of your examination. Incidentally, on referring the matter to the students I have had both types chosen without heavy preference. Fortunately, investigations carried on at such centers as Teachers College of Columbia have tested and compared the effectiveness of different types of examination questions and provide helpful information as to their general utility and special applicability.

You will consider also the two main attitudes toward the tactics of examinations, the school of thought which regards the examination as yielding a representative sample of sausage stuffing and the "make 'em think" school which endeavors to obtain the brilliant electrical discharge of thought. Most examination questions are of the sausage-sampling type, and you will find that its wider applicability and greater effectiveness with the majority of your students give this type definite advantages. Also, much of one's knowledge depends on memory rather than creative thought and despite the criticisms of this type of examination, the question arises, "How else can you tell whether the student absorbed this material and made it part of his mental equipment?" If the student does give it back to you, he must have had it, temporarily at least. Granted that it will fade and grow dim at a rate dependent on various factors, yet for those three hours at least the student possessed that knowledge and could apply it effectively.

The school of thought that tries to make the student give convincing evidence of constructive thinking in his examination is led by this worthy ideal to undertake a severely difficult task. It is extremely hard for the teacher to devise a question that unavoidably requires creative thought. Usually a student who has a good memory, strong association of ideas, and the ability to express himself effectively, will assemble remembered bits from here and there, organize them to fit the pattern of your question and with some effective writing achieve an acceptable approximation of the type of answer you had in mind. Before you heavily weight an examination with this type of question you should yourself try answering the questions you have devised, noting whether the time required is well within the allotted portion of the period and having someone else appraise them for evidences of constructive creative thinking. Also, you should remember that the student taking an examination is under the strain of meeting an inexorable deadline and of working in the unfavorable environment of an examination room. Productive thought cannot be turned on like a water-faucet under even the most favorable circumstances—as all of you who have written even a brief straightforward scientific paper for publication well realize. Certainly it cannot thus be turned on during an examination.

Furthermore, in the preparation of examinations, never lose your adherence to your purpose of securing an adequate and dependable basis for evaluating the knowledge and understanding the student has gained from the course. You and the student are not playing against each other in a game involving skill, bluff, finesse, and chance; rather you are endeavoring to take an estimative inventory of what the student has in stock and of how effectively he uses it, while he is endeavoring to display as much as he can as effectively as he can in the very limited time available.

Finally, in the preparation of your examination, you will subject each question to careful scrutiny for clarity and freedom from ambiguity. You will be astonished at the unexpected interpretations which will be given the questions you felt confident were straightforwardly simple and completely clear. Each year, after you have painstakingly worked out each question until it cannot possibly be misinterpreted, some genius will give it a new twist, a derived direction for which you were totally unprepared, yet for which you can see some justification. Each year you will profit by this and render your next questions more completely free from any possible ambiguity. This process takes much time and thought but becomes rather interesting nevertheless.

By now you have begun to realize that preparing an examination is for the teacher as grim a task as taking an examination is for the student. But the most dismal aspect of this whole happy nightmare is that the task becomes increasingly difficult as the years go by. The first couple of years it will require about three hours, approximately the amount of time the average-to-slow student requires to answer it, but in subsequent years it takes longer and longer and becomes more and more difficult. This is because you have conscientiously endeavored to cover the same general subject matter with adequate coverage and justly proportionate emphasis, yet with great pains to avoid getting into the rut of using the same questions over and over until the students, after calculating study of carefully preserved examinations of the past, will offer odds of 9 to 2, with no takers, on which questions will come up this year. Of course the subject matter of your course is ever developing, changing, and progressing, but this involves chiefly the steady addition of more factual material and the altering of interpretations here and concepts there, rather than any drastic modification of basic substance and general emphasis. Even the occasional revolutionary upheavals, such as the recent one in nuclear physics, are more likely to result in the establishment of new advanced courses than to achieve sweeping changes in the prerequisite courses at a lower level.

There are certain ameliorating or remedial measures which may be helpful. You can shift the viewpoint in a question, yet still have it cover much the same ground with much the same proportionate emphasis. You can, for example, in covering the important matter of photosynthesis, in one examination stress the part played by the sun's energy, in another you can emphasize the part played by chlorophyll, in another the part played by carbon dioxide, water, and mineral salts. If you wish, you may use the provocative type of question such as, "Explain the Biblical statement, 'All flesh is grass,' in its application to the means by which the energy of sunlight is made available to animals." The answer will necessarily have the same general content, for the only way in which the energy of the sun can be transformed into the potential energy of plant substance and hence into animals is by photosynthesis. But as one examination follows another in the inexorable course of the years, you will find that, despite your ingenuity and resourcefulness, the preparation of examinations becomes increasingly an ordeal. You will understand, then, why some teachers are driven to the trick devices and catch questions which may have annoyed you in the past. To such devious devices, which are unjust to the relative weight and proportionate emphasis of the subject matter of the course, and completely unfair to the student, you will never stoop.

Grading examination books is drudgery of the most dismal depths. No consciousness of fulfilling a necessary obligation can lessen its grimness, nor can the occasional boners or the rare bits of humor do much to alleviate its severity. No interest in ascertaining the effectiveness of your presentation can mitigate its woes; no gratification over evidences of your success in teaching can alleviate the asperity of its demands. Its humor is thoroughly atrabilious without tinge of sanguine. The burden of its drudgery is increased by your conscientious awareness of your responsibility to the student, your realization that in some cases this one examination may tip the balance of decision as to whether he is dropped or allowed to continue, or whether he receives a sorely needed fellowship or not. One way out of this depressing predicament is to use the objective type of examination, whether or not this best meets the needs of the students and the course, for this type—at an appropriate charge, of course—can be mechanically and accurately graded by I.B.M. machines in about the time you require to sort out the books and start doggedly on the first question. Once you have experienced the narcotic relief of this robot rescue you will probably become a confirmed addict, at least you will understand how the tentacles of the I.B.M. Corporation have gained such a powerful hold on our educational institutions.

The other method of coping with this predicament is to do it the hard way by means of the slow and imperfect machine of your own mentality. You will find it helpful to break down the examination questions into their component parts of the essential points required, because it is far less strain to make many small accurate judgments, many single item evaluations, than to make the comprehensive and broadly discerning judicious evaluations which long complicated answers require. In other words, if you break down an examination of five questions of equal value and approximately equal length, into 100 single points, 20 to each question, you will find it less difficult and fatiguing to perform the 100 simple judgments necessary for just appraisal of the individual points than to achieve the accurate, comprehensive appraisal of each of the five long questions. Indeed, it will be helpful to you to facilitate this process by originally preparing the examination in a form that will meet these requirements. Also you will find it helpful to evaluate, correct, and grade the examination books not book by book but question by question, because to continue judging and evaluating fairly along the same generally related line of thought is less strain than to concentrate on one line of thought in question 1, then shift to another very different one in question 2, and then to another in question 3. To avoid the possibility that your grading may become increasingly severe as continued evaluation of the same items of the same question may tend to sharpen your perception of errors and to make you more exacting, you will find it helpful first to make a preliminary survey of the answers to each question in ten representative examination books and from this to formulate, point by point with appropriate values, the scope and emphasis essential to the answer, and then to use this standard as your measure in grading. Furthermore you will find it helpful to do your grading in several relatively short sessions of uninterrupted concentration, rather than in one or two long sessions of many hours of exhausting, long-continued pressure.

If your course is relatively small you will, when necessary, singlehandedly carry the full burden of grading examinations, but usually you will be able to reinforce your efforts with the help of assistants or associates. In critical cases where much depends on the examination, you will be wise to have others check your judgment and your evaluations on points that are doubtful, as well as all the numerical calculations of your grading. If the course is a large one, you and your associates and assistants will share the burden, and careful organization of the work to use the available aptitudes and skill to best advantage and to coördinate the whole effort, will helpfully expedite progress. In any case, you, as the one in charge of the course, are the one who carries the responsibility to make certain that all the calculations are checked and rechecked until you are sure they are correct. This applies to every step, from the addition of the points for each item in each question, through the calculation of the proportionate weights of the laboratory marks, the quizzes, the examinations, and any other components, to the totaling of the final numeral values and the translation of these into equivalent letter grades. If someone criticizes the distribution curve of your final grades because it does not follow the Chicago or Columbia standard but is slightly skewed toward the *A*'s, it is your responsibility to demonstrate to him that the earnest efforts of a considerable proportion of the class, who returned with definite objectives from some years in foxholes and fighting tops, have legitimately skewed the curve without benefit of any laxity in your standards. If, despite all your careful supervision and insistence on thorough checking of calculations, any errors do occur, it is your responsibility to acknowledge and rectify them. A couple of years ago such an error occurred in calculating the final total of one of the students in our large elementary course in biology, one component being omitted from the total in spite of repeated checking of all the calculations. Fortunately the intuition of the student's fiancée refused to accept the unworthy *B* of the final grade, so with this assistance from romance, the error was discovered and the necessary apologies made to the student, to the financée, and to registrars and deans. In this instance the bitterness of responsibility was ameliorated by the fact that the timely discovery prevented any serious injustice.

Year after year, as you go through the laborious process of preparing and grading examinations and carry out the even more difficult task of evaluating the student's achievement in terms of a final grade, you will inevitably give considerable thought to the function and purpose of examinations and to their utility and effectiveness. If your class has been small and you have been in such constant and close touch with all of the students that you thoroughly know not only their accomplishment in your course, but also their personality patterns and their aptitudes and potentialities, you may find the examination has been of minor and secondary utility. If, however, the class has been a large one of 300 or more, so that for your knowledge of the students you must perforce depend on secondhand information, you will find that the examinations play a very important part in your evaluation. You will find yourself wondering precisely what essential qualities and abilities are measured by examinations and how accurate is the measurement thereof. You will question whether a student's potentialities for creative scientific research can be evaluated by the customary methods of examination. You will speculate why man, who has devised instruments of exquisite precision for perceiving and recording infinitesimally minute qualities, quantities, forces, and potentialities in the external world, has not contrived comparable instruments to measure even the larger and less subtle qualities within himself. Such thoughts will deepen your philosophy and increase your humbleness of spirit, but examinations, with the persistence of the Paradox of Evil, will still be part of your teaching life.

VARIETIES OF TEACHING METHOD

ANDRÉ MORIZE

Chapter V
TEACHING THE HUMANITIES

Some vital and practical aspects of teaching the Humanities. Preparation and delivery of the vivid lecture. The Seminar a voyage of discovery. Planning a course to fit the calendar. Previews of lectures and courses recommended. Discussion of examination questions which call for critical analysis of "to what extent and for what reasons something appears to be true or erroneous."

When I look at the impressive array of titles in this book, and when I think, by contrast, of the topic I have been assigned, I experience a feeling of frustration. No chance for me to deal with profound ideas or with the philosophy of education. My task implies abnegation and the spirit of sacrifice. In fact, my role is essentially that of a "demonstrator" of the type you find in department stores when they want to present a new product to prospective customers. This is exactly the limit of my ambition in this chapter. If you ask me why I have the right to undertake this discussion, I would say that my only titles are: first, that I love teaching; second, that I am not without some experience in this kind of activity.

So what I hope to put before you is simply how to *prepare,* how to *organize,* and how to *deliver* a lecture in a classroom, especially in the field of humanities. I should like, however, to make two preliminary observations.

The first is that, at the very first minute you face your audience, your main preoccupation should be to establish a "human contact" between the one who teaches and those who expect to be taught. There must never be between your class and you that sort of empty space or chilly zone which is disastrous for the atmosphere of your lecture. You may ask, "How does one establish this contact?" Of course, there is no trick about it, no specific rule. Nevertheless, it is, to me, the very essence of teaching. Shall I dare give my true feeling in the matter? To me it is essentially a question of love, of love for our work. Our students have a keen perception of the presence or absence of this factor, and, therefore, one of the secrets of your success in the classroom is, in the first minute, to "get the spark" and establish that sort of magnetism between the teacher and his audience. Either the "magnet" works, or it does not. When it fails, God help us! There is nothing more painful than to be, for fifty-five minutes, face to face with a class when this contact is not established. The real cause for such a failure is that the teacher does not create the impression that he "loves" to be there. He certainly deserves pity, rather than sympathy, when he seems to be coming to his desk as if he were attending a funeral. Either out of shyness or for some other reason, some teachers seem to avoid that direct, immediate, and refreshing contact—and this is the end, right at the beginning. Indeed, the first requirement in classroom lecturing is to build that sort of "gangplank" between our audience and ourselves.

Now here is my second comment: there is a great difference in technique between lecturing before a large class and lecturing for a small group of students.

Is your audience large? Then, the technique is that of the regular lecture, in the broadest sense of the term, which I shall discuss later on. On the contrary, before a small group—and very often in the humanities we have to deal with small gatherings—a lecture should in fact never be a lecture. Of course, your talk must be prepared, organized, thought-out with at least the same care that you exercise when you have to lecture before a large audience. However, the method of presenting the subject is entirely different. It must be from beginning to end a collective and coöperative undertaking.

Physical details are not unimportant in this matter. If you happen to be in an institution where you have a word to say about the rooms that will be assigned to you, and if you know that your class or "section" will be very limited in number, do your best to be assigned a small room in proportion to your audience. I know of nothing more dismal and discouraging than to have before you a wide, empty space with a few students scattered here and there. Remember there is a tendency among students to sit in the back of the room, just as in most meeting places the galleries begin to fill while the front of the room remains empty. Bring your flock right in front of you. Speak not to them, but among them. When I have a small class, I often like to stand in the middle of the room, to go from one student to another and give each one, to some extent, the impression that for a few minutes he or she has my undivided attention. It is a very good way to win them.

Of course you have a clear outline of your talk; you know where you want to go, and how. This means a certain amount of "acting": by asking questions and directing the discussion, you must get the students not to follow, but to *create* the outline you have prepared. As you go, you write on the blackboard the elements of the outline, using a sort of Socratic method which, I know only too well, is not always easy. If you don't keep your hands on the wheel and your eyes on your watch, the whole thing may run away from you. But if you are careful, you will get what you want, when you want it. The students will gladly follow the path which you have decided to follow.

May I open here a brief parenthesis? It has to do with the practice of "asking questions" in a classroom. Now, there are two ways of asking questions—a good one and a bad one.

The bad one consists in addressing one of your students, individually, and saying: "Now, Brown (or Jones), please tell me . . ." Believe me, this is enough. The rest of the class will return to a nice state of indifference—for a few seconds, everybody will feel safe. Brown or Jones is the only one who is running any risk at all. This is the wrong method.

The good one is to say, "Now, I am going to ask you a question . . ." and to mention no name. There is a second of general suspense, every student on his toes. Then you say, "Well, Brown, what do you think? . . ." So everybody had to listen to the question, to get ready to answer, to keep awake. A very small but capital "trick" of good teaching.

Again, thinking of small class lecturing, when you have reached a "turning point," a partial or final conclusion, make a stop—give the impression that there is something to be summed up, threads to be gathered. "Now, we have discovered this . . . Here is a point that deserves our notice . . ." Then, in your own words, you give about the same conclusion which you would give in a more formal lecture—and everybody will feel that we have gotten somewhere together. Always reserve the last minutes for the "grand finale," for that conclusion which you must have very carefully prepared.

Now we can come to our specific subject—lecturing in a classroom. It divides itself, logically, into three parts: (1) how to prepare, (2) how to organize, and (3) how to deliver a lecture. In these three parts we shall find the basic principles of our technique.

PREPARATION

Suppose you are to give a lecture on this or that subject in the field of humanities. Do I dare say it? The first requirement is to know what you are going to talk about. How trite! How needless to say! It may be so. At the same time, I believe it is a point that must be deeply impressed upon the minds of our young would-be lecturers. To teach a little, you must know a lot. If you do not, don't try to lecture, go home and learn. If you appear before a class with material hastily gathered the night before, pilfered from various books (and preferably those which the students are not supposed to have in their hands)—if you bring along exactly what you need for one hour, your lecture will sound hopelessly thin, or empty. To be "one lesson ahead of the class" is a tragedy—

for you and for the students. They must have the impression that you draw from a reserve, a surplus of knowledge, which (without your trying to crush them!) is far above and beyond their own supply.

Moreover, remember here that you never succeed in "bluffing" the students. It may work once or twice; it may help on certain days when you are not quite "up to it." But it does not pay, and you had better foster no illusions about it. In the preparation of what you plan to offer your student audience, *conscience* is an indispensable requisite.

To prepare your lecture, you must of course use tools and implements; those you must make known to your students. In other words, as your course goes on, you have to supply them with bibliographies and useful material. This requires the utmost care and caution on your part, if you wish really to keep up the enthusiasm, as well as the esteem, of your students. Of course, nothing is easier than to deluge your class with a tremendous amount of bibliography. Anybody who has the slightest knowledge of his field can always, within twenty minutes, gather fifty or sixty titles and then give them to the class. Now, you know perfectly well that they will never touch that mass of material. Do not try to dazzle them, try to help them. Give them only what is essential. Tell them that, if they want more, you are ready to supply it; but make it clear that what you give *is* essential. Be sure also that you never recommend any book or document that the students cannot reach. The question of the "reserve shelf" is of great importance, and to watch it carefully is a vital part of your task.

Next, you have to prepare your notes for your lecture. Never write out a lecture from A to Z: to do so is the best way to "kill" a good lecture. If, for some reason, you feel that this particular lecture is so important that you have to write it out, all right, do it. But never take your full manuscript to the classroom, and never try to memorize it. In such cases, to have written it from beginning to end will help you and deposit in your memory a supply of words, phrases, imagery. But you must free yourself from your written text; use it, but never be a slave to it.

Prepare your lecture on "notes," on small or large sheets, as you prefer; but be sure that each note or sheet constitutes an independent unit, corresponding to *one* paragraph or sub-paragraph of your lecture. Never turn a page in the middle of a sentence. In short, preserve your independence, so that if you are pressed by time, you can omit one page or one fragment. This is why your notes must be absolutely clear and always in perfect order.

Never repeat in your lectures exactly what your students will find in their handbooks: a temptation to which too many teachers unfortunately yield. Some of them try to excuse themselves by mentioning "a fresh approach" to a subject. This is illusion and nonsense. Of course, we are not suppposed or obliged to bring something truly "original" to each class. But if we know exactly what the books and manuals have to offer—if we have trained our students to study them *before*, not *after*, our lecture—then we do not have to "repeat." We are at liberty to throw the spotlight on this or that point, to supplement, illustrate, submit controversial or especially interesting points. Our teaching will be creative, not repetitious.

ORGANIZATION

This problem of organization consists, in my opinion, of three different points: one is the *outline* of your lecture; the second is that of the *auxiliary aids* to classroom lecturing; the third is that of *timing*.

As to the construction of the outline, the problem is too simple, too elementary to be insisted upon. Whatever I might have to say, you heard in your first year of English composition. This I know very well, though I also know that many young teachers confuse the numbering of their paragraphs with the systematic construction of a logical outline. In short, they too often forget to give their lectures these three things that seem so natural, but are so rare: a beginning, a middle, and an end.

Some people feel a sort of physical need in respect to this principle of organization. Some others are perfectly happy without it, and you must know some of them. And so, while they are talking, they go forward, and they go backward, and suddenly they have a bright idea, and off they go in another direction. It may be charming in after-dinner conversation; in classroom lecturing it is disastrous. I have known in my career a respectable colleague who was very particular about supplying his students with a printed "outline" of his lecture; but, as he had no idea of what an outline actually means, he always used to prepare his outline *after* he had written his lecture from beginning to end. The result was rather painful. This reminds me of the story told by Georges Duhamel, when he was watching a young native mason in Tunisia, who was building a house. "That's a nice house you are building," he said. "Show me the blueprint. I'd like to see how it's going to look." "Comment tu veux que je te montre le plan?" the young Arab retorted. "La maison n'est pas finie." I have known more than one lecturer who could not show his outline because his lecture was not written yet.

Have an "introduction": a few words to connect your lecture with the preceding class or lesson; then give the "auxiliary" data, bibliography, chronology, and so forth; finally, present a clear definition of the *problem* (not of the subject) for the day. I am convinced that it is always possible to present a topic in the form of a "problem," not of a story to be told, but of an effort to go from the known to the unknown. Nothing will enhance more the value and interest of your lecture.

And then, like the preachers of years and years ago, give the *division* of your subject. Don't be afraid that your lecture, if you do this, will lose some of its artistic value. A lecture is not something to be printed; it is to be heard, and you expect your students to follow it. Therefore, do not hesitate to say, "Our talk will be divided into three parts—Part I . . . , Part II . . . , Part III . . ." And then, please, stick to it. You will notice the expression of relief on the faces of your students!

As to the contents, do not overload your lectures; don't try to give more than you can within fifty or fifty-five minutes. Learn how to "ventilate" your talk, give it "air," and give your listeners a breathing spell here and there.

Always bring the thing to a *conclusion,* which is different from an *end.* A speaker I know well always uses the same formula: "Well, now, gentlemen, my watch tells me that I must bring my remarks to an end." His watch should have nothing to do with it, if his lecture is properly constructed. When you have said what you had to say, simply sum it up, give a sort of stock-taking of what you had to offer, and, if possible, try to open and prepare the way for what will come in the following lecture.

Two auxiliary aids available to most classroom lecturers are especially important—the duplicating machine (mimeograph, hectograph, etc.) and the blackboard. Needless to insist upon them. Suffice it to say that I am a great believer in the advantages of the mimeograph. It is a timesaver and an insurance against many mistakes or misunderstandings—the best way to convey to your students your outlines, a bibliography, a list of names or dates, important quotations, and so forth. You will find on the market some very reliable small machines at reasonable cost. To acquire one is a good investment for a young instructor. As for the blackboard, it is a reliable and useful servant, provided you know how to use it. I apologize for giving such prosaic and minute details, but do you realize that most lecturers who use the blackboard do it in such thin and tiny handwriting that most of the class cannot possibly read it? Do not hesitate to write in larger, very large, letters—from four to six inches high—and you will soon discover how much better it works. And then, when you have inscribed some very precious data, do not stand with back close to the blackboard, masking every word you want your students to add to their notes. The case is not infrequent.

You always have at your disposal a perfect way of testing the efficacy of your preparation and organization of your lectures, and that is simply a look at the notebooks kept by your students. There is no better mirror of the value of your teaching. Do you see pages where the material is clearly distributed, the paragraphs well numbered, titles nicely underscored? Then you can be sure that you have done "a good job." But, alas, if the notebook exhibits nothing but messy and compact pages, no paragraphs, no "air," and a number of illustrations of various kinds in the margins, then you have the merciless proof that your lecture was not good and that you have wasted your own time and that of your students. Try the experiment on your own notebooks, and you will see!

Finally, there is the problem of timing—a most important one. Experience only will teach you how to deal with it. However, the general principle is very simple: you have so much material and so many minutes. You have a detailed outline, your quotations are ready, and so on. Now, you must fit the material within the allotted time. May I suggest a little trick which I have found very convenient. When I have in hand all my notes, I gauge the relative importance of each part or paragraph, and, using a big red or black crayon, I write at the top of the proper page: ¼, ½, ¾, or I insert a slip of colored paper bearing the same symbols. These are my "stop signals," or if you prefer, the signs which tell me where I am and how much time I still have. They tell me whether I am behind or ahead. Now, remember this: you must remain within those time-limits. Omit, abridge, summarize, as you go. But whatever you do, if your lecture lasts from 9:00 to 10:00, at 9:30 you *must* be at the halfway mark, no matter how much you may have to sacrifice. You must have *concluded* when the clock strikes, and without giving the impression that you were pressed by time. And remember that, even if you have to leave out one or two precious paragraphs, the world will go on exactly the same, while your reputation as a teacher will not increase if you have to confess to your inability to "time" your lecture.

DELIVERY

And now, "the time has come"; you must "deliver the goods." There are many things of great importance in this respect, at the same time so obvious that it will be sufficient merely to list them.

Your voice is your tool: learn how to use it. If necessary, go and get the advice of a specialist in the matter. Many young teachers, full of knowledge and enthusiasm, leave their classrooms completely exhausted, simply because they do not know how to spare and manage their voices.

Then you must, in the delivery of your lectures, avoid certain mannerisms often found in young teachers. One is to talk with your hand in front of your mouth: it does not help! Another is a tendency to lecture to an imaginary listener under the desk, instead of looking your audience right in the eye. Still another is to speak always to one side of the audience, ignoring the other side, so that a good part of the class is deprived of the light so abundantly given to the rest. And also there are those who pace up and down the platform behind their desk, like the panther in its cage, untiringly, but very tiring for the audience. We all have such mannerisms: it does not mean that we must not do all we can to get rid of them.

Learn how to use something invaluable in public speaking: I mean silence. Know when to stop; remember that silences and pauses are the punctuation of the spoken word. Just as you paragraph when you write a page, so in your public speaking you paragraph by stopping. Also silence is the best way to get back the attention of your audience if it has a tendency to relax—also to stop any interference from private conversations among students!

Finally, at times, you can very well use some harmless "histrionics," which may bring useful results. Suppose that you are standing in front of your audience, and you have in your lecture three very distinct parts. Why not, for the first paragraph, stand slightly on the left of your desk, quite naturally, and when the moment comes, say, "Well, now, so much for the first point I wanted to discuss . . ." and then move gracefully to the right, and proceed with your second point? And, when you reach your climax, I mean your conclusion, you go back to the center of the desk!

You may smile about such trifling details, and I hope you will. I have hesitated about referring to practices which you may consider very childish. However, I know from experience that they do help; and why not let you read in twenty seconds things that it may take years to learn?

It would be a catastrophe if, after giving you so much advice, I did not reach a "conclusion" to this first aspect of our problem. Here it is: in all this question of the practice of teaching, there is no mystery, no trickery, nothing that a man or a woman of average intelligence cannot discover by himself. Whether you are successful or not in that discovery, your students will teach you. You will acquire that sense of success or failure, which is, for a teacher, the beginning of wisdom. The art of teaching is a technique, just as cooking is a technique and an art. It can easily be learned by experience and by constructive thought. I hope that you will meet with a certain number of failures: each one will be a lesson, if you stop to find in it the occasion of analyzing the reasons why you have failed. Week after week, watching your own practice and that of others, you will improve both your technique and your efficiency, and you will become more and more convinced that all the essentials, all the fundamentals of our work can be summed up in two words: love for what we do, and plain, old-fashioned common sense.

And now, we turn to a discussion of certain strictly practical problems which you will encounter when you launch yourselves in the career of teaching humanities. These are the "chores" we cannot escape.

HOW TO RUN A SEMINAR

Let me say first that there is a "background problem" to this question. You will have to deal with graduate students. This means that you have to create in your teaching an atmosphere entirely different from that of undergraduate work. There is, or there should be, a complete change from one to the other, and the awareness of this difference is the first point you should make clear to your students. The seminar remains to me the very best type of graduate work. This is the place and time to impress upon your students the real nature of the work which they are to undertake. You must make them realize that their task, their goal is no longer to learn, to assimilate, to acquire general ideas, and to get acquainted with the fundamental and general trends of human thought, Western or Eastern. You must lead them to the threshold of a new domain, that of *research* and *discovery*, a very serious and fascinating adventure.

"Research" does not mean going to the library and piling up index cards. Too many of your students will have such a notion. It is your task to open new vistas to them. In our rules and regulations on graduate studies, you will find a very felicitous expression: a Ph.D. thesis, they say, should be "a contribution to knowledge." Please weigh the implication of this statement. Graduate work should mean an effort to start from what is known to reach the unknown. Piling up facts and references is compilation, not discovery. You know the humorous definition: "If you copy one book, it's plagiarism; but if you copy fifty, it's scholarship." This kind of scholarship is precisely what you should avoid, for yourself and for your students. A seminar must be an effort to *discover* and *construct* something new in the field of human knowledge.

This is why there is a profound difference between lecturing and conducting a seminar—a difference not only in "level" but in "technique." It seems to me that the essential principle is that the work must be done not by the instructor but by the students. This, of course, does not mean that the share of the teacher is easier or smaller than the student's. In fact, the teacher's responsibility is heavier than in any other kind of course.

Research presupposes a method, and the knowledge of the indispensable implements and tools. In too many places this fundamental prerequisite is not taken care of. Students wish to enter a seminar who have no idea of the general bibliography of their field, of the use of libraries, and of the methods of investigation which have proved successful in problems of the kind they will have to approach. Do not accept students in a seminar unless they have acquired this preliminary information. In some departments special courses are being provided to teach these elementary methods. If such courses do not exist, see whether you cannot suggest organizing them, or, if worse comes to worst, devote a certain number of hours to the subject and to the exploration of all resources offered by the available libraries. I regret to have to insist on this point, but I have seen too many young men and women groping about in Widener Library, feverishly copying cards from the catalogue trays, without being sure in the least that they have found what they actually need. The amount of time and energy thus wasted is tremendous. Never forget that preliminary but indispensable element—guidance.

Now, assuming, that you have a group of students satisfactorily grounded, how are you going to conduct your seminar?

First, you map out the work. At the first meeting of the group you define the problem. It is advisable to choose one limited in scope, clear cut, without too many implications in which your students may get lost. To a large extent, the success of a seminar depends upon that clarification of the purpose and limitations of the undertaking. Upon this will depend the feeling of achievement which should be the reward of all who have coöperated.

Second, you distribute the various "topics" among your students. You will have better success if you give the students you know to be more alert and better informed the opportunity to be first. They will set a standard for others and raise the level of your seminar. Be careful not to give a student "more than he can chew." It is a question of fairness, as well as of efficiency. Each meeting should give the impression of something complete, well rounded out, a finished product. If you launch your student on an unlimited problem, the discussion of his paper will lead nowhere.

Third, do not fail to have personal consultations in your office with each and every student who is going to take part in the seminar. The purpose is not to tell him what to do, but to make sure that he is on the right track and will not waste time, either his or that of others. I do not mean that you must give him his bibliography. Simply make sure that he has found the essentials and knows where to go.

Fourth, the student presents to the seminar the result of his research. Mind you, I do not say "reads his paper"! We should never allow a student to "read a paper." Let him use all the notes, quotations, facts, and data he wants. Let him have in front of him an outline of his talk—but never allow him to "read." A seminar is not only training in research: it must be also a school of teaching. Our graduate students do not receive enough of this sort of training. They often leave us with a heavy baggage of scholarly knowledge, but what do they do with it in the classroom? So do not hesitate to discuss and criticize the presentation as well as the contents of a student's report. Students will never object if you warn them beforehand and explain that you hope to train them not only in the techniques of research but also in the art of teaching.

Finally, you have discussion and arrive at conclusions. This must come at the end of each meeting, or, if you give the student more than one meeting to present his subject (which I do not consider advisable), at the end of the time devoted to a given "topic." At the last meeting of the seminar, you contribute a general conclusion, making a sort of "inventory" of the results of several weeks or months of coöperative work and setting forth the various "new" points, the "contributions to knowledge" which are the fruition of the seminar.

Once in a while you will find a student paper of real value. Have it revised, rewritten, polished, and do your best to have it or part of it printed in one of our specialized periodicals. Nothing will be, for the members of your seminar, a more encouraging reward.

PROGRAMS FOR COURSES

You who wish to become teachers are destined to "give courses," to conduct classes or "sections." Of course, I wish I could present you with a set of recipes applicable to all possible cases, but this is impossible. How could we lay down general rules in face of the extreme diversity of subjects and of the difference of levels among your students? Each institution, each department, has its traditions and exigencies: these we cannot discuss here. However, no matter what, where, and on what level you are to teach, there are some general suggestions that may not be out of place.

The first problem you will meet is: "How much am I supposed to cover?" and the second question: "How much time have I to cover it?" (I dislike this term "to cover," but it seems to be part of our professional jargon.) This distribution of a certain amount of subject matter over a certain period of time seems to be an easy matter. In reality, it presents difficulties of which you must be aware.

First, you prepare a calendar of the course, showing all the "hours" or "periods" at your disposal. Do not omit the precaution of crossing off all the holidays or recesses. Remember that there are going to be tests or "hour examinations." In short, figure out exactly how many hours are available for actual teaching.

The next step is to make your subject matter fit your calendar. Prepare a first draft of the material you intend to include in your course, without any consideration for the calendar. You divide it into "parts" or "chapters," and you try to gauge the relative importance of the various parts. Finally you "superimpose" your calendar on your general program and attempt to apportion your subject to your calendar, which is easy to say and more difficult to do than a young teacher would believe.

May I list here a few practical suggestions that may, or may not, eventually apply to your particular problems:

1. Always keep a few free or "open" hours to preserve the elasticity and flexibility of your program. You may wish to prolong a discussion, or to add some unforeseen material. It should not upset the whole schedule.

2. Remember that you will have to give tests or "quizzes," and that there will also be some registrar, or dean, or records office that will exact "grades" on a given inflexible date. So, organize your program accordingly. You must have time to read those tests, to return those grades. Also try to subdivide your program in such a way that tests or examinations will come at the end of a definite chapter of your subject; it will be easier to tell your students exactly what you expect from them. As far as possible, avoid setting examinations or quizzes on a Saturday, for various reasons into which I shall not enter. But why insist? All these details experience will teach you when the day comes.

3. On the first page of the program, explain in very clear terms the purpose of the course and the method you intend to follow. Give the time and place of your consultation hours, the location of the reserve shelf, and whatever practical details a student may wish to know. Finally, set forth exactly what you expect of your students—in short, the general discipline of the course. For instance, give the dates on which you expect to receive themes or course papers and then "stick to it" without mercy. This training in promptness and order is part of an education.

4. Have your program mimeographed and give a copy to each student. Make sure that the student inserts it in his notebook. Post one in your classroom and deposit a few others in the library.

Once more I apologize for dealing with such minute details. But I believe that you will some day discover that good and efficient teaching comes not only from scholarship, deep thinking, and oratory, but also from the patient, unglorious, and obstinate application of these modest technical recipes.

PREPARING EXAMINATION PAPERS

I have great misgivings and hesitation when I come to discuss this last point. Tests and examinations are an immense question, which to a large extent is the cherished domain of the Schools of Education. Go there if you want to know everything about it, find an overwhelming bibliography, listen to courses devoted to the problem, read thousands of articles—very scientific—on the subject, and discover that there exist machines to correct tests, quizzes, and examinations. Waiting for the day when you have mastered all this material, you will have, just the same, to prepare and to correct with your own hand, in your courses in the humanities, examinations of various kinds.

1. There are forms and types of examination that I am extremely reluctant to accept—for instance the kind in which a student is required to answer a more or less unlimited number of questions simply by "yes" or "no" or by "true" or "false." In some cases he is expected to punch a nice little hole in the examination paper to express his opinion about Truth and Error. At the head of some papers of this type, I have read this, to me, very tragic line: "Do not waste your time writing; simply state 'true' or 'false.' " Whether this makes sense in geometry, physics, or other "exact sciences," I am in no position to say. But I am convinced that, in the field of humanities, it is a very dangerous practice. What we want to teach the young human beings entrusted to our care is to "think," not in terms of "true" or "false," but in terms of to what extent, and for what reasons, something appears to be true or erroneous. To conclude a course, or a college curriculum, with that mechanical and inhuman sort of examination seems to me a very dangerous practice. So let us discuss only the traditional —old-fashioned, if you want—type of examination which we use in most of our courses.

2. Do not ask *too many* questions. Keep in mind the exact length of time given to the student—one, two, or three hours— and be sure that you are not exacting more than he can actually produce. May I confess that I am simply terrified when I read some of the examination papers offered in our own university— fifteen, twenty questions, some extremely wide and comprehen-

sive. No human mind, no genius, is in any position in three hours to cope successfully with such a test. No reflection, no organization of one's thought, no style, are possible, and too often the results bring the proof of this.

3. Be very careful about the way you phrase your questions. Ask only those which the student is supposed to be able to answer. This may sound obvious, but it is often lost sight of.

Especially in literary courses where a large amount of reading is required, remember that it is hardly fair to ask questions the answer to which depends entirely upon the knowledge of *one* minute fact, *one* date, *one* title.

Be sure that none of the questions you ask duplicates another question on the same paper, even if the angle of approach appears to be different. If you let this happen, the student is likely to feel somewhat lost or worried. He may feel that there is a "trap" somewhere, and that you are trying to "catch" him. This must be avoided. An examination must always be a perfectly loyal affair.

4. Do not ask questions that can be answered simply by "yes" or "no"—a fault which you often find in examination papers. Each question must be a *problem,* which the student has to define clearly and solve—a challenge to his analytical and critical ability.

5. I am not a warm partisan of a certain type of examination which seems to be in great favor in certain departments. It consists simply of a certain number of "statements," within quotation marks, and nothing else: not a word to define what is expected from the student, not an inkling about the author or the date of the statement (sometimes there is a very good reason for such omissions). And so the student starts writing, and writing, and writing, without knowing exactly where he is going: a good chance for loose thinking.

6. There is a general tendency among students the world over *not to answer* the question as it is asked, but to write about something else more or less connected with the real question. If the question is well phrased, limited, "foolproof," the student should be expected to answer it and nothing else. I strongly advise you to be extremely strict in this respect. The word "irrelevant" in the margin of an examination book should be considered the most

damning remark to appear there. No matter how beautifully written the book is, how original and talented all the "hors d'oeuvre" presented to you, if the question is not exactly treated, I count all the rest against the student. In a scientific examination he would never change the terms of a problem or example. Why should he be allowed to do so in the field of humanities? This discipline I believe to be one of the most important chapters of the intellectual training to which our students are entitled, and one of our gravest responsibilities.

The practices and methods discussed here cannot really be "taught"; they have to be "learned," and the only school in which you can learn them is the experience of your classroom. There you will invent, explore, improve and there is no greater joy than that freshness of exploration and invention. You will also make mistakes and have useful opportunities for self-examination. But some day the feeling will come to you that you have done well and succeeded in a small measure in contributing to the great work of building up young human beings.

May I risk a last, personal word? Later on, after years of teaching, some evening in the quiet atmosphere of your study or of your home, when you are reflecting on your work and the methods you apply, if you happen to think: "It seems to me I remember that, years ago, when I was at college there was an old French teacher who told us something of the sort, and perhaps, after all, he was not entirely wrong"—well, if that happens, I shall be very happy.

WILLIAM H. WESTON

Chapter VI

TEACHING THE NATURAL SCIENCES

The natural sciences are endowed with certain advantages for teaching—direct contact with material to be studied and the possibility of experimentation, often with living material. Methods of presentation, useful apparatus and equipment. Special function of laboratory, the use of manuals, the importance of competent assistants. Advantages and limitations of field work. Obligation which rests on both teacher and student to achieve conclusions which are dependable.

The natural sciences, by their very nature, have several notable advantages over other fields from the viewpoint of teaching. One advantage is direct contact with the material. You can deal with the material itself and from it you can derive your information at firsthand rather than through intermediary agencies. You are not impeded by the handicap of the historian who is unable to relive and recapture at firsthand the glory of Greece in the age of Pericles. Rather you are using the material itself for investigation and for teaching and from precise examination, analysis, and interpretation you are drawing dependable conclusions and generalizations.

From this follows the second advantage that through experimentation you can deal more effectively with material than is possible in some other areas of academic activity. The experimental method is one of the strongest attributes of the natural sciences, and the notable contributions of this method to progress and development are familiar to you. The principles of experimentation constitute a most valuable asset for teaching. To recognize a problem, analyze its essential features, and formulate a procedure which will question the material so precisely that an unequivocal answer is obtained; to employ adequate controls in order that comparison of the control series and the experimental series may reveal the factors which caused the results; to repeat with enough material enough times so that the results are adequate for dependable quantitative evaluation by appropriate statistical methods; to absorb these essential principles into his processes of thinking—all these contribute greatly to a student's development.

In addition to these advantages inherent in dealing directly with the material itself, biology, of all the natural sciences, possesses one more characteristic which is its distinctive attribute: it deals with living materials, with things that are alive. From the viewpoint of teaching, the effects of this vitality are outstandingly helpful. The student, himself a living being, in studying the qualities and activities of life, is studying the very attributes that make him what he is. The realization of this and the fascination of working with material that is not inert but has vigorous dynamic vitality have the power to kindle the interest and arouse the enthusiasm of the student to a sometimes startling degree. Furthermore, the diversity and range of living things is extraordinarily wide and in some organisms the mechanisms and activities of life are reduced to the simplest possible terms. This facilitates studying such vital activities as photosynthesis or respiration in simple organisms without the hindrance of the structural and functional complexities of more highly elaborated creatures.

TOOLS FOR TEACHING

The material itself is a basic tool for teaching in the natural sciences. In this field the student gains much of his information directly from the material itself, most of the subject matter is concerned with the properties and structure of things and with their reactions and behavior under various conditions, and even the most abstract theories and concepts can hardly be considered by themselves apart from the stuff or the activities from which these concepts have been formulated. In your capacity as teachers you will realize that material which is inadequate or unsuitable can be a liability rather than an asset, much as a blurred lantern slide may be a liability as a visual aid and ill-chosen words may be a handicap by causing misunderstanding. Therefore, in any of these sciences you will ensure that the material is the most effective possible from the teaching point of view, and you will enable the students to study it in its active functioning and, if possible, under natural conditions in the field as well as in the laboratory.

Another teaching tool comprises the apparatus and equipment used in studying the material. These range from the simplest traditional implements, such as the dissecting sets of elementary biology, to the most modern, complicated, and expensive apparatus of investigation, such as the electron microscope, but they all have in common the function of subjecting the material to increasingly precise and intensive manipulation, examination, analysis, and evaluation. While some types of teaching require less equipment than others, and while ingenious makeshifts may in some cases be made to serve, yet adequate and suitable apparatus will be important in your teaching. For the student working under your guidance, the determination of weights, volumes, dimensions, and temperatures with precise, dependable, and reproducible accuracy is a valuable educational discipline; the study of the structure and activities of the most minute forms of life by means of a high-powered microscope is a significant and instructive experience. Furthermore, the instruments used in science have a fundamental significance that is very important for the student's development, for they are the means by which he gains the many-valued attitude of the mature mind. The two-valued, "either-or" attitude natural in childhood thinks in terms of either hot or cold, big or little, black or white—and unfortunately this attitude all too frequently persists in those of far greater age. Experience with instruments which attain precise evaluations of quantity or intensity helps to develop in the student the many-valued perception which is not restricted by the "either-hot-or-cold" limitation but comprehends an extensive range, from beyond the temperature of the sun to absolute zero, and appreciates the significance of such precise designations as 212°F. or 37.5°C. or 32°F.

Visual aids represent an essential tool for teaching and your suitable use of them will strengthen notably the effectiveness of your teaching. Whether Confucius said it or not, "one look is worth a thousand words," at least in the natural sciences. One look at a formula, a curve, a graph, a diagram, a chart, or a map communicates more than many words. In one well-executed lantern slide you can present effectively complicated material that would defy presentation by words alone. A motion picture can unfold, in the twenty-five minute projection of two reels, a vivid, logical, and unforgettable sequence of a development or an activity which has required months of intense work by experienced investigators to reveal—a development or an activity impracticable for class study in the laboratory and impossible for adequate communication solely by means of words. Three-dimensional scale models, especially those which can be taken apart to show relation of parts or looked into to observe interior construction, can make clear to the student structures so complicated as to defy adequate description by words alone.

From your experience as students you will remember that the blackboard provides a valuable service. Hence you will use it effectively making your diagrams, calculations, formulas, symbols, and words large and bold enough to be easily comprehended by those in the rear rows and shunning chalk colors that have only dim visual luminosity. In this, as in all aspects of your teaching, you will be mindful of your obligations to the student and never stand in front of a complicated calculation or formula you are contriving and then erase it before the whole class has ample opportunity to record it. You will never swiftly work out a detailed diagram of a complicated structure and at the same time rapidly pour forth the long descriptive analysis that is essential to comprehension; for you will realize that you are using two means of communication, the drawing and the voice, while the student is at the disadvantage of being able to record only with the one facile but overburdened pencil.

From years ago I still remember the comparative anatomy lectures in which the professor, with consummate ambidextrous skill drew marvelously beautiful and complicated two-fold diagrams of cross sections of the dogfish, using his left hand to fill in the skeletal and muscular systems on the left half and his right hand to fill in the internal organs on the right, accompanying this simultaneously with appropriate detailed and carefully organized descriptive discussion! My companion and I worked as a team, one recording the drawings, the other the description and explanation, and later we combined these and studied them until we knew them thoroughly. Incidentally, we had the strongest admiration and respect for this man for he was an outstanding lecturer and a superb teacher in every respect and we rather took pride in keeping up with his gifted presentation. Only when you are equally outstanding and admired teachers, will you be justified in thus taxing the capacity of your students.

In lantern slides you have an aid whose utility you appreciate from your experience as students. To make the most of this utility you must bear in mind certain requirements. The number of slides must not be excessive or they will overwhelm the student and defeat your purpose. Certainly, if the slide needs explanation or descriptive comment of any extent, you must allow two minutes or more for each slide. The nature of the slide is important and in the natural sciences the slide that is not excessively complicated but shows clearly distinguishable features and obviously presents its essential message is most generally effective. Even these, however, although they can be comprehended by the student while you are describing them, cannot usually be recorded also in the brief time of showing. In such cases, if it is important that the student record as well as understand, you will do well to refer to book illustrations which can be studied at leisure or to have available charts which remain on view for longer scrutiny. I have even tried having the lecture slides available in the laboratory so that the students could give them more careful examination by means of a short range projector; on the whole this was worth while when the class numbered twenty-five instead of eighty-five, even though some breakage occurred.

Slides in color, in cases where color has significance, are very effective, and their rapidly growing popularity in certain of the natural sciences should lead you to explore their possible application to your own needs. You may even find it advantageous, despite the drawbacks of more complicated apparatus, to use recently developed processes which give a marvelous illusion of three dimensional quality in the projected image. Finally, you will be scrupulously careful to have your slides in the correct order and correctly marked so that they will appear in the right sequence and in their right position and you will develop your technique of skillfully pointing to important features on the screen without interrupting your direct attention to the class.

The preparation of your lectures imposes requirements which are familiar to you. Already, in preparation for seminars, discussions, or reports, you have had adequate experience in assembling suitable material and organizing it with effective unity, emphasis, and continuity. You realize that this necessitates intense concentrated work which requires a disproportionate amount of time, in a ratio of at least ten to one, as you will remember from the five or more hours you devoted to preparing for a twenty-minute seminar. You will be resigned, therefore, if your first teaching has a crowded schedule, to working far into the night and will find new implications in the Biblical statement that "day unto day uttereth speech and night unto night sheweth knowledge." Nothing more need be said about the preparation of lectures except to remind you that if you have not thought out and prepared the lecture clearly, you certainly will not present it clearly.

In the pronunciation of the scientific and technical terms with which the natural sciences abound, do not let any feeling of insecurity lead you into hurrying over, or slurring or murmuring such words. On the contrary pronounce them clearly and distinctly in the manner to which you are accustomed. The important thing is for the student to get that term in that context, not for you to salve your insecurity. If you do pronounce the term adequately even though differently, he will understand it, indeed he may even cherish the difference for the vividness which makes it memorable.

LABORATORY WORK

In the natural sciences, laboratory work is the most valuable and effective of all teaching procedures because it involves direct study of the material itself. This direct study of the material through careful examination and unprejudiced comparison, through precise purposive experimentation and honest analysis—this patient and persistent adding of fact to fact to gain an understanding of objective truth—these are the essential attributes, the fundamental strength of the natural sciences. In your teaching never forget that this direct study of the material was the original source from which came the content of books, the subject matter of lectures, the substance of group discussions and of examinations. Always remember that this was the source from which came the facts that led to the interpretations, concepts, and theories that yielded the fundamental laws and basic truths by which humanity has advanced.

Therefore the primary function of laboratory work as a teaching procedure is to enable the student to learn from the material itself directly, and your function as a teacher is to foster, expedite, facilitate, stimulate, and otherwise aid this important process to the utmost of your capacity. In relation to lectures, textbooks, discussions, or other aspects of your courses the function of laboratory work is to exemplify, strengthen, support, corroborate, extend, and supplement the knowledge and understanding gained through those other means. Yet the versatility of laboratory work is such that the elements of lecture, discussion, and quiz, already inherent in it, can be extended and the laboratory procedure can be modified and adapted to fulfill effectively a large proportion of their functions. If your teaching in the natural sciences were to be limited to one procedure only, you could teach more effectively through laboratory work than through lectures or discussions alone. Indeed, if you think over the laboratory work of your own experience, you will probably find that it partook of the functions of lectures, discussions, and quizzes to some extent at least.

To consider the advantages and disadvantages of laboratory work, already appreciated to some extent from your own experience, may be helpful to you. The advantages for the student are strong. The knowledge he gains directly from the material has a vividness and force which make it more vital and personally important than similar knowledge gained from books or lectures. His realization that he is not wholly dependent on the authority of others but can work things out for himself gives him a feeling of personal achievement. To carry through a process or work out a complicated structure is for him his own discovery, even though many others may have preceded him. If his laboratory work is in biology and he observes the activities and vital processes of living organisms, there is for him an especial stimulus in this enlightening experience; to watch a phase of development progress, not as a series of pictures or as a paragraph of descriptive words, but as a dynamic continuous process, has a peculiar fascination and arouses in the student those powerful forces of intense and enthusiastic interest so vital and indispensable for learning and comprehension. To learn techniques and to develop skill in the use of instruments and apparatus have for the student the advantages not only of a highly practical utility, but even more of the enlightening realization that these tools contribute to man's progress by enabling him to measure, evaluate, and observe with precise accuracy and exact dependability. One of the strongest advantages of laboratory work is that it enables the student to understand the scientific method and make it part of his intellectual equipment, to comprehend the method and the fundamental significance of experimentation.

For you, in your capacity as the teacher in charge of the course, the advantage of laboratory work lies in your opportunity to help the student to profit from the advantages which we have noted. Your students will differ widely in their receptivity to the things which laboratory work can contribute to their development. For some, who show strong preference for talking about things rather than working with things themselves, the requisite precision of observation or procedure or recording may seem a bore, the experimental method may seem an empty procedure devoid of enlightening significance. For others these will prove to be the exact tools they have been seeking, the very things they need to foster their development. For some there may be far greater mental certainty in turning to the authoritative words of a book or even of a companion than in studying the material; for others, the experience that they themselves can obtain dependable answers from the material adds greatly to their surety of purpose and strengthens their maturity of mind. Laboratory work typifies the procedures, methods, and approaches which have enabled us to reach our present stage of human development; whether or not you feel that our present civilization represents real advance you cannot help but profit, as teachers, by the advantages which laboratory work offers you.

The disadvantages of laboratory work are obvious. The equipment, supplies, material, facilities, and maintenance necessary to provide adequately for the laboratory work of large classes in such fields as physics, chemistry and biology represent a total cost that is formidable. The salaries of laboratory assistants, one for each section of twelve to twenty students, add greatly to the inevitable expense. Even for small classes, in colleges whose tradition demands long hours from an inadequate but devoted staff, the cost is severe. It is small wonder, then, that officers of administration and finance are impressed by this disadvantage, especially when they contrast it with the inexpensive needs of other fields in which outside reading and the preparation of term papers take the place of laboratory. You are fortunate in that your teaching falls in a period when the importance of laboratory work is generally recognized as being worthy of adequate support, rather than in the pioneer era of less than a hundred years ago, when the struggle to secure recognition and support for laboratory work was severe.

For you in your capacity as teachers laboratory work has the disadvantage of adding greatly to your responsibilities. In addition to your own teaching and your supervision of assistants, you will have to do considerable laboratory housekeeping and keep track of innumerable troublesome details. The situation becomes tinged with irony when a woman graduate student, whose choice of teaching has unconsciously been influenced by an abhorrence of the drudgery of the kitchen, finds that many types of laboratory work require meticulous attention to essential activities that closely resemble the despised dishwashing of her rebellious adolescence. Similarly there is irony in the disillusion that comes when a young man, who has thought of himself as one of the chosen men in white whose research is destined to push back the frontiers of science, starting his first teaching in a small college where he himself must perform all the tasks previously performed for him by skillful technicians and preparators, finds that for his class the refulgence of his shining example is somewhat dimmed by the burgeoning contaminants of the culture medium he has prepared.

The essential requirements, on which will depend the effectiveness of laboratory work as a means of teaching, are generally familiar to you. Adequate facilities, equipment, and material, a suitable laboratory manual or guide, and, if the class is too large for your single-handed guidance, competent and enthusiastic assistants, comprise the major needs. The adequacy of the equipment and material will vary with the strength and activity of your department in the college where you teach. Probably you will be teaching in a department in which ample budgets are traditional, with bountiful provision for material and with beautiful and expensive equipment. Perhaps, however, you may start your teaching in an institution which has emphasized fields other than the natural sciences and has done very little toward supporting the subject which you have been asked to teach.

In such a situation, until you can convince the administration that the value of your courses merits adequate support, you will use your ingenuity and resourcefulness, obtaining essential apparatus and equipment by begging, borrowing, purloining, scrounging, finagling, promoting, and liberating suitable items from other more adequately equipped laboratories and departments; manufacturing makeshifts with the help of skillful students; and adapting to your needs various items from the ubiquitous but uncatalogued laboratory supply houses of Messrs. Kresge and Woolworth. The janitors will be your friends in need, revealing articles forgotten in attic and cellar storerooms; the Department of Buildings, Grounds, and Maintenance will be your very present help in trouble by unearthing and reconditioning other useful items. Although in times of discouragement you may find yourself feeling something closely akin to envy when you observe, in other fields of learning, colleagues whose essential facilities are a desk and an easy chair and whose equipment and materials are two textbooks and a fountain pen, yet your reward in watching the students develop under the stimulus of laboratory work with you will be ample compensation.

Another requirement is a suitable manual, guide, or outline for laboratory work. Fortunately, in the natural sciences at least, there is available an ample range of outlines, well planned and executed and, in many instances, well coördinated with suitable general texts; from them you can select the one best suited to your purpose. Their suitability will of course depend largely on your viewpoint and on the objectives you feel the laboratory work in your class should attain. Two extremes are represented. One, typical of some courses in high school science, uses a manual which describes, illustrates, and explains in detail thus: "The spherical, finely granular body in the center of the cell, is the nucleus, spelled n-u-c-l-e-u-s; draw and label the nucleus." Given such detail, the student has little difficulty in acceptably representing the nucleus whether he has seen and understood it or not. The other extreme is the Agassiz approach of shoving a fish at the student, saying, "Study this," and walking away—expecting, on returning a week later, that the student will have every detail of structure meticulously worked out, recorded, and illustrated. The former has certain advantages for a large, overcrowded, understaffed elementary course; the latter for an advanced course of three or four graduate students. Somewhere between these is the golden mean of the laboratory outline which effectively stimulates and helpfully guides the student to work things out successfully himself with some help in interpretation from the laboratory instructor. Probably, finding that not one of the laboratory manuals available precisely meets your needs, you will prefer to work out your own outline, using it in mimeographed form and revising it from year to year. In any case you will realize that no outline, however complete or skillfully contrived, can take the place of personal guidance by the teacher and the assistants.

One of the chief requirements, therefore, is that there shall be laboratory assistants adequate in number and suitable in teaching ability to give the students the guidance and help that is essential to effective laboratory work. The number will depend on the size of the class and the nature of the laboratory work; the proportion of one assistant to about sixteen students, for example, is regarded as practicable in biology. The qualities which distinguish an able laboratory assistant are the contagious enthusiasm, the interest in the subject and in teaching it, the sense of responsibility toward the course and of obligation toward the student. In seeking your assistants you will be wise to be guided more by their fundamental philosophy, attitude, and point of view toward teaching and toward the students than by their formal training in educational methods or their extensive knowledge of the subject, because, as you know from your own experience, the personality of the assistant or section man can make or break the course for the student.

Finally, as by now you have realized, your own part in ensuring the effectiveness of the laboratory work is a highly important one, as it is in all the component procedures of your teaching. Yours is the responsibility of making certain that the facilities, equipment, and material are adequate, that the laboratory outline is effective, that the assistants have the most favorable qualities. In addition you are the one who ensures that the spirit and atmosphere of the laboratory contribute to the objectives and ideals which you consider essential to the integrity of teaching. If your college teaching lies in small advanced and specialized courses you will be able to manage all of the aspects of the laboratory work yourself and will derive greater satisfaction from the effective progress of the work in this single-handed integration. If, however, you give the elementary course to a class of four hundred or more students you will find yourself harassed and beset by innumerable routine details of supply, organization, coördination, administration, and personnel relations even though you delegate many responsibilities to your laboratory assistants. As a result it will be impossible for you to keep in close personal touch with the laboratory work; you will know only a few students by name and none as individuals; you will find yourself functioning as a director rather than as a teacher in the full sense of the word;

your only personal satisfaction will lie in lecturing effectively; your sense of achievement will be only general and objective. Let us hope that at first your courses will be small so that in the laboratory work you may make the most of the opportunity for effective teaching thus afforded you. When the growth of your courses and the increasing demands of your service on various committees and boards force you to delegate the laboratory guidance largely to your assistants, let us hope you may still be able frequently to spend at least short periods of time in the laboratory. Thereby you will be able to keep a guiding hand on the course of the work, to see whether the rate and amount of work required are suited to the average capacity of this year's class, or whether the experiments would be more effective if carried out by pairs rather than by teams of four students. Also you will be able to sense the interaction between the students and the assistants so that you may make certain that the spirit of the laboratory is congenial and productive. It is through the closer and less formal contact of the laboratory that you really get to know the students not only by their names, which you will take pains to learn as soon as possible, but by their characteristics, which you gradually come to understand.

If you really enjoy teaching it will be the laboratory which gives you satisfactory opportunity to teach effectively. Here at this table in your biology class is a student, obviously keen, who takes one look at the specimen under his microscope and then barrages you with questions. If you convincingly show him that he, by himself, could have answered each of those questions from careful study of the material, you have given him something more valuable than any verbal answers, and the next time you see him he will probably demonstrate this by asking you some very penetrating questions which arise from thorough study of the material but are quite beyond answering through such study. At another table is a student who, in defense of his drawing, insists that he has seen the essential features and understands them perfectly, but he just can't draw them. If you can show him that he, as the one who has explored the territory and understands its salient features, is obligated to draw a map which makes those features correctly understandable for those who follow; if you can show him that it does not have to be a beautiful map or an artistic map but that it must transmit the truth as he saw it; if you can show him that if it does not communicate the truth either he did not observe correctly or he was willing to draw an incorrect map which would mislead and endanger those who follow—then you have given him something far more valuable than merely pointing out the inadequacies of his drawing. You will use all your skill and enthusiasm, all your ability as a teacher, in your laboratory sessions, and you will derive unceasing satisfaction from their progress and find an unending fascination in the extraordinary diversity which the supposititious type of the "American college student" may represent.

FIELD WORK

The purpose of field work is the direct study under natural conditions of the nature, activities, and interactions of the living and nonliving components of our environment. Since it is concerned with the study of material in the out-of-doors, it is limited in the natural sciences to geology and to certain aspects of biology and does not apply to such subjects as chemistry or physics. Because of these limitations, its applicability as a teaching procedure is rather restricted, hence we need consider it only briefly.

You should, however, note the outstanding advantage of studying the material in relation to its surroundings. In the ecological aspects of biology, for example, field work demands consideration of trees not as mangled remnants of a branch with a few leaves and buds, or of a trunk or root cut in transverse, radial, and tangential sections, but as a complete and living being, growing in characteristic stands in complex interrelation with the many plants and animals that are the living components of its environment, and with the sunlight, rainfall, wind, temperature, soil, and other nonliving factors of its surroundings. Similarly it vividly impresses the student with, let us say, a fish, not as a drab and dismal specimen gazing with an alcoholic leer from a dusty jar, but as a vital creature with a life of activity that is closely interrelated with the aquatic plants that furnish shelter, the living things that serve as food, and the water that supplies or denies the dissolved air necessary for respiration. The advantage of its vividness is especially clear to those of you who have had the memorable experience of following the natural succession of vegetation in the Harvard Forest, or of tracing the fascinating story of the part played by the great glaciers of the past in the formation of drumlins, eskers, potholes, and kames.

The urban location of some universities is a handicap, as it requires undue time and extensive provision for transportation, but some of the institutions in which you may teach, institutions such as Cornell, Wisconsin, Dartmouth, Bennington, and many others, are situated so that field work is readily available. Within the limits of its applicability you will find field study, as a teaching procedure, a very effective and useful adjunct to the more widely useful laboratory work.

On coming to the end of one of your courses you will naturally look back over it in critical review. Probably the course as a whole will seem adequate to you, but undoubtedly you will note certain aspects which should be modified and improved in the following year. Probably your records will show reassuring evidence that the students as a whole have "learned" what you have endeavored to "teach" them, and that the factual content of the course has been adequately absorbed and understood. You have, therefore, met your obligations to the students and to the college and have attained the main objectives of your teaching. With this you may justly be content. You will realize, however, that unless the student continues in some field that constantly refreshes this subject matter, it will inevitably fade and grow dim as time goes on. Even though this subject matter will not, as a whole, persist in the form and substance of your presentation, you will hope that some of it has been assimilated into the intellectual equipment of the student to contribute to his knowledge and understanding. From your own experience you realize that, in many cases, it is not the store of facts gained from a course which in the long run proves most valuable, but rather the perspective, the attitudes, and the interpretations. Yet it would not be practical to attempt to have your course consist solely of these, for these attitudes and points of view are attitudes and points of view toward the factual substance of the course content. You will, therefore, emphasize the factual content of your courses, and it will depend on the maturity and the needs of your students whether you feel they will profit most by having these valuable intangibles left to their own selective absorption, or by having at least some of them emphasized for direct consideration.

In your own courses, in whatever field they may lie, there will be many of these intangibles which will seem to you to be potentially valuable for your students. In my own field there are many such and perhaps it may not be out of place if I mention a few which seem to me especially important. The unique power of chlorophyll to transform the energy of sunlight into the stuff on which all life depends is worthy of the thoughtful contemplation of any student. The realization that without this the superiority of man would find an ignominious end should contribute to his perspective. The complex interdependence of the many diverse types of living things demands the student's serious consideration. The parallel interdependence and interlocking between the many branches of learning demand his attention; his viewpoint will be significantly broadened by his realization not only of the obvious interlocking of chemistry, physics, and geology with biology, but also of the less obvious, but none the less valid, interrelation among the natural sciences, the social sciences, and history. These and many other potent realizations are intangible by-products which can enrich the student's understanding.

No course in the natural sciences should fail to awaken in the student the realization that certain obligations must be met and that faith is not a dream but a necessity. The results of scholarly work must be maps that are dependable so that others may go forward through that territory with the certainty that the indicated trail will be free from quicksands or quaking bogs. The considerable progress we have made has been proportionate to our agreement on things we can trust. Betrayal of this faith results in destruction. If your teaching, in addition to transmitting to the student the essential factual content of your courses, also contributes to his intellectual self fundamentally vital attitudes such as this, then you will have attained the ultimate objectives of your teaching.

JOHN T. DUNLOP
ELLIOTT PERKINS

Chapter VII

TEACHING THE SOCIAL SCIENCES

Indoctrination in the social sciences is easier than teaching. The aim should be analysis and appreciation of factors involved in a problem rather than the finding of an immediate answer. Objective study of actual problems will show students the relation of theory to fact. The teacher will further relate these theories and facts to questions of ends and of social values.

ECONOMICS AND GOVERNMENT

John T. Dunlop

The first problem for the teacher in the social sciences is the attitude he is to take before his class and with his students on matters of public policy. I have special reference to the fields of economics and government, which very frequently involve you in questions of the day or with public policy issues of the past. It is my conviction that students come to have an overadoration for their teachers; you have therefore to guard continuously against influencing their views.

It is much easier to indoctrinate than it is to teach. In the fields of social sciences, and particularly in economics and government, you should therefore be continually on the alert to teach in a way that gives the student an appreciation of the *problem,* rather than the "answer" which you may have evolved from your own personal convictions. Teaching tactics ought to be directed almost entirely to posing and analyzing the problem rather than to reaching any conclusion. It is typical for the undergraduates to want a definite answer. What ought to be done to monopolies is much more interesting than any analysis of imperfect competition. The question of what laws ought to be passed regulating labor unions is much more appealing to a student than any analysis of the evolving relation between the parties in collective bargaining. In my experience, posing the problems in as challenging a way as possible secures more response from students than any other method of teaching.

I do not hold, however, that in the community teachers should not take sides on public issues—a number of my colleagues, as an illustration, issued a public statement on referenda affecting union security in a recent election in Massachusetts. In the classroom, however, the important thing is to get the student excited about the problem rather than to get any set of answers. I like the suggestion made by Mr. Allport of ending the hour with a couple of questions. That is a practice of mine.

An illustration from my own experiments with the "problem approach" may be helpful. Three years ago, on return from a government assignment, I felt depressed by the results of trying to teach labor economics solely by the lecture method three times a week. The students were doing their work, but they seemed to gain little understanding. So I experimented with breaking the class up into small sections once a week and presenting problems and cases to them. I first mimeographed a series of cases and later published some seventy such cases in book form for class use.

Let me be quite specific. One of the most important aspects of industrial relations is to understand the range of interests of unions and management. These different interests are conveniently illustrated in discharge cases, instances in which employees have been fired. These cases are relatively simple in many ways, yet they raise fundamental questions. Suppose we look at a particular case. It is an actual case, not a hypothetical question.

The United Automobile Workers of America, the organization of which Mr. Reuther is president, and the General Motors Company in their Buick Motors, Melrose Park Plant, had this dispute: Two colored employees became involved in a fight with a white employee and a member of his family outside the plant. After the white employee had brought the situation to the attention of management, the colored employees were discharged, and the union protested their discharge. The union based its protest on the ground that, since the entire situation occurred outside the plant, the company lacked authority to impose discipline. It therefore requested that the two men be reinstated with back pay. Management's position was that, although the incident occurred outside the plant, it gave rise to a latent racial issue which had already evidenced itself in several ways within the premises of the plant. Management claimed that it was within its rights in discharging the complainants whose actions outside of the company resulted in the existence of dangerous tendencies among the company's employees while they were actually on the job.

Now, you are the arbitrator and the question comes before you. Are the two men to remain discharged or to be reinstated? If they are reinstated are they to receive pay for the time they were out of work? I really do not care what decision the student makes. In fact, one of the complaints I get, and try deliberately to capitalize upon, is that there are in the back of the book no "right" answers to which you can turn instead of thinking through the problem. To the student it is exasperating at times, but the important point is the nature of the problem rather than an answer. In this particular case, the idea is to get the student to think about the contention that this particular dispute took place outside the company property. Is it a valid conclusion that everything that happens outside the property is irrelevant to rights under an agreement? May an employee be fired for a crime or for an unsavory reputation? You get the students thinking about drawing distinctions and they begin to understand something of the problems of reconciling the rights and interests of unions and managements. Collective bargaining becomes more than an empty phrase.

You will find that students generally come to courses in this field with highly emotionalized attitudes about these matters. In my experience, at the outset of a term, about 50 per cent of the class will say that management is right and another 50 per cent that labor is right, simply because the students have brought to the classroom emotionalized reactions to this type of problem. One of the tasks of the teacher is to pose the problem as a way of de-emotionalizing many of these situations in the field of government and economics. By presenting these cases to people you begin to get a more detached and thoughtful approach to questions.

The second main problem I would like to pose involves teaching the relation between theory and fact. In the teaching of government and economics it is most difficult, and yet it is most essential, to show the interrelation between abstract principles and theory on one hand and facts on the other, the relations between tools of analysis and practical situations. I think you will find that most of the students who come to these fields at the outset may be classified into two groups. One group has a very great interest in particular facts and in particular situations. They are unable to generalize. They have no apparatus with which to look at a larger world. On the other hand, the other group comes with one of several types of preconception or generalized views which explain all problems. There may be a person with an extreme Marxist background who thinks all of these policy problems are settled by a few dialectics. Or you may find some students who come to these problems with another extreme view: free enterprise is the simple formula. The phrase not only answers all policy problems, but is also a description of the way the world really works.

The task of the teacher is to relate particular situations to a general theoretical apparatus. In the field of economics that is most difficult on the college level because the undergraduate is normally not interested in a general theoretical system. He does not understand the necessity or role of theory. So again, it is suggested that the way to tackle this problem is by demonstration. Let me briefly sketch an example intended to illustrate the importance of the relationship between theory and fact.

Consider the hosiery industry in the United States. You are trying to explain supply and demand, the type of subject which tends to bore the undergraduate. You say, "We had a change in tastes in the United States, to use the technical economic term, as a result of the change in fashion." In the 1920's, as a result of women's skirts becoming shorter, the hosiery industry boomed. The great expansion in the hosiery industry is a shift to the right in the demand curve. This shift in demand resulted in an increased profit to the hosiery firms making women's stockings. These profits attracted new firms, which led slowly to a great overcapacity. Since skilled knitters cannot be trained overnight—it may take four or five years—wages of knitters rose sharply. You have a fall in demand with the decline in income during the depression. You can trace in terms of this theoretical apparatus all the major developments of the industry in the last twenty years, down to the changes in tints and color in women's stockings, a form of product-differentiation. You can even discuss the competition of paints and the effects of summer tans. The whole story can be presented in accurate statistical terms.

Such an illustration may help to bridge this gap between theory and fact. It can make the tools of theory, which are absolutely indispensable in this field, more meaningful. Theory is transformed for the student from just memory work to the actual tools of analysis, which it is supposed to be. In this area lies one of the most difficult problems that confronts a teacher in the social sciences—how to relate for the student theory and fact.

As a third major problem, the teacher in this field must face more than the very difficult task of relating theories and facts. Issues of public policy raise questions of ends and of social values. For example, you may say that economic analysis, by itself, leads to the conclusion that monopoly of a certain kind is harmful. Now you cannot just leave the matter there for most undergraduate students. Neither, as a matter of fact, can or do most economists leave it there. Their interest is not merely on the level of abstract thought. Most of them are interested in translating these ideas into guides for the problems of the day.

Here, it seems to me, the teacher must be most explicit in separating several different things: the level of analysis, the level of facts and institutions, and the value judgments and social judgments that influence conclusions for policy. Take a field like taxation. You can say a lot on the level of analysis about the effects of taxes. Soon you are sure to come into the realm of certain value judgments. If you are to discuss public policy, you will have to make judgments about equity among individuals and groups in the community.

A major great problem for the teacher in the field of social science is to search his conscience as he prepares each lecture to be sure that he has identified for himself and for his students those statements which he makes which are of this value judgment sort. He should try to be explicit about them. I do not happen to think that it is possible to hide completely from your students your value judgments. If you ever did, I think you would be a most uninteresting teacher. But you should try to separate value judgments from fact and theory and thus leave the way clear for the students to form their own conclusions about values.

HISTORY

Elliott Perkins

A liking for history necessary if one is to teach it successfully. What should a history teacher's main objectives be? Practical hints on the teaching of history.

Any discussion of the teaching of history must, I think, touch upon the three questions of why teach, why teach history, and how to go about it.

The initial question is one that you should ask yourself now and continue to ask yourself as long as it is possible to change your career. To all of us comes the day when we must answer the question of why we are teaching, or whatever else it is, by saying that it is that or starve; we are too old to learn a new trade. If we were wise, or perhaps just lucky, in our choice, the closing of the door to change will not bother us. But it is a sad thing to see those who went into teaching because of misapprehension, and stayed there because of inertia, dragging out their lives. By all means try teaching, but keep an open mind. The facts that it is respectable, that it offers considerable security, that it offers long vacations, will be poor compensation for the mouthfuls of ashes that will be your daily fare if you are, instead of a teacher teaching, a pedagogue going through the motions.

That is true because teaching is one of the inspirational occupations. Probably no one makes a *marked* success in an occupation which is, to him or to her, simply a livelihood instead of a way of life; but in most occupations to earn a living is to enjoy a sufficient success. Teaching is different. It was summed up by Owen Wister's cowboy, the Virginian, when he said, "A middling lawyer is a poor thing, and a middling doctor is a poor thing; but keep me from a middling man of God." A teacher is very much a preacher, and when he is middling he is a failure.

The only way to find out about teaching is to try it. I had an illuminating talk with a man a few weeks ago. He has been teaching a few years and he has his doubts. He likes to learn but students bore him. He does not find, as I think all good teachers find, that anything he reads or hears, on duty or off, is instinctively subjected to the test, "Can I use that for illustration, clarification, or further exposition?" He is in the wrong box. Teaching is not the only intellectual occupation. There are any number of other ways of using your mind that pay as much or more in money, and more in that other thing that many people want so much—power, influence, a part in current events. Watch teaching and be sure that you like it.

The other question, "Why teach History?" is more simply answered. Probably most of you, if history is your chosen field, have answered it already, for you have done enough studying to know that history is what you like. That is the touchstone. If you do not like history—or any other subject, for that matter—you will not be capable of the drudgery that is an inescapable part of mastery of the subject. However, you will probably find that a more intellectual justification of your choice is desirable and I suggest to you, as an introduction to the considerable literature on the subject, the recent book by A. L. Rowse, *The Use of History*.

So much for what might be called background. Now, how

about the business of teaching? Let me make one point at the start. If you cannot speak, learn to; and if you cannot learn to, don't teach. An assured, decisive speech is essential whether you are lecturing, conducting a section, or simply having an individual conference. It is not a matter of being assertative or bellowing. Two of the greatest teachers Harvard ever had, Bliss Perry and C. H. McIlwain, appeared almost apologetic when taking a class and spoke in the gentlest of voices. But they were always audible and always conveyed a sense of competence that a class demands. You will attain to their stature after long years, if ever, but an adequate degree of voice control is essential and can be easily acquired with the aid of an instructor in public speaking.

Let us now consider other aspects of the business of teaching. We may assume that your first independent undertaking will be to give a course. That is the point at which you really start out on your own, with full responsibility.

The first step is to decide what you want the course to teach. You will not, at first, be teaching a graduate course and it is well to remember that after your years of graduate training. Most, if not all, of your students will be undergraduates, only a few of whom will carry on into professional scholarship. Your course is a contribution to what used to be called the liberal education of future citizens.

What, then, are you trying to give these students? Certainly not the professional techniques that you would be teaching in a graduate seminar. Certainly, also, you are not trying to give them the facts as an end in themselves. Very few students carry the facts they learned in college very long. You are, rather, trying to teach the historical method, the historical discipline, the habit of reasoning, as far as possible, from ascertained facts and of laying on those facts no more than they will bear. How do you go about it?

One thing is settled for you by your department, the subject of the course. But within that frame, you will have freedom of action. Your frame, to take the Harvard half-course as an example, is about one hundred hours of the student's time; thirty-five classroom hours, and, at least in theory, two hours in the library for each hour in class. In that time you must deal with the history of the Middle Ages, or Medieval England, or America since 1789, or whatever you have undertaken, in such a way that the class will take away a certain skill in the historical method and, despite what I have said about not teaching facts as an end in themselves, some memory of what the segment of history studied was, and meant, and means.

You must form for yourself some concept of what is to be learned from the field covered. You will get nowhere by running off a chronicle. People study history because it has meaning, relevance to the problems of their own place and time, and you must decide what you think that relevance is. So you give the course a direction, a core around which to wind the exposition of those happenings and aspects that you have elected to present. For example, in my own course I use as a core my opinion that the lesson of lasting meaning to be gained from eighteenth-century British history is the development, by that people in that time, of effective representative government. Around that I wind the history of the century, or as much of it as I can include with coherence. That, of course, is the old, or political approach to history, and other people would not necessarily use it. The important thing is that you should have a definite approach, an interpretation, and that you should present it to the class, simply because it gives form to what is otherwise a confused mass of material. Need I add that one should avoid "indoctrination"? The political interpretation should not be presented so categorically as to obscure the social and economic interpretations that so many people hold to be more valid, nor should the students be discouraged from espousing the other interpretations, if they want to. All that I want to convey here is the importance of having for yourself an intellectual interpretation of the segment of history that you are teaching.

There is another point that I would make. Remember that in the light of time the important thing about teaching is not the teacher and his opinions but the student and his education. All of us are likely to feel, and feel sincerely, that we owe the class the fullest possible amount of our time, and we find that the thirty-five or so lectures possible in a half-year are too little for development of the subject. The result is that we cut down on the interruptions that come from hour examinations and other methods of making the student express his knowledge and ideas. It is quite as important, if not more important, that the student learn to formulate and present opinions as that he absorb the instructor's. Few of us are that close to Aristotle. So let the students write (this amounts to saying *make* them write) sacrificing some of your precious lectures to that end. If you find that you have a small class, you may be able to organize discussion sessions, and those are very effective, being a test of the instructor as well as of the class.

Some practical hints may be in order. It is a good idea to chart your course. Take a cardboard sheet, rule it off into squares, each one representing a class period, and plan your term's work. You will find, in some years, that holidays and festivals make quite a hole in your available time. A course must run on something akin to railroad schedule. You must reach the end at term end, and you must in advance decide how much time is to be allotted to the various episodes that you must treat. You will find, when you sit down with a clear and unemotional chart, that a lot of your interests cannot be presented.

In this connection, remember that the collective mind of the class cannot be stretched more than so far. To you, the course is of prime importance, the chief concern of your life, at least for that term. To the class, it is one of four or five courses, possibly preceded by a course in French literature and followed by one in organic chemistry. Students' attention must be treated with some respect. You cannot effectively discuss, or even mention, all the facts that you know and that have significance to you because you are so soaked in the subject that you perceive significances. You must cut, and cut, and cut; cut material that you think really should be in. Remember, too, that the lectures are accompanied by reading, and depend on the class to follow allusions to what is in the reading.

An older man told me, when I began lecturing, to notice that the class attends in waves, and that a wave cannot last more than twenty minutes. At the end of that time, everyone relaxes, and if you have picked the moment of relaxation for one of your high points, it flops. His advice was to lay out a lecture in three sections, with short "breathing spells," which you fill by some form of anecdotal material.

Similarly, don't indulge in "detective story" lectures, building up a case without telling the class what the case is, and springing the solution on them at the end. If they haven't followed, they don't appreciate either the conclusion or the build up. Tell the class where you are going, and they will be more appreciative of the signposts that you point out along the way.

I may have given the impression that lecturing is the whole show. It is the backbone of American formal instruction, but it cannot stand alone. Reading assignments are of almost equal importance—without good reading, the lectures are crippled. Pay attention to that, and, when selecting reading, try to think as an undergraduate would. Good solid monographs may impress the professionals, but they are likely to put the amateurs, who are most of your class, off.

Another point, often neglected, is adequate criticism of students' written work. To mark a bluebook or an essay *A*, *B*, *C*, or lower, with perhaps such comments as "confused," "inadequate facts," is not teaching. If you can, sit down and write out, quite fully, your reasons for the grade you give. There are only two grades that can be given without comment, the *A* and the *E*. All the others call for explanation, for the earnest student will want to know what he should do for a better grade. So take the time, and the trouble, to do that job, which by the end of a term is likely to be most ungrateful to you.

The late R. B. Merriman, one of the greatest lecturers of the generation just passed, was a firm believer in what actors call "business," particularly when dealing with a large class such as History 1. It was his contention that to stand in one place, laying out a well conceived lecture, invited the immature mind to wander. If, on the other hand, the lecturer walked about the platform, made full use of wall maps when relevant, and used a pointer a good deal, the class would watch him, instead of gazing dreamily at the ceiling. Unconsciously, what was being said would sink in. I remember that when I first went in as a guest lecturer in History 1, Professor Merriman urged me to walk a good two miles during the hour. The point is a good one, and while "business" will not fool anyone into thinking that a bad lecture is a good one, it can be used to good effect. But here you should remember that the class is not interested in you, but in the subject, that anything that you may do is important only in relation to the subject.

SOME INSTRUMENTS OF TEACHING

SCIENTIFIC AIDS TO LEARNING AND RESEARCH 134

VERNON D. TATE

VERNON D. TATE

Chapter VIII

SCIENTIFIC AIDS TO LEARNING

Modern scientific aids to learning involve new processes in printing, reproducing documents, pictures, and sound, and in the mechanical selection of facts from a rapidly increasing store. Scholars and teachers will find these new devices useful supplements to older libraries.

Communication provides the medium whereby the experience of the race can be drawn upon by an individual. We are now more immediately sensitive to great events as well as to many small ones because the vast improvement in the art of communication has reduced the time lag between event and news from years, months, and weeks to hours, minutes, and even seconds. It is salutary to reflect that there is scarcely a corner of the earth where anything of note may happen without knowledge of the event becoming household gossip everywhere in a matter of hours. Communication, therefore, is the key to much of our knowledge. Scientific aids to learning derive largely from the methods and devices of modern communication.

Through a generous grant of funds from the Carnegie Corporation it has been possible to establish at the Massachusetts Institute of Technology a Center for Scientific Aids to Learning, devoted to the accumulation and dissemination of data and to research. Five general fields have been selected for emphasis. These include *printing,* which embraces all variations of *edition* processes, although no one has ever been able to define exactly what an edition process may be; the most usual estimate at the present time is anything over a hundred copies, although anything over one copy is an edition and even a single copy is an edition of one. Letterpress, offset lithography, and many other less pretentious forms of duplication such as the mimeograph, hectograph, and the like, are being studied. The second field is *documentary reproduction,* including all methods of reproducing material by photography, microphotography, microcard, miniature print, and similar techniques. The third is *visual education,* defined as the use of visual techniques in instruction—whether the medium be lantern slides, motion pictures, or other methods for textual and nontextual material. The fourth field is *sound-recording,* that is, the full exploitation of the sense of hearing. The fifth embraces *mechanical selection* or principles of coding and mechanical methods for assembling, arranging, and supplying data of all types through punched cards and other media. These five categories overlap in many ways and the list itself is more exclusive than exhaustive.

The vast output of printed material is largely volume production by machine, but even the machine has limitations that are increasingly evident. Large scale letterpress or offset printing requires volume production which diversification and specialization often cannot provide. "Duplicating" and other cheap reproduction processes are widely used. Mimeograph, hectograph, multigraph, planograph or office offset, are attempts at what have been called near-print techniques. They are designed to bring within the reach of small-edition publishers methods of reproduction that may eliminate some of the obstacles to publication that are now in effect.

The former director of the King's Crown Press at Columbia is conducting a survey under foundation auspices of the use of typescript reproduction in low edition formats. He is investigating other aspects of scholarly publication as well. Publication may be the only reward many scholars and scientists receive; sometimes it is less a reward than an obligation. The scholar must publish, but he has to face severe financial competition. Offset reproduction may be one solution. Miniature facsimile or the reproduction of pages at varying degrees of reduction may lower costs. As a sample, a copy of the *Bulletin* of the New York Public Library has been reduced by printing sixteen pages on a single sheet. A magnifier or some type of optical magnification device must be employed to read it.

An entirely new approach to printing is provided by a new process called Xerography which has not yet been placed on the market. It is a significant development, resembling offset lithography but using quite different principles. Offset lithography is based on the fact that greasy ink and water will not mix; consequently greasy ink on a moist plate can be used to print on an "offset" blanket, which in turn transfers the text to paper. Xerography uses another material and utilizes the electrical properties of attraction and repulsion. An image is placed on a plate by photographic printing—incidentally from microfilm—and dusted with a powder which takes the place of ink. Paper is then given an electrostatic charge and brought near the plate. The powder passes over the intervening gap between the prepared plate and the paper, and is rendered permanent by heat. The result is a new kind of printing which has many possibilities.

Another new development promises photo-composition at extremely low unit costs. A machine now in operation but not yet ready for the market will enable a competent typist to produce material that is precisely similar in appearance to conventional printing and allows great flexibility in choice of type size and font. The end product is a "printed" page in the form of a photographic negative or positive. It is only necessary to make a photo-offset plate from the negative and run off the required edition. Since composition accounts for a considerable percentage of the expense of printing, this new labor-saving device, when available, should materially reduce the cost.

A second field, photographic reproduction, deals with the many applications of photography to documentary work. Photography all too often means full-size techniques such as the making of photographic plates for large prints—reflex prints and photostats or, more accurately, photocopies. Although such "copies" are included in the program of the Center for Scientific Aids to Learning, greater emphasis has been given to miniature photographic techniques—to microfilm, both sixteen and thirty-five millimeters wide in long ribbon-like lengths and in sheets. High reduction submicro reproduction is a promising development. The higher the reductions, the greater the number of pages that can be accommodated in a particular area, but also the greater the required precision of operation. A single sheet about 4 by 5 inches in size can suffice for reproducing an entire book. A small volume can be further reduced to a film about the general dimensions of a pinhead with the text intact and readable. A reduction of this size would produce a submicro print. During the war, application of submicro reproduction, known as the microdot, was used by German espionage agents. The microdot was made photographically from a page of typewritten manuscript, sometimes in code and sometimes in text, reduced to about the dimensions of the period or the dot over the letter *i* on a typewriter. The transparencies were then colored and affixed to a letter. The recipient would clean the microdot of the color and read through a microscope. The system was used also in Latin America with some initial success.

Of more immediate importance is a photographic development known as the microcard. As an edition technique, it resembles microprint and miniature offset. The microcard can reproduce about seventy pages and must be read in a special reflection reading machine.

Microfilm is a method of reproducing current material for preservation without using long or bulky files. Current and past files of some four hundred daily papers in this country are being preserved on microfilm. Banks and insurance companies and the federal government make microfilms by the millions; all war bond stubs are microfilmed for record purposes. Microfilm is also a method whereby a scholar or scientist may secure required documentation at a nominal cost.

At the Massachusetts Institute of Technology a bibliography

of micro techniques is being compiled. There are thousands of titles and the greater number relate to articles or monographs. Once compiled, the bibliography will be reproduced in the form of microfilm negatives. This work illustrates an important field for scholars and scientists. It is possible now in compiling a bibliography in a relatively restricted field to secure microfilm copies of all the items. In the history of shipbuilding, for example, there are perhaps one thousand significant titles between 1587 and 1800, including different editions. A bibliography, accompanied by microfilm negatives of each title represented deposited at a central point, obviously creates a special and functional collection. Anyone interested in the field may then write to secure a positive microfilm copy of any item.

Reading machines for use with microfilm or any other miniature reproduction are as yet the most troublesome hindrances to widespread adoption of the technique. By definition, a microfilm is a miniature textual image on film, reduced so that it is not readable by the unaided eye; some magnifying or other device must therefore be used to read the text. The cheapest really good reading machine costs approximately six hundred dollars. Others range in cost from seventy-five dollars to almost a thousand. An instrument which would fit into a brief case, suitable for the average scholar or scientist, costing nearer twenty-five dollars, would be of real service.

A third field of interest, visual education, involves the use of motion pictures, film and other slides, and pictorial materials generally in the processes of instruction. At the Center, interest is restricted to material of university grade, since many other societies and individuals are working effectively on material at other levels. Some interesting hypotheses have been developed. Some distinction between visual education and entertainment has had to be drawn. If it is true that a motion picture "teaching film" is predominantly instructional only for the first three to five minutes, and if subsequently it becomes predominantly entertainment, the implications are obvious. It might be desirable to develop a type of medium designed to project teaching films for short periods. If one desired to illustrate a lecture, for example in physics, in such a way that the demonstrations would always work, and so as to avoid the instructor's having to crawl about the room connecting up equipment, the result would be much more effective. The fact that there is a direct drop in the efficiency of visual education when the lecturer turns his back to the audience to point out something on the screen, has lead to the development of equipment which will allow him to continue to face the audience while referring to the projected image.

The fourth interest is sound-recording, and the use of various types of sound material in instruction, in the preservation of information in communication, and in the work-patterns of the individual. Facilities at the Massachusetts Institute of Technology range from the Acoustics Laboratory through the many electronic and related laboratories, to the departments of Modern Languages, English, History, and the library. The new Charles Hayden Memorial Library will feature a carefully worked out center for the use of sound. Efforts are also being concentrated on the development of a sound-spectrograph, an instrument developed initially by Bell Laboratories during the war and used for various purposes, among them reproduction in the form of a frequency or energy pattern of sound as it is spoken, for phonetics research and other purposes. The sound-spectrograph is a basic research tool that may even prove useful in measuring comprehension in reading.

The fifth and final field is mechanical selection. As the fund of general knowledge has grown, the difficulties of gaining access to information have increased almost in a geometric ratio. We do not now know with certainty how to lay hands on facts that should be instantly at hand. Punched cards used with the I.B.M. punch card selectors, the Bush rapid selector, and other solutions have been offered, but no definitive large-scale experiment has been completed. A project undertaken in coöperation with the American Chemical Society has been organized as a test. Structural formulas in chemistry will be reduced according to the "Dysonian notation" to symbols that can be punched on cards and selected by machine. Dyson, a distinguished British scientist, developed a code book which will allow structural formulas to be converted to characters and figures that can be punched on a punch-card machine and then sorted. A new alphabet must be learned, but the results may justify the effort. A full-scale test set of cards is now in process. It is not as easy to make the cards as it is to use them, that is to say, to machine-sort a date file for material of particular properties. The file is cumulative and if used widely will be economically feasible. There is, too, a definite similarity between a structural chemical formula and an electrical circuit. If the experiment relating to chemistry succeeds, subjects in electrical engineering may be the next field.

Another approach to the problem of access to voluminous data is illustrated by the Bush rapid selector. This incorporates a large file of material on microfilm that has been carefully indexed and can be searched with great rapidity. As an inquiry is set up, the film is fed into the machine, and the result is a copy of all the related material contained in the master file. There is a machine of this sort now being built in Washington which will be used to provide access to seized enemy technical information files.

Some discussion of a radical new development which has only recently become public knowledge may be of interest. The Radio Corporation of America recently previewed Ultrafax at the Library of Congress in Washington. Ultrafax is one of the most interesting developments in the transmission of information to appear in the postwar period. Essentially it is a television by-product whereby material, either in the original or in microfilm, may be televised with great rapidity and transmitted within a circle of about three hundred miles. The receiving machine uses a microfilm camera to reproduce the televised images. A special fast processing machine develops them for projection on a screen in a very short time. At the first public demonstration of this particular technique, *Gone with the Wind* was televised in 2 minutes and 14 seconds. It was not televised from the original book because the pages could not be turned sufficiently fast, but from a microfilm copy which passed across the scanning plate and was reproduced in the form of microfilm at the receiver. The importance of Ultrafax lies in the fact that it would allow the great libraries of the future to become centralized depositories equipped with Ultrafax, or something like it. Instead of readers coming to the library, the inquiry could be dialed to the library from a portable or fixed Ultrafax set, and the required material would be televised and recorded, ready for immediate use. The only hitch in Ultrafax at the moment is the cost, which is still about two thousand times the price of a telephone call.

These notes may provide an introduction to some aspects of scientific aids to learning. They detail concepts and equipment designed to help the research worker, the student, and even the more or less casual reader, to make his way in a sea of documentation.

What then of the actual and potential uses? In the humanities, the library is the laboratory; in the sciences, documentary research has come to be fully as important as laboratory research. Library and documentation policies therefore are of a vital interest to both humanists and scientists. Yet it is surprising to find neither group devoting as yet sufficiently serious attention or effort to understanding or utilizing the new facilities. In this formative period there might well be, in every institution, a specialized course of instruction stressing the use of the library and all its tools. Micro-reproduction as a tool for research, and as a vehicle for publication and communication, should be explored. At this time, while the student is developing his own methods of research, he should be brought into contact with all the known scientific and library aids to learning. The effort will be rewarded in many diverse fields. Should the student enter business or industry, he will have knowledge that can be widely applied. The same situation will prevail for law, medicine, engineering, or virtually any profession, trade, or occupation. Finally, if the student decides to devote himself to an academic career, he will possess the background for maximum utilization of the resources of our present civilization. Scientific aids to learning are fast becoming essential tools for the scholar. Remember the proverb: a workman is known by his tools.

SPEECH MECHANICS FOR THE TEACHER

NEILSON CAMPBELL HANNAY

Chapter IX

THE INSTRUCTOR AND EFFECTIVE SPEECH

Speaking as an aspect of personality. The teacher must himself desire to use speech effectively. This involves elements of his physical and emotional mechanisms; health, posture, poise, proper use of the breathing and vocal apparatus, modulation, articulation, pitch, inflection, tempo, emphasis, spontaniety, drama, general bearing, and zealousness to serve rather than obstruct communication through speech.

Personnel evaluation for positions of importance is receiving increasing emphasis. In academic circles this emphasis is especially apparent. As competition for college teaching positions becomes more intensive with the growing number of available candidates, the sifting of these candidates becomes more and more thorough. The prospective instructor must expect to meet a qualification standard which includes, besides character, such criteria of fitness as ability to coöperate with departmental and other faculty members, scholarship, experience, intellectual honesty, pedagogical aptitude, health, generous liberality in expenditure of himself, and, preëminently, that complex asset we call *personality.* With this latter asset I shall be especially concerned at first because it conditions the effectiveness of one's speech; later I shall treat of speech technique.

The technique of effective speech is elaborate and exacting and is made up of innumerable details. To master this technique requires patient and persistent discipline. It is not enough to be *interested* in speech improvement; if you desire to attain speech effectiveness, you must *want* it and want it very much. The fact that you have spoken articulately for many years is no guarantee that you are utilizing your vocal resources at their best. Ordinarily a person becomes a qualified speaker as a potential poet becomes a master, namely, by learning the rules and the restrictions and the disciplines implicit in the art; thus he finds release of power within law.

If you want to be effective in the personality that conditions speech you must start by being a good animal. A student may be allowed certain cuts, but the teacher cannot take cuts. He must be on his job five or six days a week and for extra hours; he must not miss; he must not be late; he must not be half ill when at work—in short, he must be, or appear to be, physically competent. The teacher needs health because he needs to be at maximum efficiency, cheerful and happy and buoyant when teaching, and you cannot be cheerful and happy and buoyant without good health. He needs health and endurance for certain qualities of personality and for essential qualities of voice. As the case of a violin is as important as the strings, so the body is as much the instrument of speech as are the vocal organs. You speak, or you should speak, from your head to your feet. The whole body is the soundboard through which speech is transmitted and qualified; therefore you need good health.

To be a good animal you must have good posture, for good posture is the condition of proper breathing and consequently of good health. Within the body there are two large cavities separated by the diaphragm, the thoracic and the abdominal. If you slump and slouch, you shorten the capacity of the thorax from two to three inches; if your posture is correct, your heart and lungs and liver will function freely and your general circulation will improve. If you will sit and stand and walk with correct posture, within perhaps a matter of three weeks you will be able to note an improvement in health and spirits. Whether in an auditorium or in a classroom, a speaker impresses people by what he appears to be as truly as by what he says, for people listen with their eyes as well as with their ears. You are always communicating something to the group before you, either overtly, by willed and purposeful action, or covertly, by the physical intimations of the effect of your thought and feeling upon yourself. Good posture will say the right thing; bad posture may suggest an inferiority complex; but the posture *will* speak.

Inseparable from posture is that asset we call poise. It is perhaps as much mental as it is physical. Essentially it is the introduction of control into the physical and the mental. Such control is pedagogically invaluable. A teacher controls others to the extent that he controls himself, and no more. If you have physical and mental control so that you are not flustered or excited, so that you do not do things you do not intend to do, so that you do not make meaningless or grotesque gestures, you have poise. If students become excited or contentious or unruly, you cannot react in the same way or you will lose the game; you must introduce control into your mentality, and your control will be an intimation to them that they should govern themselves accordingly.

More positively, the teacher ought to be dramatic. Remember that people listen with their eyes. If you want to teach effectively you will need to give your students cues, to intimate how you think and feel about the subject matter of your teaching. If you do not do that, your students will probably develop an attitude of indifference, possibly of boredom; but if you are interested, if you reveal the animation that is sincere because you think and feel very keenly about the material you are considering, if you are intellectually incandescent, somehow the spark within you will ignite your students, and they will glow with interest and enthusiasm. Don't be afraid to be dramatic. Be dramatic to the extent of being memorably individual.

When you stand before a class you face a group that expects things of you. You are supposed to know more about your subject than they know. They expect you to lead. When you meet a person a little contest takes place. He has his background, his experience, his information, and he values them; you have yours, which you likewise value. Then you two meet, and one personality impinges upon the other, and there is, often unconsciously, a minor psychic struggle for mastery. Which one is going, for the time being, to lead the other? Your function is to dominate.

Vigorous health, good posture, poise, dramatic action, individuality and sovereignty of bearing will do much to effect this dominating influence; but your major reliance, to express your thinking, will be upon speech, upon your ability to do yourself justice through the medium of expressed language.

You will be judged in large measure by your ability to requisition your mental resources and to express them adequately in words. This desideratum President Eliot emphasized in his often quoted statement: "I recognize but one mental acquisition as an essential part of the education of a lady or a gentleman, namely, an accurate and refined use of the mother tongue." If you are to have an effective use of your mother tongue you will need a good vocabulary. By "good" I mean extensive, accurate, selective, and contemporary. Today you as a teacher need a working vocabulary of about 30,000 words, double the number you probably now possess and utilize, so that when you want to say something you have the requisite verbal resources. To make this addition requires hard, persistent discipline, but the reward will be mental growth and power. When you increase your word stock you push back your mental horizon a little farther.

Even so, however, if you are to maximize your personality as a teacher, you will require skillful vocal technique. The human voice is a marvelously complex instrument. You have a mechanism consisting of tongue, lips, palate, sinuses, larynx, lungs, and so on, and you have a brain capable of thinking. The instant you think or feel, you can at will connect the thinking and feeling instrument with the sound mechanism in a perfect synchronism so that the two coöperate as a unit. But the functioning of the mechanism will be no better than the ideals of functioning you keep in mind. You cannot expect to go far in the perfecting of vocal technique unless you set before yourself high ideals of vocal efficiency and then feel that it is worth while going out to achieve these ideals. If speech is to function at its best, the voice must be trained to please and to impress.

To have a voice that is attractive you must begin by learning how to breathe; that is as fundamental as anything in the art of speaking. If you don't breathe satisfactorily, you will not speak satisfactorily, and you will not have much vocal endurance. You have been breathing for a long, long time, but, unless you have been instructed and have adopted the technique taught, you probably have been breathing incorrectly. When you were an infant you breathed correctly. Little babies and animals, as I have often observed with fascination, have admirable breathing technique. Adults do equally well when they are asleep, while the subconscious mind is in control, but as soon as they take over with the conscious mind they function wrongly.

There are certain disciplines to which even teachers may need to devote themselves. How do you breathe correctly? You must expand the chest, because correct breathing means deep breathing and economical breathing. To get the chest up where it ought to be, raise your arms perpendicularly above your head; that pulls the ribs up off the hips and spreads them out. When you get your ribs up, keep them up, thus shortening the neck. Keep the chest hanging up on the shoulders. That is a fine start for good posture and good breathing. Next, having expanded the chest so that you have plenty of depth of breathing, use your diaphragm. This conical muscle that divides the thorax from the abdominal cavity is a voluntary muscle. To introduce diaphragmatic breathing, start your breathing with the abdominal muscles, which you have brought to tension by correct posture, and keep the shoulders perfectly still. Expand the abdomen and take in breath; then expel it by allowing the abdomen to collapse. The process is just like the working of a bellows. Probably you will need weeks, possibly months, of patient training to overcome your improper breathing habits, inveterate through long continuance, and to reëstablish correct automatic breathing technique, but the end result will justify and reward the self-imposed discipline; you will be able when speaking to breathe deeply and tirelessly as you should do. To test yourself, place your watch before you and take a deep breath; then say "ah," and prolong the sound for twenty-five or thirty seconds. If you can do this without taking a breath, you have reasonably good deep breathing. But you may not have economical breathing. Most people not only breathe as they please, but they waste breath when they talk. These breathy tones are unpleasant tones and tend to exhaust a speaker quickly. Sometimes it is highly important to be able to utter a long sentence without halting for breath in the middle. A simple test for economy of breath is to hold a lighted candle about three inches in front of the mouth, inhale deeply, open the mouth and say "ah," prolonging the tone evenly for twenty seconds without causing the candle to flicker. If you can do that, you are economizing breath.

In mastering the technique of deep, diaphragmatic, economical breathing you will have gained another indispensable speech asset, resonance. Resonance yields two invaluable vocal properties, carrying power and what are known as covered tones, both the effect of supplementary vibration. The carrying power of a tone does not result mainly from its loudness but from the amplitude of the vibration of sound waves, rounded fullness of volume or sonority rather than loudness. Other factors being equal, a resonant voice of mild intensity will be heard, directly or by telephone, farther than a forced, high-pitched, nonvibrant voice. Likewise, covered tones, which contrast so pleasingly with thin, bare, metallic, fundamental or pitch tones and which convert voice into music, are but overtones, the intensifying enrichment which resonance supplies. These are precious vocal values which a speaker cannot afford to disregard.

Furthermore, although ever mindful of tonal values of voice, you must remember that you speak primarily to communicate ideas, pleasingly if possible, but certainly intelligibly. If that communication is to be adequate, it must be characterized by distinctness. The problem of distinctness is mainly a matter of articulation and phonation and of the correct use of the relevant speech organs. Unless you do a neat job in your enunciation you will depreciate yourself to a marked degree and create an impression of intellectual slovenliness. To avoid giving such an impression, you will need to build up auditory ideals and school yourself in habits of deliberateness and accuracy of speech. Thus you may avoid defects of slurring, such as "gov'ment" for "government"; syllabic interpolation, such as "athalete" for "athlete"; and rhotacism, as in "fah" for "far" and "idear" for "idea." Furthermore, you will need to pronounce correctly all your vowels and diphthongs and consonants. As for the consonants, one of the most common defects is the tendency to omit them in certain relations, as in the pronunciation "wen" for "when" and "thas right" for "that's right"; another is excessive prolongation of some letters, such as *s*, resulting in sibilancy. The vowels, however, are often mispronounced, as when one says "gurl" for "girl," and they are usually slighted, to the great loss of carrying power, of beauty, and of impressiveness. And so I urge, DON'T—BE—AFRAID—TO—PROLONG—THE—VOWELS; if you exaggerate your vowels somewhat, you will improve your speaking.

For all these defects there are corrective exercises for those who patiently and persistently discipline themselves. In many instances the defects are due to wrong position of the organs of phonation and articulation. You cannot produce the correct sounds unless you know how and where to form them. As we have learned through photographs, there is, for instance, a requisite distance to open the mouth and a proper contour of the lips necessary if one is to pronounce the vowels correctly. For short *e* as in "met" the distance is one third inch, but for broad *a* as in "ah" it is two thirds of an inch. In the main, poor phonation and articulation are due to hurry, indifference, and downright laziness. We Americans have the laziest voice apparatus of all the English-speaking peoples—lazy jaws, lazy lips, lazy tongues, lazy laryngeal muscles. If you have these, you cannot enunciate clearly. You need to learn how to activate, to control, and to train your speech organs so that without your conscious effort they will function with precision.

Even when your phonation and articulation and use of the speech organs have been corrected, you will need to watch your pitch. This is especially a feminine hazard, inasmuch as the female voice averages about an octave higher than the male voice. Seldom is a voice too low. Perhaps you have assumed that your individual pitch of voice is fixed, is what you were born with, and that you cannot do anything about it. While it may be more difficult for persons having a certain physical structure than for others to alter their pitch, you must remember that the human voice is remarkably tractable; you can train it to a desired level just as you have trained yourself to raise or lower your hand at will. Each of us has a normal pitch. To ascertain yours, start with your usual pitch and go down the scale, sounding "ah" until you reach the lowest note you can sound fully and without strain; then run up the scale four whole notes, and you will reach what should be your pitch median. If this median is found to be too high or too low to meet with general approval, use your will and practice daily whenever you speak until you establish a pitch level that is moderately low and sonorous.

Pitch must be varied to avoid monotony and to adapt the voice to the idea to be expressed. You may have a thoroughly acceptable voice, well-controlled, resonant, pleasingly pitched, but if you harp on one string you will have at best magnificent monotony. How wide should one's range be? The average untrained person uses a range of only three notes, occasionally four. That is too narrow. If you can command five or six, you are fairly capable; if more than that, you are vocally superior, and you can continue to speak almost without limit and people will not weary. Otherwise, no matter how delightful your tone and how valuable your subject matter, you will tire your audience. All speakers who hold the attention of their hearers at length and who stimulate interest and awaken admiration on the platform or in the classroom make use of an extensive variety of tone. If such variety is wanting, it can be developed. You can extend your range by such a simple exercise as finding your median note on a piano, and then, following the diatonic scale, stretching your voice gradually note by note up or down as desired. But you must continue the practice frequently, regularly, and with determination.

Of equal importance with avoidance of monotony by range of voice is the ability to adjust the inflection to the sense you would convey, for the expression of meaning is largely contingent upon inflection. If, for instance, you wish to convey the idea of cheerfulness or optimism or buoyancy or hopefulness or encouragement or uncertainty, your voice should ride up to an appropriate height like a cork upon a rising wave; if your desire is to impress your hearers with the notion of seriousness or importance or futility or repugnance or refusal, it should drop to an appropriately low level. It should play through the scale of variance, not at random but with nice discrimination. As an illustration of this technique consider the following from Proverbs xv : 13–14:

> A merry heart maketh a cheerful countenance; (↑)
> But by sorrow of heart the spirit is broken. (↓)
> The heart of him that hath understanding seeketh knowledge; (↑)
> But the mouth of fools feedeth on folly. (↓)

Inflectional technique, be it ever so discriminating, can be impaired and even ruined by an unsuitable rate of speaking. What is a desirable rate? There is a tradition that 130 words per minute is a fairly satisfactory tempo. No standard should be so rigidly fixed. As some persons think rapidly and others slowly, a safe principle to keep in mind is never speak more rapidly than you can speak well; that is, adjust your tempo to your individuality. Having done that, do not forget that a deliberate rate—probably much slower than that you are accustomed to use—is essential to giving attention to the quality of your voice and to the control of your speech mechanism responsible for your breathing, your phonation, especially your vowels, your volume, your articulation, and the management of emphasis. Moreover, tempo, however deliberate, must not be unvarying. You should learn to accelerate and to decelerate according to your subject matter and the emphasis you desire to make. You should not glide into your sentences, falter through them with confused repetitions or with spasmodic spurts, and then glide lingeringly out of them. Like an expert musician you should attack promptly and finish abruptly. A certain crispness in speech is an intimation of intellectual tidiness and acuteness. To the prospective teacher, rate control should be a prime consideration. If you talk too fast, your slow-thinking students, who can't digest rapidly, will be unable to follow you; if you do not control your tempo to the point of effectiveness, they will not be impressed.

To a considerable extent, tempo is regulated by rhythm, and so you must learn how to manage that also. The average untutored speaker drives along at random speed, pausing anywhere he pleases in the middle of phrases and clauses, like a motorist blissfully indifferent to traffic lights and rules of the road. And yet all good speaking is characterized by a certain measured and proportioned motion, a designed flow of cadences, a grouping of tones in an accented pattern. Inasmuch as you as a speaker have no punctuation marks to guide you, you need other assistance. Some such aid derives from an observation of Robert Louis Stevenson. In his essay "On Some Technical Elements of Style in Literature" he affirms: "Each sentence, by successive phrases, shall first come into a kind of knot, and then, after a moment of suspended meaning, solve and clear itself." This node, or climactic point, is the key word towards which the mind rides up, and then declines. To speak a simple sentence with fluent rhythm, the voice should slight the unimportant words and with springy movement run up liltingly upon a rising curve to the node, pause on the key word for a perceptible instant, and then slope down from it to the end. If the sentence contains phrases and clauses, each of these will have a very small vocal node; if the sentence is compound or complex, obviously it will have two or more major nodes. Some types of sentence, such as the interrogatory and the exclamatory, may end climactically at the node. Of course, your hearers will not be aware of your technique any more than the amateur listener may be aware of the principles of a musical composition he enjoys. But your auditors, like their ancestors through the ages, have learned rhythm from the pulsations of their own heartbeats and from nature's undulating voices, and when you violate rhythm in your speaking they are uncomfortable; they feel that something is wrong, and they depreciate you. So, watch your rhythm.

If you do that, you will gain some assistance in mastering another troublesome speech technique, emphasis, or, to give it its technical name, ictus. The prevailing tendency is to overdo accentuation by giving vocal prominence to most of the words in the sentence. If this is done, rhythm suffers, and the sense, often wholly contingent upon stress, is obscured. In speaking and in reading, you should emphasize only those parts of a sentence that carry a heavy freight of meaning or require attention. Any word may call for emphasis if you want to summon special attention to it, but in general, verbs, nouns, adjectives, adverbs, and occasionally pronouns, but chiefly verbs and nouns, are of prime concern; the other words, prepositions, conjunctions, articles, and interjections, are for the most part just insignificant connective tissue, and as such are to be slighted. If stress is excessively frequent and you rely upon it exclusively to produce force of utterance, you will offend by your monotony; indeed, the stress by virtue of its very frequency will cease to be emphasis at all. Accordingly, it should be restrained. You can gain attention and stimulate interest by varying your rate, by altering your pitch, by nicely calculating the frequency and the duration of your pauses. In addition, you can employ the subtle and difficult technique of visualizing the *meaning* of your key word and pouring into it the emotional content which the image demands. If you can *feel* the value of the word in question, your voice will register the intensification, somewhat onomatopoetically, and the suggested image will become impressive.

At its best, this characteristic of voice quality, or timbre, may be regarded as the crown of vocal virtues; it is the distinctive property most likely to determine a speaker's success. You will readily admit that, whatever the temptation or provocation, a teacher cannot afford to allow his voice to intimate that he is discouraged or listless, cynical or sarcastic, conceited or browbeating. But what overtones *are* indispensable? In replying, selectively rather than comprehensively, I would stress three: spontaneity, authoritativeness, and friendliness. A teacher to be successful must at all times make it evident that he is very much alive. This is often difficult. He has worked over his material so long that it is almost contemptibly familiar to him, and this material he may be injudicious enough to read, or he may utilize it as notes. He may be obliged to teach two or three divisions of the same subject on the same day. He may teach at the fag end of the day when he is jaded or below par, when he had rather do almost anything but teach. To seem to be fresh and cheerful and buoyant and animated at such a time and to register this spontaneity in the voice will be taxing, but I know that it can and must be done.

If you can solve the problem of vocal spontaneity, you will have less difficulty in commanding the other indispensables, albeit you may be perplexed to harmonize them. Once a student has been awakened by his teacher's spontaneity, he is to be impressed by that teacher's note of positive authoritativeness—that dignified, courageous, judicial quality of tone that not only expresses dominance but convinces the student that the person before him is utterly fair, independent, and dependable. As a teacher, you need to create the impression that you are worth while and reliable because you know that you know. If you can do that, you have but one other hurdle to surmount: somehow you must contrive to mingle a tone of warm friendliness with your cool authoritativeness. You will want your students to be happy, for you know that only in the atmosphere of happiness can learning be at its best.

To recapitulate, our whole consideration comes to this: you must start by being a good healthy animal, with good posture and poise; you must go on to be somebody, such a dramatic and individualized personality that you impress yourself upon your students; you must lead both by your manner and by your command of the verbal resources of your mother tongue; you must discipline yourself diligently in the varied techniques of breathing, resonance, distinctness, pitch, range, tempo, rhythm, stress, timbre. All these assets you must seek to harmonize and to the harmony add a certain accentuation. In a word, as a teacher zealous to be successful, you must train yourself with long patience in the skills that enable you to reveal your thought through the blended qualities of competent and appealing speech.

THE INSTRUCTOR'S MANY-SIDED RELATIONSHIPS

PAUL H. BUCK

Chapter X

THE COLLEGE TEACHER AND FACULTY ORGANIZATION

The fledgling instructor and his development into a full-fledged professor. The proper balance between teaching and research. What parts these play in appointments and promotions. Types of institutions. How they are administered. The place of trustees, administrative officers, the faculty, and students.

Some twenty-five years ago, when I was a graduate student, I heard an address by Professor Haskins, then Dean of the Harvard Graduate School. He got off a remark that rather surprised me at the time; he said a graduate student is an academic hobbledehoy. I must confess that I had gone through that portion of my life without ever having heard or read that word "hobbledehoy" before. I went home and looked it up in a dictionary and found it defined as "a youth between boy and man; an awkward, gawky fellow." I must say that definition rather put me back a little. It rather dismayed me to hear the Dean of the Graduate School so describe his students of whom I was one. But as the years have passed, I think I can understand somewhat better what Dean Haskins had in mind. The adolescent scholar, like the growing youth, has his awkward age. The years of graduate study constitute a sort of in-between period. The individual is no longer a student in the undergraduate sense of the word, and he is restless under the many restraints and practices in our graduate training which persist from the undergraduate college. He is becoming a professional in scholarship and yet he is treated so often as though he were something less than this. The mature scholars who are his graduate instructors are not ready to say to him, "You have become one of us." When he is invited to participate in instruction as an assistant or a teaching fellow, the apprenticeship relationship is strongly emphasized. A good deal of this awkward in-betweenness cannot be avoided. I presume every professional man experiences it in some manner. Graduate training is to our profession what an internship is to a doctor of medicine and what a law clerkship, or secretaryship to a judge, is to the newly fledged lawyer. But those of us responsible for graduate instruction have not given enough thought, if indeed we have recognized its existence, to this aspect of the graduate student's experience. It does create situations, tensions, uncertainties that affect both the quality of graduate study and the future degree of success achieved by the individual. I wish to discuss some aspects of this subject.

You will find that this discourse will not be highly intellectual and I shall purposely keep it on quite an informal level. This is no talk on the philosophy of education, the inner meaning of physics, or causality in history. My subject is the prosaic one of problems we live with in our earnest effort to become teachers and researchers, the bread-and-butter sort of problems which sadly enough have as much to do with success in this sorry world as intelligence and application. A psychologist might say it was a matter of individual adaptation to the highly complex social organization of education.

From the days of the first graduate schools in this country, men have debated the issue of whether research and teaching conflict. And every individual who has passed through a graduate school and embarked upon a career in scholarship has pondered this issue in relation to his own future. Our graduate schools themselves reflect the unresolved debate. Does the graduate school exist to train teachers or does it exist to advance learning through research? If the answer is that the graduate school should do both, then we have the difficult questions: In what proportions? How maintain a balance? And the individual still wonders whether teaching skill or early publication will advance him more. Here as in so many aspects of American life we attempt a combination of aims. Our energies are required for adjusting the resulting conflicts, and we expose ourselves to the risk of individual frustration.

Graduate instruction as organized in graduate schools is a very recent addition to American education. The schools came first into being in the latter decades of the nineteenth century and reached their present position of influence only within the living memory of the older members of our present faculties. Not only is graduate instruction a youthful phenomenon; it is also a revolutionary one. It, more than any other influence, marked the transition from colleges concerned mainly with the teaching of boys in relatively elementary subjects into the modern university with its great complexity, its emphasis upon the advancement of learning, and its concern with great professional schools, as well as with the undergraduate college. So it is quite natural that the first great influence that the graduate schools had upon our colleges and universities was to establish research as an essential function of the university. A story from the early years of President Eliot's administration well illustrates this point. A young chemist had just returned from Germany, where he had found professors in German universities not merely teaching but also engaged in research in university-supported laboratories. This impressed greatly the young Harvard chemist, who accordingly explained the matter to President Eliot and requested funds for establishing such a laboratory here. President Eliot turned down the request for the reason that the work would not relate directly to teaching and hence had no place in the university.

Eliot, of course, changed his attitude very quickly and later, as everyone knows, vigorously supported research in universities. But the very fact that so great a champion of research held contrary views when he first became president of Harvard all the more graphically illustrates my point of the newness in American education of the university concept of advancing learning through research. The American college of the pre-Eliot era lived up to its purpose of training youth, but the ancient concept of the university as a conservator, transmitter, and advancer of learning did not exist in any vital sense.

The first great mission of the graduate schools in this country was to establish research as an integral part of the university. Consequently the early graduate school had to emphasize method, giving much attention to the seminar and the laboratory. It had to plant and carefully nourish among faculty and the student body the curiosity of the investigator. It had also to preach to society the relation of research to the well-being of the country so as to win from donors and from legislatures financial support.

The task has been well done. So much energy had to be devoted to its accomplishment, however, that the concept of training youth was more or less taken for granted and has accordingly suffered from lack of emphasis. Research especially came into its own during the recent war and was widely publicized. Today in our graduate schools research is dominant, it is glamorous, and in some fields like physics and medicine it has become big-business in the size and complexity of its organization. Teaching may appear, in contrast, drab and uninviting. Hence the appeal of teaching and its rewards need stressing today. More attention needs to be given to the methods of teaching. Its place in the university needs recalling. And certainly there should be given some preparation in the art of teaching. It is certainly an anomaly of the times that our graduate schools with their seminars and laboratories in research methods are entirely devoid of similar methods for training teachers. This situation is all the more indefensible in that the great bulk of our graduates must earn their living by teaching.

If the graduate schools have not successfully adjusted themselves to this conflict in aims, one can readily understand why their students suffer from confusion in their efforts to balance research and teaching in their individual equations. It is true, of course, that a number, and perhaps an increasing number, of our graduates enter research institutes or industry and never teach. But by far the great majority do devote the major part of their time and energy to teaching. And this group must face the problem of research and teaching.

Speaking bluntly, you cannot get a Ph.D., much less a job, unless you have demonstrated your ability to do research. You cannot hold a job unless you show some skill in teaching. By the nature of things it is easier to assess the quality of a man's intelligence from a published article or book than it is from the always more or less vague description of his teaching. Hence more often than not the research performance is the more influential factor in getting the young man his first job. But then the teaching factor immediately has its innings. Nothing shows up more painfully than early failure in the classroom. Our academic history is full of such episodes.

Ideally a graduate training should provide for training in research and practice in teaching. There should also be some conscious effort made to explain the relationship of the two and what each will exact from the individual. One's first job in teaching should not be so burdened with classroom duties that the interest in research is lost. If so, you will end in having a teacher whose mind is dead to future growth. Nor should the individual enter his first classroom to neglect its proper demands so that he can give all his best efforts to research. If so, he will secure for himself a sorry reputation among colleagues and students. It is always difficult to approximate an ideal. But certainly the first step is to face the actual facts. Confusion and frustration tend to disappear when students are given the facts with which to work.

The basic point to remember is that there is no necessary conflict between teaching and research. Research keeps a subject alive. It rejuvenates the researcher. One of the most tragic things in academic life is the middle-aged man whose subject has gone dead on him. With approximately twenty-five years behind him and a similar period ahead, he is teaching by rote, repeating lectures and ideas which once had the stimulation of life but today lack the spark of living fire. He has gone to seed. His subject is dead. His students are listless. The only way I know of avoiding this tragic fate is to live always with the new ideas of your subject. Give attention to those who work on the frontiers where new ideas are discovered and assessed. Be one of those who are sharing this exciting venture. You need never worry then about what you have to carry into the classroom. There are, fortunately, many kinds of research and hence many ways in which the individual can adapt his own interest and aptitude to the process of keeping himself intellectually alive.

On the other hand, in this country at least, I believe that the researcher profits a good deal from teaching. We express ourselves largely in terms of a living society. Kinship with that living society gives insight into the basic aims of research. Such kinship can be realized most directly in our academic world through contact with students. The classroom, the seminar, and the laboratory serve both as a source of ideas and as a testing ground for their validity. The researcher who closets himself frequently finds himself out of touch with the living environment and the energy of democratic society. Since the days of Solomon, some people have fancied a sort of research institute with no students to divert the research staff. I question whether such institutes are as productive or as meaningful in this country as what we have—the university faculty with its dual responsibility.

I personally doubt whether basically there need be a conflict between teaching and research, although I readily admit that both the institution and the individual have a problem in keeping them in proper balance. Each can facilitate the work of the other. Research will keep teaching alive. Teaching will keep research meaningful.

The phase of the problem which concerns the individual graduate student most is whether research or teaching counts more in appointments and promotions. I have already alluded to this. The truth of the matter is that this particular problem is only a phase of the much larger problem of appointment and tenure and that the whole subject is unnecessarily encumbered by too much mystery and secrecy. At Harvard we have given a good deal of thought during the past decade to evolving criteria and procedures which are both searching and fair. We expect men to have both teaching skill and research interests. We do not expect to find them equally represented in every man, but we do expect a man to excel in one and be adequate in the other. And we believe that in a faculty like ours there can be a career open to a man who excels in either, provided he, at the same time, does not ignore the other. Thus a man can be an excellent teacher and a good researcher, or an excellent researcher and a good teacher, and we should be interested in him. If he were excellent in both, as a few notable individuals are, we are more than pleased. We are not interested in a man who is excellent in one aspect and poor in the other. This because, let me repeat, our faculty has a dual function: teaching and research. It can neglect neither. Now, just as there are varieties of research, so also are there varieties of teaching. Part of the problem again is giving the individual the type of teaching task for which his interest and aptitude best equip him.

It is extremely difficult to secure an objective, impartial, and searching assessment of any individual who is a candidate for a position. How significant is the research? Was it his own idea or did it proceed from someone else? Has he a continuing interest in research? What will he be like ten or twenty years hence? Can he teach? Will he overcome this or that defect in lecturing? Will he coöperate with his colleagues? These are only a few of the bewildering problems most of which cannot be answered without the help of a crystal gazer. Then enter other factors which proceed from the human equation. Is the man as good as his sponsor suggests, or is it the not infrequent story of a professor pushing a protégé? Is the man on the scene getting a better break because he is known than the outsider who may be abler but not so well known? Has the young man with the new idea stepped on some tender toes, or has he caused offense in older circles by the not uncommon tendency of youthful brilliance to be brash?

The only solution to these problems is a procedure which makes use of multiple checks. The assessment should be vertical in that it brings into play the observation of students, all members of the department, the dean, and the president. It should be horizontal in that it seeks opinion outside as well as inside the university. And while the opinions themselves must be kept in confidence, the essential features of the procedure should be well recognized and observed in each detail in every case. Gradually the system will grow in perfection and win the confidence of the candidates, thus removing one of the most serious of the tensions in the life of the young scholar.

So much for one large aspect of my theme. A second aspect is the approach to the type of institution in which the young instructor finds his first teaching job. The diversity of American education is a truism. We have a wide variety of institutions all calling themselves universities and colleges. It should be an obvious corollary that these variant types need variant types of individuals on their teaching staffs and that an individual who might be happy and successful in one place will be unsuccessful and unhappy somewhere else. Nevertheless, I know of no graduate school which adjusts its program with this variety in mind. The same Ph.D.'s in economics are thought equally well prepared to teach at Columbia, Oberlin, Tulane, Temple, Sarah Lawrence, Chicago, Texas, Beloit, California, Denver, Cincinnati, Minnesota, or Agnes Scott. Most students in our graduate schools think too much in general terms, as though wherever you went and whatever job you found, it would be pretty much the same thing, requiring the same preparation, the same adaptation, and the same qualities. There is nothing that could be further from the truth.

Individuals are unlike in their range of abilities, habits, and interests. Institutions vary greatly in size, structure, program, locality, and type of students. Hence happiness and success depend quite a good deal on the individual's being placed in the type of institution best suited for him. Some few individuals are either so outstanding in ability or adaptable to any environment that they get along anywhere. Likewise some others are so lacking in brains and personality that they would fail anywhere. But for the most of us the old adage of one man's poison being another man's meat is good. Each of us experienced in this problem can cite innumerable instances: as for example, a son of Alabama trained at Harvard failing at North Carolina and then succeeding at a small college in Iowa; a son of Chicago failing at a small eastern college and succeeding in a great state university; a farm boy from Nebraska failing in Oregon and succeeding at a great urban university in the East. I have never believed the problem was one essentially of migration from one section to another. Our history is too full of the success of migratory individuals. Rather it seems to me essentially two things. First, our graduate schools do not prepare the students adequately to meet the diversity either intellectually or in attitude. A man going to a small college will certainly require a different preparation from one entering a large university. In the latter, for example, he may teach only a special phase of his subject. In the former he may well find himself the only man in his field and expected to teach quite generally all phases of the subject. The second is that our graduate students must be disabused of the idea that the only place a successful career can be achieved is in a half-dozen or so "prestige" universities. We have been very remiss in our failure to present to our graduate students the wide range of opportunity which exists in the rich diversity of American education. The result has been a timidity on the part of the students, a narrow horizon, and unnecessary unhappiness.

There is much to choose from. All sections of the nation have all types of institutions. There is bigness, medium size, and smallness. There is the complex program of Minnesota and the simple program of St. John's, and all varieties of combination in between. There are high standards and low standards, communities that are impersonal and others that are neighborly. Some colleges are urban and others rural, some offer liberal arts and others vocational training. Some have two-year curricula, others four, others merge into graduate and professional schools. A good deal of study should be given to this diversity. The individual should give much thought to the preparation and the adaptation which will be required of him in terms of the actual community he is entering.

There are advantages and disadvantages peculiar to each type of institution. This is true of the small liberal arts college as it is of the urban university, and of the state university as it is of the church-related college. The impact of entering a different environment upon graduate students trained at Harvard, Columbia, Chicago, and California can produce situations which are both tragic and ludicrous. Some of the humor of academic life would be lost if graduate students were more intelligently advised of what confronted them, but if such were done the potentiality of each institution would be better realized and its peculiar hazards more frequently avoided.

An evil which exists in virtually every type of institution is the tendency to force the young instructor to teach too much on too many subjects, to make him responsible for a wide variety of programs, and not to protect himself sufficiently from his own youthful enthusiasm and generosity to students. More often than not bright young people in such instances are stifled, not only as researchers, but as buoyant teachers by far too much teaching in the first ten years of their tenure.

A related evil is that in these early years of preoccupation with the problems of the new job and the responsibilities assumed in the new home which comes with marriage, the young instructor unconsciously falls into habits which isolate him from centers of thought and the ferment of ideas. The richness and stimulation of his graduate-school days disappears. He ceases reading the new books and articles in his fields. It is too expensive, so he feels, to attend the meetings of his learned society. After a decade of this isolation and overwork of early teaching, the instructor, no longer young, is found to be intellectually stagnant. The promise of his early years is gone. He seems destined to mediocrity. If you wish to remain alive, you must work especially hard to keep alive during the first decade you leave the graduate school. This is the individual's responsibility. No less important is the institution's responsibility of protecting, as a matter of conscious policy, the young instructor's growth. If it wishes to avoid a great deal of middle-age dead wood and old-age dry rot, on its faculty, the time to begin is in that first decade of the instructor's tenure. The remedies are quite obvious: a teaching schedule that is not too heavy or too routine (90 per cent of all young instructors' teaching schedules are both), an occasional semester off, and encouragement to participate in the professional activities of the learned society in his field.

The third aspect of my theme is the place of the young instructor in the government of his college or university. This is a much misunderstood subject. It surprises me how little students, or even members who have spent a lifetime on the faculty, really understand how their particular institution is administered. You hear a lot of gossip that So-and-So runs Such-and-Such and usually that he is running it badly. If you actually look into it, there is no common pattern of how any institution is administered. The man who holds a particular title in one institution might be doing something quite different from someone with the same title in another institution. How are our educational institutions administered anyway? There is no one answer. In any institution that I know anything about there is always a great deal of illogicality in the arrangement. Inconsistency and variety appear in every direction. The great philosopher, Alfred North Whitehead, who came to Harvard, fortunately, after a career in England and spent here many years, said that if anyone was shown a diagram and told that Harvard was run the way it seems to be run, he would say it would not work. It was so illogical, the lines were so mixed up and confused, yet, said Mr. Whitehead, "The place does run surprisingly well." Traditions and personalities have a great deal to do with it. One president or one dean would accomplish something in the same office with the same authority beyond what a predecessor or a successor might or might not have done. Tradition and personality mean a gread deal; but in every institution there is, I think, a give-and-take among five elements: trustees, administrative officers, faculty, students, and alumni.

What is the range of trustees' activities? You have to have them. Sometimes they are a small group; sometimes they are a large group. At Harvard it is a combination of both. We have two governing boards. One is the so-called Corporation, made up of the President, the Treasurer, and five Fellows, who are very active, who meet regularly, own the property of the institution, and vote major appointments and decisions of policy upon the recommendations from the Provost or dean of the school in question. Then we also have a Board of Overseers who are elected by the alumni and are very widely representative of all interests in America. A group of about thirty men, they do not meet very often; but they have the final authority to investigate, if they wish, any part of the university. The range of activity on the part of these two boards of trustees, or governing boards, is quite different. I think that in the more stable, enlightened universities the governing boards have come to realize that their main function is not to meddle too much in the details of internal administration, or of educational policy. Insofar as selection of personnel and the shaping of educational policy is concerned, those people who are spending their lives in the university know better as experts than do a group of men from the governing board, distinguished as they may be. Those more enlightened boards, it seems to me, have come to define certain procedures which are proper and which, if followed, safeguard the major interests of the university. These boards insist that such procedures be followed. If followed, they usually abide by the results; if not followed, then they quite rightly interfere. I think that is roughly more or less what the Harvard governing boards preoccupy themselves with. And yet this does not completely solve the problem. Much as we properly cherish academic freedom, the faculty of any university must recognize its responsibility to society. Like any human institution, if left completely to itself it may be irresponsible in the discharge of this responsibility. Its educational policy may become inadequate; its appointments unwise. It is at such times that the governing boards must be prepared to speak for the prior interest of society that the universities live up to their great responsibility. The governing boards do represent, as a faculty cannot represent, the public's stake in the university. This is a sobering responsibility. The board that discharges it must realize the nature of universities and be aware how easily the power can be abused. We have had both wise and unwise boards in the United States. Fortunately for us at Harvard, our two governing boards have acted with wisdom.

In a more mundane way the governing boards must protect the property of an institution. The teaching faculty take too much for granted. But the financing of an institution, whether privately or state supported, is an exceedingly arduous task. The income of any institution must be translated into living resources. When you are appointed to a position that has tenure, someone has to be concerned with the problem of having resources sufficient to pay your salary until the day of your retirement. This is one headache faculties have quite readily left to their governing boards.

Secondly, there are the administrative officers: the president, the deans, the department chairmen, and so on. I have no interest in discussing this except to make the personal observation that I believe all college and universtiy administrative officers (other than the business and financial officers) should be selected from the teaching staff and should have come up the professorial ladder. Universities are such peculiar institutions that I doubt whether they can be wisely administered except by one who thinks and acts like a professor.

Then there is the faculty. What should the faculty be primarily concerned with? Here you have a very difficult matter. We like to have democracy in our faculties, but a member of the faculty is also a professional in some line of work. He may be a chemist, he may be a physicist, he may be a historian. To master his specialty as a teacher and as a researcher takes a lot of time. If he gets up in a faculty meeting and takes a stand either for or against something, it usually ends by a committee being appointed to study the matter, and some officer then appoints him to that committee. Then he has to spend a lot of time on it and that time has to be taken from his professional work of scholarship and teaching. In other words, there is a clash all the time between the individual's own work and its details, and the time that is required for self-government. Democracy is a form of government which involves service on an endless number of committees composed of individuals who have an inviolable right to talk forever. In a democracy you talk a problem either to death or to a solution. This is time consuming. It is wearing on the individual. Consequently it is very distasteful to many people. So on every faculty a goodly number of men avoid committee work, which means that the burden is heavier on those who either like it or are too conscientious to avoid it. There is a good deal of joking about faculty committees. But the fact remains, faculty committees are the only way the self-governing of a faculty can be exercised. And if any semblance of democracy is to prevail, membership on such committees must be a matter of rotation.

It seems to me that there are three major policies which the faculty should handle rather than delegate. The first of these is the policy in respect to admissions. The decision as to who comes to a particular college and on what terms is so central to the future of the institution that no self-respecting faculty will surrender its interest in the matter. At Harvard each faculty determines the broad aspects of admission policy and delegates to a committee of faculty members the application of the policy.

The second obvious matter of faculty concern is educational policy. The governing boards at Harvard have authorized the various faculties to award certain degrees. The Faculty of Arts and Sciences thus awards the degrees A.B., A.M., and Ph.D. In doing so it defines the requirements for the degree and the course offerings in the curriculum. Every aspect of educational policy should be an active and continuous concern of a faculty. Not the least of its concerns should be an awareness of the broader aims of education to which its particular program should be related.

The third major aspect of faculty activity should be concern for and participation in the procedure by which individuals are appointed to the faculty and the tenure rules which govern their continuance on the faculty.

I shall say nothing about the role of students in the governing of a college except this: they are the guinea pigs of the educational process. They are fairly mature. They have been so carefully selected that their innate intelligence probably averages somewhat higher than that of the faculty. Hence, my suspicion is that a good deal can be learned from students and I urge you to do what you can as teachers to make their weight felt.

President Lowell once said that Harvard had, in its three centuries, accumulated a great store of knowledge because each freshman brought a little learning and the seniors took nothing away. If this be true I do not know what we can expect from the alumni in the governing of an institution. If, however, the college has been successful, the alumni will be loyal, and if loyal, will know best how to serve the institution.

A. BAIRD HASTINGS

Chapter XI

THE COLLEGE TEACHER AND PROFESSIONAL SOCIETIES

Professional societies the modern version of the eighteenth-century learned society. Their contributions to the teacher are many: they provide a platform where the novice can be seen and heard, they offer a forum for criticism and discussion, they usually publish journals, and they maintain an atmosphere congenial to friendships within one's chosen profession. International societies represent the universal company of scholars.

I assume that all of you who are going to be teachers will join one or more professional societies sometime during your professional careers, hence the reason for a discussion of this particular subject. When I became interested in what were the facts about scientific societies, I found they were rather hard to get. My secretary wrote to various potential sources of information and finally obtained from the United States Office of Education what to me were some rather staggering figures. There are about 100,000 teachers, distributed in 2,000 colleges and universities. Those teachers belong to about 500 national professional societies and to many additional state and local societies. From a sampling of over 20,000 teachers in the north central states, it was found that each teacher belonged to an average of 1.8 societies. Professors belonged to the most, 2.2 societies per person; instructors to the least, to something less than one per person. These teachers, however, did not attend the meetings of their societies very frequently. The figure is, on the average, about one meeting per member every five years, so that, roughly speaking, members attend only about one-tenth of the meetings of the societies to which they belong. Now, I have no profound moral to draw from these data save to point out that there are probably enough professional societies to meet the needs of the college teacher and that what we need are more good teachers rather than more professional societies.

Our modern societies date from the academy founded by Plato for his philosophical school. Scientific societies in this country began with the foundation of the American Philosophical Society in Philadelphia by Benjamin Franklin in 1743, closely followed by the American Academy of Arts and Sciences in Boston in 1780. Both of these societies served the advancement of the arts and sciences in this country by being forums for the presentation of discoveries resulting from observation and experiments and for the debate of theories, and both are flourishing today. As far as I am aware neither of these societies felt any overt responsibility toward education, but their influence on what was taught and how it was taught was far-reaching and continues to be so.

Although the American Philosophical Society was modeled on the Royal Society of London, whose stated objective was the "improvement of natural knowledge," Benjamin Franklin gave it a more practical objective, "the promotion of useful knowledge." In 1780 this objective was more fully worked out as follows:

> Its objective is for the cultivation of knowledge, the advancement of the liberal arts and sciences in the interests of the improvement of agriculture, the enlargement of trade, the ease and comfort of life, the ornament of society, and the increase and happiness of mankind. . . . The experience of ages shows that the improvements of a public nature are best carried on by societies of liberal and ingenious men, writing their labors without regard

to nation, sect, or party, in one grand pursuit, alike interesting to all, whereby mutual prejudices are worn off, a humane and philosophical spirit is cherished, and youth are stimulated to a laudable diligence and emulation in the pursuit of wisdom.

Modern societies seldom take the pains to spell out their objectives so clearly.

In the nineteenth century the scientific societies multiplied prolifically, coincident with the luxuriant growth and multiplication of the various natural and applied sciences. Following this century of diversification, the pendulum is now swinging back toward unification of many of the scientific disciplines which, in my scientific youth, were thought of as separate and distinct.

As an example of what I mean I shall use biochemistry, my special interest, as an illustration. At the turn of this century there was a national chemical society, a national physiological society, and a national medical society, but no biochemical society. Chemistry was, however, coming to be recognized as of greater and greater importance in the study and understanding of physiological and medical problems. Departments of biochemistry—called physiological chemistry at Yale and biological chemistry at Harvard—were formed and the subject became one of the important required courses of the medical student. Now biochemistry is assuming importance even as a college course of study. It was natural that there should be formed almost at the same time, in 1906, the American Society of Biological Chemists. It was composed almost entirely of teachers, but professionally, only a few of them called themselves biochemists. They were chemists, physiologists, pharmacologists, biologists, and physicians. Today it is difficult to be elected to the Society unless you are not only a professed, but an established, biochemist. However, there are so many different kinds of biochemists and so many different facets of the subject that this limitation has not in any way decreased the pressure for membership.

This society today has a membership of less than a thousand and it still retains as its primary responsibility that of being a forum for outstanding advances in biochemistry. One of the features of the American Society of Biological Chemists is its close association with other societies in related fields, with the physiologists, the pharmacologists, the nutritionists, the pathologists, and the immunologists. Together they comprise the Federation of American Societies for Experimental Biology, and they hold their annual meetings at the same time and at the same place. Thus is achieved cross-fertilization of ideas, so important for scientific progress.

I would suggest that some attention be given to the extent to which you can participate in your professional societies before joining them and that you consider whether you want a permanent file of the professional journals before subscribing to them. Like all things, it is not so much the original cost—it is the upkeep. If you once get a journal started on your shelves, you hesitate to give it up. I would not want to leave you with the impression that membership in professional societies should be weighed in mercenary terms. I should, however, feel that you were justified in evaluating them in terms of the extent to which they are a forum for "discursive debate and the expression of opinion." All too often this aspect of their function is lost sight of.

The history of all societies and clubs is about the same. They start as a small group of congenial souls who like each other and have common intellectual interests. Often their origins have been in the members' dining and wining together. After a time these small groups want others to share their good fortune and comradeship. They then become formalized with officers and stated meetings, fussy about whom they will elect to membership, and soon they find themselves saddled with new responsibilities toward their profession in particular and the public interest in general. I do not decry this evolution of supper clubs into social forces, but I am glad that it has continued to be the Boston tradition that supper clubs remain supper clubs.

What then can be said to summarize the contributions which a professional society makes to the teacher? First, there is the very practical contribution which it makes to the young scholar. It provides a platform where he can present a paper on his research, and be seen and heard by professors who are seeking junior staff or by senior investigators who are looking for colleagues and assistants. Second, and more important, it provides a forum where he can get the benefit of discussion of his results by his peers. He will, furthermore, often get a valuable idea from listening to the papers of others on subjects having no direct bearing on his own immediate interest. Third, professional societies usually publish or sponsor the publication of a professional journal. This, of course, is one of the most important contributions which a society can make to scholarship. And journals which are the responsibilities of societies are on the whole better edited and more critical of their contents than those which are published under private auspices. Fourth, and by no means to be ignored, is the opportunity which the societies give all scholars, young and old, to be members of a community of scholars with common interests. Most of us don't care for the ivory tower; we are friendly souls who like to share our disappointments and successes with others. The professional society can be a way to friendships which serve as catalysts for our teaching and research. Fifth, there are those who regard the professional society as a proper agency for initiating and, to some extent, directing economic and social reforms in the professional fields. When called upon to do so, a professional society should be willing and able to assist those concerned with such matters by giving professional advice within their competence. Sixth, and finally, professions throughout the world have societies in the various fields of scholarship comparable to ours. What is a better meeting-ground for international understanding than a community of scholarly interest that knows no national boundary? For these reasons, I regard the professional societies as a most important adjunct to progress in scholarship, and without progress in scholarship there can be no progress in teaching.

BERNICE BROWN CRONKHITE

Chapter XII

THE COLLEGE TEACHER AND STUDY ABROAD

Is there special value for the teacher today in study and travel abroad? What is the best time, what preparation is useful, and how can it be financed? Post-college foreign study should be preceded by scme study of the language, history, customs, and intellectual resources of the foreign country and of its universities. Special values for teachers of languages, history, or fine arts. The public and private sources of grants to aid foreign study.

Not so very many years ago study abroad was regarded primarily as a delightful luxury, something that one could enjoy if he were a person of means and leisure. With changes in the world situation and with the growing interdependence of one country upon other countries, that valuation has changed. It has become vastly important that we should, so far as possible, know how the rest of the world lives, what it is thinking, and how it is working. Ideally we should all go abroad often, but since not all of us can do so, it is useful that at least our teachers should go and bring back to their students whatever they have been able to learn. We may well consider at what period students and teachers can best go abroad to study, what preparation is desirable, what advantages can be expected, and how such undertakings can be financed.

As to when to go, the instinct is to say, "whenever you get the chance." Other things being equal, however, later is better than earlier. While the popular plan of spending one's junior college year abroad has some advantages, a student who waits until he has finished college and then goes will know much more what to look for and will have gained a more mature view of what he wants to do. It seems better advice to wait until you have your master's degree, or, better still, wait until you are gathering material for your doctor's thesis. You may then be received abroad as a young colleague by the faculty members you meet, instead of being looked upon as another young American student in search of himself.

If summer is the only feasible time, go in the summer. A student of the classics here who went to Rome last summer spent three months in the American Academy at great profit. Another in psychology went to London for the meetings of the International Conference on Mental Health, and a third, an anthropologist, went to Morocco for field work. One can accomplish a good deal if he has adequate preparation to go, but at best a summer is too short. To go for one year or two is much better. Spending longer than two years away at a time may result in losing touch with possible openings at home, and is generally not wise. If, when you have taken your doctor's degree, you are offered a good position here, but could, perhaps with difficulty, finance a year of study abroad, I would say "go abroad." When you come back, as good a position or a better one is likely to be open to you, and you will often find that promotions will be more rapid because of the advantages that study abroad will have given you.

What preparation for foreign study is desirable? First, of course, comes some knowledge of the language of the country in which you plan to spend most of the time. While English is spoken in many parts of the world, and while it is true that in most countries there is at least a little island of people who will be able to talk that language, you will be limited very much in moving about and in gathering all that can be learned if you do not use the language of the country. As a preliminary, go to a language school, buy a phrase book, and practice. Try to find people of the country in which you intend to study and practice the idioms with them. Bravely go ahead and speak. Americans are shy about trying other languages, but foreigners are extremely kind and courteous and ready to help.

Learn the library and other resources of our own country in your special field. If, for instance, one is working in the Elizabethan period, it would be well before going to England to visit the Folger Library in Washington and to know as much about its contents as possible. It would be embarrassing to discover in England that the manuscript you ask for is here in the United States.

To know something of the foreign country's past and present is valuable. Know a few of their great names. Know some of their great events. Every country has its own history, to it very precious, and sharing this knowledge is a bond. One of our French professors, on the first day in a beginning course in French, presents twenty questions to his students; for example, "Into what sea does the Rhone flow?" "Who built the Arc de Triomphe?" "Do French women vote?" Many of his students realize at once that although they know something of French grammar and French words, they know very little about France itself, as an entity or as a culture, and that this vocabulary of ideas is as important as the vocabulary of words.

It is useful, too, to learn something of the country's customs. That may be very important if you are going to Latin or to Oriental countries. You may have seen the excellent little books which were prepared for our forces going overseas in the last war. Stress was put on the fact that "wherever you go people are going to judge the United States by you. They'll watch you, listen to you, and then say, 'So that is what an American is like, is it?' "

I would correspond ahead of time with the professor under whom I hoped to study. Make sure that he is not going to be on leave, and incidentally make sure that he does not object to teaching women, if you happen to be a woman student. Also find out what he has written. It is only courteous to go with some knowledge of what his ideas are and what he has published.

Choose your foreign university with care and be sure to decide early. Students who come to consult about going abroad, in nine cases out of ten, say that they want to study at Oxford or Cambridge. These are great universities, but there are many others of first rank in Europe as well as in Great Britain. Many great institutions are operating in spite of heavy war damage. I would be careful in choosing my central institution, and then plan to branch out and visit others as well. The American Council on Education has set up what is called a Foreign Universities Project. A handbook is being printed to be ready some time in 1950 giving information about all the universities of the world outside the United States.

A few letters of introduction can be of great help. We give at Radcliffe, as doubtless Harvard and other universities do, to any student going abroad an official letter bearing the seal of the college. The letter recommends the bearer as a distinguished student of the college and asks that she be given friendly consideration by those to whom she may present the letter. That letter does wonders in getting one into libraries, or private museums, or other places not open to the public. Show that "pass," and generally the doorman will let you in.

In these days of continued shortages, I suggest that you take along not only things that you will run out of and not find it easy to buy, but things that you would like to use as little gifts. To be able to give a weekend hostess something to make up for the rationed food that you have eaten during your visit is a pleasant courtesy.

What advantages, academic and otherwise, can be expected from study abroad? For a teacher of languages obviously nothing can be more helpful than living for a period in a country where the language one is going to teach is native. To live with a family where that language is spoken, and if possible where no English is known, is important. Eschew the pleasant but inhibiting company of other American students when going abroad to learn the language of the country. In selecting your family, take good care, lest you find yourself learning what would be the "cockney" of Hungarian, say, or of some other language not familiar to you. If you went into an English cockney home, you would sense that the English spoken there was not the English you wanted to speak, but if you went to China you might not be as aware of the local deviations from the accepted literary standard. Get advice from the cultural attaché, or the consul, or someone else who knows.

If a teacher of fine arts, you will want to see the cathedrals and works of art that you are going to talk about later. If you are to teach history, that history will come alive when you visit the places where history was made. If you are to teach geography, you will want to cross some of the great mountains and see the rivers that have influenced the life of mankind.

If your field lies among the sciences, or mathematics, or philosophy, you should make your choice of locality on the basis of your prospective teachers. You may ask, "Where is the man or woman who is strongest in my chosen field?" An English student at Cambridge University became interested in astronomy. She investigated the observatories of the world and decided that the one man in the world best qualified in the branch she wanted to study was here at Harvard. So she walked into my office one day with no warning and said, "Here I am. I want to study with Dr. So and So." Another wrote us last year from France. She had been using in a course in economics a book by one of our economics professors, and she wrote, "I feel I must study with that man." We managed to find money for a fellowship so that she could come.

Dean Briggs once said, "When you go abroad don't study all the time. Soak up the old world." Visit the country's schools, visit parliament, visit the hospitals, visit the courts. Find out how they do things. Dorothy Canfield Fisher describes a Vermont girl who, after being taken on the Grand Tour, came back to her Vermont village and was greeted eagerly by her neighbors. They asked her, "How do the people in Italy, where it is so hot, keep their milk sweet?" She didn't know. They asked about the schools, "How do they pay their teachers? Do they have a tax for the schools, or do families pay only if their children go?" She didn't know.

About all those matters which would be of concern to a Vermont housewife she had learned nothing.

The opportunity to collect books and other material useful in your field is not to be missed. If you know what you want and are on the lookout, you can often gather source material that does not cost much and that will be a great pleasure to own.

The really important part of this story is often the finding of the wherewithal for study abroad. It is fortunate that the value of foreign study is being widely recognized and that funds are becoming increasingly available. Newspapers, women's clubs, and business houses are giving money for this purpose as they never did before. Even congressmen grasp now the necessity for this interchange of ideas—the Fulbright Act is a good example. Senator Fulbright of Arkansas, who was formerly a Rhodes Scholar, had the bright idea of selling our surplus war property abroad and making the proceeds in the foreign currency available for American students going abroad. The sum thus made available will be nearly a hundred and fifty million dollars. At this date the countries that have signed an agreement to act under this Fulbright plan are Belgium and Luxembourg, Burma, China, France, Greece, Iran, Italy, the Netherlands, New Zealand, Norway, the Philippines, and the United Kingdom. Students who want to go to any one of these countries apply for the necessary funds to the Fulbright Division of the Institute of International Education, 2 West 45th Street, New York. If you are a professor, or a specialist, or an advanced research scholar, apply to the Conference Board of Associated Research Councils, 2101 Constitution Avenue, Washington. There are also other sources of government aid. You can use your G.I. money abroad as well as in this country. The United States Office of Education combines with the State Department to finance study in South America. For the year 1950, for instance, it is possible to go to Brazil, Chile, Costa Rica, Colombia, the Dominican Republic, Haiti, Honduras, Mexico, Paraguay, Peru, or Venezuela. The country which agrees to receive you gives a monthly allowance and tuition, and the United States pays your transportation down and back.

Many foundations make grants for study in a particular country. There are, for instance, the American Institute of France, the Belgian-American Educational Foundation, the Netherlands Foundation, and the American Scandinavian Foundation. The Harvard-Yenching Institute which sends some Americans to China and brings Chinese here has its American headquarters here. There are certain foundations making grants for which one must be nominated by others—your professor or a board. Among these are the Rockefeller Foundation, the Dreyfus Foundation, the Kellogg Foundation, and the American Council of Learned Societies. There are other organizations to which you can apply directly. For instance, if you are a woman you can apply to the American Association of University Women, which gives twenty-five fellowships a year. The National Research Council and the Social Science Research Council finance advanced students. Rotary International and many women's clubs are now awarding money for travel or study abroad. There are associations which sometimes finance special work, such as the College Art Association, the Bivin Foundation in Child Psychology, and the American Philosophical Society. At Radcliffe we have a few fellowships for travel: the Agassiz, the Longfellow, and the Ireland. At Harvard there are a great many more. UNESCO has published an excellent handbook (1949) entitled *Study Abroad—International Handbook of Fellowships, Scholarships, and Educational Exchanges.*

There are also loans to be had from graduate schools and from certain foundations. One should not hesitate to take a loan if it is the deciding factor in going abroad for serious study. There are ways of saving on travel expenses. "Student ships" have been running the last few summers. A free ticket on the airways to South America is usually available to a student having a fellowship, and often a large discount is given on government-subsidized steamship lines. Savings in living costs are possible by using student hostels instead of hotels. The Women's Rest Tour Association, which is concerned only with young women traveling unchaperoned, can prove useful. It publishes every year a little handbook of addresses of good places to live, several places in each city with description—as "inexpensive, with a garden, hot water," and so on. Teacher exchanges are becoming popular by which one occupies a teacher's room abroad while that teacher comes here and occupies yours, no money needing to be passed. The English Speaking Union will help arrange these exchanges in Great Britain.

Sometimes money can be earned on the side. Magazines or newspapers in this country will sometimes accept articles. Talk with the editors in advance; tell them what your specialty is, where you are going to be, and ask if you may send them articles. Sometimes business houses will employ you to send back reports on prices, or crops, or strikes. Students can arrange in some cases to buy foreign goods on commission.

Plan, if possible, a year abroad before you begin to teach. Then have a refresher summer whenever possible, and a sabbatical whenever opportunity offers. The returns to teaching can be very great indeed. Keep a diary, and a scrapbook, and an address book. You will find that over the years you will want to keep in touch with many of the people you met abroad. Out of such small ties grow bonds between nations. Professor Jones once said, "There is no such thing as a French cloud or American capillary action." Both as students and teachers we are grateful to find that there are, in the last analysis, no frontiers in knowledge.

WILBUR KITCHENER JORDAN

Chapter XIII

THE COLLEGE TEACHER IN RELATION TO RESEARCH AND PUBLICATION

Research by a college teacher may represent the difference between a professional life of dying embers and one of brightening fire. Writing monographs and articles and beginning a book in the first teaching post. Advantages of a small faculty. Sources of financial assistance. Inter-library loan. Microfilm. Finding a publisher. Launching your first book.

It is generally agreed that the college teacher lies under a direct responsibility to share in the advancement of knowledge. For many centuries past the teaching and research functions have been conjoined in collegiate education, in those ages when Western universities were in a state of health and when the frontiers of learning were being widely extended. Consequently, the whole of graduate instruction is based on the assumption that the college instructor will be at once a teacher and a productive scholar. This is the ideal which we set for ourselves as graduate students, even though many of us who later become college teachers do not fully attain this goal.

The college teacher who somehow manages to maintain a lively, even if not a consuming, interest in his research is likely to remain through the whole of his teaching career an alert and happy person. It may even be suggested that a college teacher must continue with his research and writing, though perhaps at a modest pace, if the wellsprings of his inspiration as a teacher are not to run dry. Those who have observed college faculties know all too well the frequent tragedy of the well-trained and promising teacher who, though well advanced in some piece of study, gradually abandons his work while sinking slowly into a morass of personal frustration. With very rare exceptions such a teacher also gradually withers in the classroom, since it seems to be true that advanced instruction cannot be separated for long from the active pursuit of knowledge. It is possible to draw for a good many years on the store of knowledge and inspiration one has received in graduate school, but with the passing of time these resources will become exhausted. Instruction, then, if it is to be good and vigorous, must itself be quickened and enlivened by a pertinacious interest in the pursuit of research.

Qualitative differences in students proceeding to the doctorate in any large university in a given year are not as marked as one might suppose. All these graduates will have been soundly trained, all will have given evidence of ability to proceed independently with investigation, and all will have made at least a beginning in studies which may be broadened after a few years into some significant contribution to knowledge. Yet observation suggests, while statistics in my own field of history confirm the fact, that not many more than one in four of these graduates will continue actively with research and publication once the degree has been gained and the first teaching post obtained. This is a depressing fact which represents a tragic waste of human materials and a very considerable loss to the advancement of knowledge. Many reasons conspire to produce this unhappy result and many rationalizations are advanced to explain the unwritten books from these college teachers. But all these explanations may in most cases be reduced to the fact that relatively few, even of college teachers, possess the sustaining drive and the intellectual curiosity required for productive scholarship.

In these chapters we are seeking to consider the problem of the young college teacher under normal conditions. We should therefore think of the possibility of maintaining an active interest in research and publication in the circumstances that are likely to confront one in his first college teaching post, since it is almost axiomatic that the first four or five years test surely the devotion of the teacher to the life of the scholar.

The young scholar's first appointment after leaving graduate school will almost certainly be to a small department in a college, or as a very junior member of a large department in a university. In the very nature of the case there will be no possibility that the young teacher can devote himself exclusively to instruction in his special field of knowledge; he will be fortunate indeed if he may offer one course in his specialty. All of us during the first four or five years of our tenure are obliged to do the hewing of wood and the drawing of water for our departments. The large introductory courses which undergird the instruction of every department provide the apprenticeship for the young teacher, and it is not until these testing years have been passed that he comes to enjoy the opportunity to become the specialist he thought he was when he left graduate school. Moreover, since not more than perhaps ten universities in this country are really fully equipped in terms of libraries, laboratories, and traditions for the prosecution of advanced research, the young instructor coming from one of these centers of learning will at first be confused and depressed as he adapts himself to the necessity of carrying on with his studies under conditions that are far short of ideal.

These are roughly the facts as the young college teacher is likely to find them, and these are the facts which are usually cited by the three in four who, after a short struggle, abandon, save for an occasional pious gesture, the life of the scholar. How are research and publication to be carried on under these seemingly unfavorable conditions? This is a fair and it is also a very important question, not only as it relates to one's happiness as a human being, but also for the very pragmatic reason that if one does not like his first academic post, the most certain way of securing a more advantageous appointment is by enhancing one's reputation as a productive scholar by impressive publication.

Shall we, then, address ourselves explicitly and in some detail to the question of how *you* as graduate students should prepare for the life of the teacher and scholar under the apparently adverse conditions likely to be met on your first appointment to a small college or university not well equipped for the prosecution of research?

Preparation ought ideally to begin in the graduate school itself. Many professors try to arrange for the publication of particularly interesting and fruitful papers done by students in their advanced seminars. It is rare, in fact, when there are not in a given year two or three reports in a seminar which, if somewhat extended by additional research, might not after careful rewriting appropriately be offered to one or another of the learned journals in the field in question. You will do well, therefore, to consider this possibility when you choose your seminar topic. If the professor expresses himself as highly pleased with such a report, you may quite properly ask whether with some more work there might not be a publishable article in the paper, and you can expect the professor to assist you in placing the article. When a student has been able to secure the publication of one or two articles before taking his degree, he will have gone far towards mastering techniques of scholarly writing, and he will likewise have made it much easier for his department to place him in a satisfactory post after graduation. This, I would suggest, is the first rung on the ladder of research and publication.

The second rung should also be grasped when one is still in graduate school. I would earnestly suggest the high importance of choosing a dissertation topic, some segment of which can be completed for the utilitarian purpose of the degree in a relatively short time, but which can then be opened up as a considerable field of investigation in which you can work fruitfully for several years after that academic exercise, the Ph.D. thesis, has been completed. There is an almost shameful waste in the too narrow and highly technical doctoral dissertation which completely exhausts a small and unimportant piece of investigation, thereby robbing the young teacher of the momentum which the thesis itself should impart. If, on the other hand, the thesis does open up an extensive field of research, you will go out to your first academic appointment with a good start on your first book and with that enthusiasm which is required if the first book is ever to be written. You will find that you can talk very frankly with your professor about these matters and that there are many topics suitable not only for the dissertation but also for the first half-dozen years of your career.

The first book—the first monograph—if planned as an extension of the research for the dissertation, is then relatively easy to complete, and it is that book which will establish "the early reputation" of the young college teacher and very possibly secure for him his first attractive academic offer or more probably his promotion in the faculty in which his first appointment was made. The testing point—the point where the academic saints are divided from the sinners—comes, however, with the publication of the first monograph and the planning and execution of the second. It is precisely here that the weak falter. The first book is normally a by-product of the thesis, and its paternity must in part be attributed to the senior professor who in graduate school supervised at least the early stages of the research and planning. But one is on his own in the writing of his second book. It is, I think, axiomatic that teachers who write a second book continue as productive scholars for the rest of their lives, since they will by that time have become completely infected with that incurable virus which is research.

We are therefore especially concerned with your problems as they are related to the publication of the first book and to that critical stage in your career when the decision is being taken to begin research on the second major work. Let us now be as specific as possible as we discuss your problems. We are assuming that you are going to find yourself a junior member of a small department in a small college or university, that you have published an article or two while in graduate school, and that your doctoral dissertation has laid open for you the materials and the conception for your first book. Just how should you proceed as a junior member of this hypothetical faculty, assuming always that you are deeply and seriously interested in becoming a productive scholar as well as a successful teacher?

You will find that a considerable prestige will quite properly accrue to you in such a faculty if you say that you are interested in research and if you begin to implement this assertion by sustained effort. You will also discover that in certain fields and in many specialties in others it is actually easier to find time and money for the prosecution of research in smaller faculties than in the larger institutions where, as the scholar grows older, administrative responsibilities and the load of graduate instruction begin to exact heavy tolls on his research time. It may in point of fact be said that the vigorous and promising young scholar in most smaller faculties can gain more concessions in the coin of teaching load, research leaves, and very possibly research grants than he can in a major institution where everyone is engaged on research as part of the responsibilities of his tenure. There are positive advantages at this stage of your career in having gained your first appointment in a smaller faculty.

You should, I think, discuss your research plans and aspirations fully with the chairman of your department before accepting an appointment, in order to gain the support and full sympathy of your senior colleague. It is also well to talk with the president or academic dean of the college as soon as you have made substantial progress towards the completion of your research and well before it is necessary to ask for research or publication assistance. It is normally helpful at this stage to sketch out in a carefully drafted prospectus the plan you are pursuing in order that it may be presented for mature consideration. Needless to say, these conversations and representations should present your plans modestly and simply, and you should always be quite sure that you are fully prepared to carry them to completion. You should also remember that college administrative officers like to know about the research activities of their faculties, and that it is very much to their advantage that they should be fully informed.

You will find it stimulating to join one of the shop clubs that you will probably discover flourishing in your faculty. There you will find men and women of about your age, or a little older, who are working with problems of the mind, who are probably those members of the faculty actively interested in research, and there you will receive the needed criticism of your own ideas and the opportunity to criticize the ideas of your colleagues. If you do not find that kind of shop club in the institution, set about organizing one after you have been there for a full year. The opportunities for lively and informed discussion, which is of course enormously stimulating to research, are much greater in a small academic community than in a large and sprawling university where one's contacts are normally limited, at least as a junior faculty member, to instructors in one's own department.

If you carry on with your research stubbornly and persistently at a pace which the teaching load permits, you will find in time that you are going to need some financial assistance, since it is improbable that you can save considerable sums from your salary. In most circumstances your need for research assistance will not be large. I feel, perhaps a little too strongly, that in the social sciences and humanities at least, a research grant should very rarely cover more than typing costs, necessary travel, purchase of materials unavailable locally, proofreading costs, and the like. There is doubt about the propriety and the value of research grants which permit the hiring of research assistants for the young scholar, or, for that matter, for the older scholar. But even though it may be relatively small, the sum that you require may well mean the difference between continuing with your work at a time when it is well in hand and having to put it aside almost indefinitely. When that critical time does arrive, it should mean that the manuscript of your first book is very nearly in final form. It will then be the direct obligation of your college to provide the necessary funds or to assist you in finding them. One first step is to apply to one of the numerous research committees and agencies set up by foundations interested in the various fields of knowledge. The chairman of your department or the president of your college should be able to suggest the one or ones to which you might most appropriately apply. If your project is carefully conceived and well advanced, you will almost certainly get the money you require, because these agencies are quite properly much more interested in helping young scholars in the smaller universities than they are those in the heavily endowed universities, which they feel and probably quite correctly, should carry their own normal research loads. If for any reason you are unable to secure a needed grant from such an agency, the president of your college will lie under an obligation either to raise the money independently or to appropriate it from college funds.

There is high importance in keeping yourself well informed about developments and writing in your own field of special interest during these early years of your scholarly career. You should see that your college library subscribes to all the leading learned journals in your field and you ought to read them regularly and promptly. Not only are the articles important, but the book reviews will serve to keep you in intimate contact with the ever-expanding field of knowledge with which you are concerned.

It is also well to try to gain from your department or president at least a small library appropriation which you may use at your discretion for the purchase of books, microfilms, or other materials which will assist you in the pursuit of your own research. You will hear a great deal of grumbling in all faculties about inadequate library facilities; in fact, the inadequate library is, next to the too heavy teaching load, the favorite rationalization for those who have forsaken scholarly work. It is rarely ever a sufficient excuse. In many fields of knowledge, especially in the social sciences and humanities, there may be in the neighborhood of your college really priceless opportunities for research in local or regional materials. Then too, you must remember that there is a great system of inter-library loans in this country which enables you to borrow almost any reference or secondary work not available in your local collection. Finally, there are illimitable resources which microfilm opens up for the scholar who finds his sources scanty in his own library. These films are cheap, they are now easy to use, and they will open the whole world before you. Most college libraries are enthusiastic about microfilms and it will be relatively easy for you to secure a special appropriation to cover your own research needs.

We are assuming that during the first three or four years of tenure in your appointment the manuscript of your first book will have been completed. Shall we now discuss the problem of securing the publication of your first work?

The prime rule is to try to submit your manuscript in really final and polished form to an appropriate publisher. Any publisher will testify that not one manuscript in four that comes to his desk is more than a good rough draft of a possible book. Be sure that your work is submitted in the form in which you want it published and that you will be proud of that form ten years later. Revise your manuscript, rewrite it, work over undigested materials until they are really incorporated in the text, and then polish that text. Reduce the documentation to defensible limits, remembering that footnotes and critical apparatus are expensive to print. I would also suggest that you read aloud what you regard as your final text, if possible to some friendly critic who will stop you at every turgid passage and lift his eyebrows at every grammatical slip. Work on your manuscript with the ever-present reflection that this is your work, that it is in a true sense a permanent and unalterable monument to yourself. You ought, in these final stages of polishing, to apply this rule: the manuscript which you submit to a publisher ought to be so finished in style, grammar, and technical details that the publisher can proceed immediately to page proofs and the errors which you correct in proofs ought in all cases to be those of the printer.

When the manuscript is ready for submission under these rigorously applied rules, you will have given your work a fair chance with the most critical of publishers and you will then be quite certain that it will receive careful consideration. You will then have to decide to what publisher you will submit the work. If the first book is a monograph, you will find that a university press usually is the best publisher for this kind of learned work. The university press has more skill in publishing and marketing this kind of book and in arranging for its review in the various learned journals in your field. It is always wise, at this stage, to ask the senior professor under whom you carried on your research for the doctorate for his advice in deciding on the list of publishers to whom you will submit the manuscript. You should remember that all publishers have their own special fields of interest—just as do scholars—and that there is no point in sending a book to a publisher, however renowned, who is not publishing in your field. Secure the current catalogues of all the publishers who might conceivably be interested in your work, and then prepare a list of those who have recently published books in the general area of your own manuscript. Every publisher likes to have three or four books in his current list that are grouped around a large special topic and it may well be that you can find several niches in which your own work will fit. Draw up a list of such publishers—university presses and commercial publishers alike—and then submit your manuscript to them in what seems to you to be the order of logical desirability.

You must also remember that relatively few books are accepted by the first publisher to whom they are submitted and you should resolve not to be discouraged if this should happen to your own work. If the manuscript is declined, always write to the editor to ask if you may have the privilege of seeing the readings of your manuscript. He will have sent it to one or two eminent specialists in your field and these anonymous reports will often give you the most brutally honest and helpful criticism of your work that you will ever receive. Revise your manuscript in the light of these criticisms, insofar as you think them just, and then send it on to the second publisher on your list; although not infrequently the first publisher, impressed by your willingness to accept criticism and to work with your manuscript, will reopen the subject of publication.

At some point, if the manuscript is good, if it makes a substantial contribution to knowledge, it is going to be accepted. There will be a glorious first paragraph in the letter from your publisher setting out that fact, and then you will come to the second paragraph, which will very probably say that "because of present conditions" a subsidy ranging from $500 to $1500 will be required. That should not be upsetting news; it happens to all of us. It will simply mean this: that some time is going to be required to find the money. I am sure I am right in the suggestions I am going to make now. Try your own college, the one in which you are teaching, first. The smaller the college, the more probable the subsidy. The president will almost certainly make it his business to go out and find the money, if he cannot put his hands on it in his current budget. When you take your problem to the president of the college, always through the chairman of your department, take with you any outside criticisms that you may have from the publisher so that he will have full and formal judgment of the press on your work. This will greatly assist him in getting the required subvention. If your college fails you, and it rarely will, you will then want to try for a grant from one of the numerous learned societies. In making application to these groups, your publisher will help you and he will frequently make the application for you. He will know much more about how to approach a learned society than do you. Use your own funds only as a last resort, and I implore you to use caution in this respect. Many of us as young teachers and scholars get so impatient in the search for funds that we are too likely to injure our economic status by borrowing the money or by trying to get it from relations who can ill afford to pay a substantial sum. With just a little patience, money will be found from other sources. In fact, I think I can say categorically that so far as my knowledge goes I have never seen a manuscript, carefully edited and written, making an original, even though a minor, contribution to knowledge, not ultimately published without expense to the author, though three or four years may have elapsed before the money was found.

One of the great joys of publishing your first book is the reviews that you will receive. These will be exciting and rewarding reading. They will very often be intensely critical; they will sometimes seem to you to be almost direct assaults on your character. But they are not. They are written by men and women who are endeavoring to be helpful and who are trying to point out improvements that you can make in your next volume or in the next edition of the first. You should take these criticisms seriously, but you should not take them personally.

With the publication of your first book, you will have laid the foundation of your scholarly career and you will then want to begin to think of the scope of your next piece of investigation. You will have attained the habits and the attitudes of the scholar and you will bring to your teaching a finer and a richer mind. You will have created for yourself a good and a fruitful life.

THE SEARCH FOR A TEACHING POSITION

EDITH G. STEDMAN

Chapter XIV

THE USES OF A COLLEGE PLACEMENT BUREAU

The function of a college placement bureau and practical hints on the use of its facilities. How to be interviewed. How much is the teacher worth? Is geographical location or the type of institution more important? Positions abroad. Administrative posts combined with teaching.

The head of a college appointment bureau feels sometimes as if she were the manager of one of the First National Stores with a variety of goods to sell. She looks around on her shelves and sees some commodities that move easily—tomato soup and macaroni and cheese—and she knows that she is going to sell them without much effort. Then she looks around further and sees little pots of caviar and crêpes suzette and wonders who is coming along to take them. She feels that eventually she will dispose even of these, but she hopes not to have too many of them on her hands for too long. To carry the analogy any further as to what fields of intellectual concentration constitute tomato soup and what caviar is a subject which is better left alone.

What does an appointment bureau do? In the first place, it can act as the link between employers offering positions and students seeking them. Last year we received between five and six hundred teaching calls, ranging from the primary grades to college professorships. When each call comes in, we try to think of what students are available to suggest as candidates. We collect all the information we can from letters and credentials and send out pertinent information about candidates. We also make available to students information about institutions, through such a source as the directory of *American Universities and Colleges,* which gives the names of all the accredited institutions in the country and a description of them, the size of the institution, the size of the faculty, the number of books in the library, and so forth. For those interested in secondary schools, there is the Porter Sargent *Handbook of Private Schools.* The United States Office of Education publishes a directory which is useful if one is interested in a particular geographical area and is not sure of the names of the educational institutions in each state. That directory lists colleges, junior colleges, and teachers' colleges, giving the names of heads of the institutions.

The Appointment Bureau of Radcliffe College does a great deal of general vocational counseling. There is a certain stage in studying for a master's degree, when a low point in morale seems to be reached by a good many people. Girls to whom Cambridge is as dust and ashes in their mouths come to us and the one thing they want to do is to get out of it as quickly as they can, taking an A.M. degree with them. After they have gone through that period, there usually follows another stage in which they cannot bear to leave. They walk lovingly over the crooked sidewalks of Cambridge and think, "When shall I see these again?" Both stages are bad!

The Appointment Bureau continues working with the student after she leaves college, for a degree does not by any means terminate connection with the bureau. In fact, you the student are much more valuable to us, let it be said, after you have your degree and have acquired a little experience than you were when you were in college.

Apart from the things that a placement bureau can do for the student, there are things that the student necessarily must do if the bureau is to function successfully. At the beginning of the year a post card is sent asking graduate students to come in and register. The bureau wants to know who is present and who is going to be actively interested in a job. To know at what stage your studies are and when you are going to be available for placement is essential. If all concerned register in the office, we then know these answers and are better able to help with plans. The blanks which are to be filled in are tiresome; they are long and detailed, and they may not seem to make much sense, but the information gives a basis for later placement. Many students have difficulty in getting professors' names to use as reference. In some fields this presents a real problem, but every effort should be made to know at least one or two professors. References from them are invaluable.

Personal records need to be kept up to date. Many times a student may have taken a job and then have forgotten to notify the bureau. Or we do not know the most recent addresses and are obliged to telephone and telegraph madly in an effort to locate the supposed candidate. The placement business is a two-way affair. The bureau can be useful to you, and you can be useful to the bureau, but there is necessity for thoughtful coöperation.

There are many ways of getting a position. Candidates do well to be registered at their own undergraduate college, as well as in the graduate school bureau. Calls sometimes come through department heads and some professors are more actively concerned than others. The writing of letters of application, accompanied by one's history and references, frequently is valuable. If you do write, having chosen the part of the country and the institutions where you would like to teach, address the chairmen of the department in which you are interested. Six or eight letters, well written and judiciously distributed, can bring in very good results. It is better not to go into great detail. Names, addresses, and telephone numbers, the different degree institutions, the fields in which you have majored, the subject of the thesis and any teaching experience—these are the data wanted. At the end, it is useful to add, "My complete credentials are on file at the Radcliffe (or other) Appointment Bureau and will be sent to you on request." Enclose a stamped, self-addressed envelope. The timing of such letters is important. Since most contracts are closed between February and April, one should not wait until too late in the season to present oneself.

There are also commercial agencies, although few are concerned with college placement. One is the American College Bureau in Chicago and another is the Coöperative Bureau for Teachers, at 1776 Broadway in New York. Notices of vacancies will sometimes be found in professional journals. Another way of helping oneself to find a position is to attend professional conferences, where a polite form of teacher swapping often takes place.

A great many graduate students feel that unless they take a senior college job, as contrasted with teaching in other schools, they have not fulfilled their mission in life. It would be good if there were enough college positions to go round, but there are not. The important thing, particularly for those with an A.M., is to get some teaching experience. That is what is needed more than anything else, and if one can get into a good secondary school doing college preparatory work, or into a junior college, one will be better served in many ways than by teaching in an inferior senior college. The work will be with a group of good students and the teaching experience will be valuable.

Being interviewed for a position presents some minor, as well as some major, challenges. It is important that one dress suitably for such interviews. Any appointment that is made should be kept, or if anything does interfere, immediate notification and rearrangement with the persons involved is essential. After the interview with the head of a department or the head of a school, it is a good idea to write a letter of thanks, regardless of the outcome or your decision for or against the place.

The heads of departments or schools have a way of asking what salary will be accepted—a very difficult question to answer. What one would like to say is, "All that can be got," but there has to be some more practical way of getting around the problem. To name too low an amount may undercut what the school may have intended to pay. At the same time one does not want to put oneself down for a sum which staggers the prospective employer. The safest way, it often seems, is simply to say that it is assumed that the institution has a salary scale for people with experience equivalent to yours and that you would be very glad to be considered at that rate.

When in one's career should a "job" be sought? Is it advisable to take a position after an A.M., provided you are going on to a Ph.D.? Is that a better time than after one has finished the general examinations for a Ph.D.? There is no clear answer to such questions. In some cases it is best to stay and see the whole degree process through from A.B. to Ph.D. On the other hand, many students seem to reach a point at which they could benefit greatly by working for a year or two before continuing study. In many cases, money is a consideration. In a great many college jobs, only a teacher with a Ph.D. will be considered, but sometimes positions can be obtained after the Ph.D. "generals" are passed. The difficulty is to save time enough out of the teaching routine to work on the Ph.D. thesis.

Geographic location presents more of a problem to women applicants than it does to men. Since up to about 40 per cent of women students, as in the Radcliffe Graduate School, may be married, communities where husbands and wives are not allowed to teach in the same institution raise a very real problem. The married woman graduate student may be obliged to decide whether she will give up teaching and consider other jobs such as are to be found in larger institutions in a library or in research laboratories or projects.

When jobs are to be found, there are often objections from candidates as to the geographical location. There seems to be a rooted objection to teaching positions in certain sections of the United States. Yet it is well to remember that not all virtues are vested in the eastern seaboard, and very often there are good jobs elsewhere. The most important thing is to think of the institution itself—what it has to offer and what opportunities there are for a young instructor—rather than the section in which it is located.

Teaching positions abroad are of interest to some people. There are not too many, but the Near East College Association is almost always interested in promising graduates. There are also occasional openings in the Far East. There are some positions with the Army. Except for the latter, foreign positions as a rule do not pay very well, but generally the salary is enough for transportation, for living, and sometimes for holidays.

Some graduates want to teach to the exclusion of all else, abhorring the thought of taking any kind of administrative responsibility. Others are very anxious for administrative work, saying in substance, "How can I be a dean?" There are all kinds of deans —indeed a hierarchy of deans; there are academic deans, there are social deans, there are deans of residence, there are freshman deans, and so on. There is not the slightest use, in my opinion, in expecting to be an academic dean without a Ph.D. and some college teaching experience. Those who are getting A.M.'s and want to go into administration could very well take a position in a college as head of a house or dormitory, continuing academic work if desired. That is a very good way of beginning. It gives opportunity to learn something of student behavior, from the other side of the fence, and to develop gifts as an advisor and guide to students.

To aid in all such hopes and activities is the business of a college appointment bureau.

DAVID OWEN

Chapter XV

THE GRADUATE STUDENT IN SEARCH OF A POSITION

Many variables and changes can affect the "market" for teachers. While the active demand continues in elementary and secondary schools, there is postwar contraction in many college and university fields. Your qualifications—do they fit you for secondary school, junior college, or college teaching? Value of the appointment office, supplemented by independent search. Varieties of institutions. Salaries in liberal arts colleges. Placement of the research specialist. General acceptability and adaptability may be important. Identifying oneself with the employing institution without sectional or Brahminic prejudices.

It is probably both unnecessary and unkind to put before you the broad outlook for gainful employment in the teaching field. It is almost impossible to make any comments that will hold good for the whole range of academic disciplines, and that is especially true because the future seems to me to be dependent on a good many variables that cannot be assessed at this time. For example, the continuation of Federal aid in substantial amounts, the ratio between graduate school enrollment and college enrollment—such things are clearly going to affect the vacancies in the teaching field. During the 1930's college enrollments remained almost static or possibly even declined, while the number of graduate students, who had nothing else to do but to continue their education, continued to mount. Not only that, but new graduate schools which drew chiefly on a local clientele developed amazingly, so that the total number of Ph.D.'s given in the 1930's increased enormously.

Although there are many questions unanswerable at present that will have a good deal of effect on the volume of teaching vacancies in the future, I am afraid that it is a rather sad song that I must sing. No one ought to be unduly optimistic about the future, at least in the disciplines that I pretend to know about. The fields that had a big expansion in the two or three years immediately after the war, I gather, are rather contracting now. That applies certainly to the social sciences, and I infer that it applies to English. I have no information about the natural sciences. I doubt whether it applies to history because we did not have much of an expansion after the war. As far as I can discover, the situation this year in history is neither much worse nor much better than it has been for the last two or three years. Just to impart a really cheerful tone to these proceedings, I should like to report one pair of jobs that I heard about three or four weeks ago, jobs in an extremely good liberal arts college in the Middle West—two jobs, one in American history, one in European history. The college was hoping to get candidates at $2500. I am afraid I replied rather cynically, knowing, I thought, our candidates here. The dean wrote back and said he realized that it was not very much money, but that they had had thirty applications for the American history and one hundred applications for the European history job.

Now, the dean may have been a fisherman for all I know. I don't for a minute suggest that as at all typical and you can put down at least two-thirds of those applicants as practically unemployable from any rational point of view. Nevertheless, it is clear that those jobs were considerably oversubscribed. My point here is that there seems to have been a good deal of nonsense in the last two or three years about the demand for teachers, and the public hasn't been at all clear on the point. I'm afraid a good many of our applicants for graduate school have not been aware of what kind of shortage exists. No doubt there is a critical shortage in the elementary schools. No doubt there is a serious shortage in the public secondary field. But colleges and universities, it seems to me, are a rather different matter.

Well, how does a student go about getting one of these jobs that I am so bearish about? It seems to me the first thing is to decide what kind of job you are qualified for. What degree are you working for? Is it the master's degree? Do you expect to stop with the master's degree? If that is the case, you are probably destined for junior college or secondary school work. On the whole, it seems to be inadvisable for our graduate students to take a college teaching appointment after the master's degree, although in some cases an institution will be more eager to have you at that stage than after you get your Ph.D.—because you can be more easily disposed of after the rush of students subsides. Also, presumably you come cheaper. Yet the college job you get with only the master's degree is going to be, at best, temporary; at worst, a blind alley. Are you more interested in teaching on the whole than in scholarship? What kind of work would you be most interested in doing in this non-existent ideal academic world? In other words, analyze yourself.

Your job may, of course, come through a member of the department. It may come through the department office; many of the better jobs do. Some of the jobs come through the appointment office. In many cases the president, or dean, or chairman of a department—whoever happens to be in charge of filling a vacancy—will write directly to the appointment office, and it is only fair to you to explain what happens to a request that comes through those channels. In the Harvard office it is always referred to the department concerned. The particulars come to the department office in duplicate. We make the recommendations and return the carbon to the appointment office. If it seems a particularly good job or if we have an individual that we are particularly anxious to place, I, as chairman of the department, write a personal letter to the institution or ask a member of the department to do it. On that point, I should like to emphasize the desirability of getting your papers on file in the appointment office. I grant there is a certain amount of cynicism among the graduate student body as to what good all that does, and it is important, therefore, to know what the appointment office conceives its function to be. The Harvard office does not go out on the road beating the bushes for jobs. Perhaps it ought to, but it is not at present staffed for such activities. The appointment office is primarily a clearing-house between the department and a potential employing institution. Having returned to the appointment office our recommendation for a particular job, we then ask the director to send the formal papers to the institution. You will find it hard to credit this, but in one fortnight when we asked the office to send the papers of eight different individuals to various institutions, it was discovered that not a single one of those graduate students, some of whom had been nagging us to death for jobs, had filed his papers with the appointment office. Our secretary had to chase around and persuade these gentlemen to go over and sign up. In short, even though your job may not come directly from the appointment office, it is extremely important to have your material on file there so that it can be sent out without delay.

Although the department and the appointment office will do their best for you, don't exclude the possibility of finding a job for yourselves. The best single job which has come to a graduate student in our department this year (and I am a little bit embarrassed about it) came as a result of his own letter. The student's letter produced excellent results, partly because the institution happened to be looking for a man with precisely his training.

Let me just give you one example of how not to apply for a job. This, I blush to say, was a letter written by a certain Ph.D. to the director of a summer session in a middle western institution and was sent by the director of that summer session to one of my colleagues. It was written several years ago and runs something like this:

> The world situation may make it desirable for you to offer in your summer session this year a course on the British Empire, either historical or contemporary. I am admirably qualified to teach either. I am regarded as a competent teacher, as you may find by reference to Professor ——— of this department and to Professor ———, president of this college during

the three years I have been associated with it. I might add that I am thirty-four, Anglo-Irish in descent, Protestant [there was no FEPC in those days], married, and without idiosyncrasies or physical defects of any kind. It is possible that you have already decided on your summer session faculty. Otherwise, you will not regret having given this application favorable consideration.

Most institutions will want a personal interview with you. Always make the appointment in advance; don't simply happen in one day and ask to see the dean or the chairman of the department. Show up on time, of course, and I will say this to the men, since they are presumably not addicted to bobby sox: don't appear in your sportiest and most collegiate tweeds. In an interview of that kind it is always hard to strike the right balance between assertiveness and modesty, and if you can't strike the balance yourself, nobody can tell you how to do it. But don't be a shrinking violet, and don't go without some ideas about what you want to teach and how you would like to teach it. In other words, it is useful to have some ideas about teaching before you are interviewed about a job. I know of one rather good job, in fact, that was lost by an individual who was worried about the specter of unemployment and decided he would agree with everything. When they asked him how he wanted to teach the course he said, "I'll teach it any way you want it taught." The whole interview went in that way, and he did not get the job. (I've got to destroy the point of that affair, though, because he got a better job two months later.) I do think you will want to have some notions about teaching and not be afraid to offer them—in all modesty, of course. Still, don't give the impression that you will do everything that the head of the department asks you to.

How about the salary? Again I speak only of teaching history—I don't pretend to know what the story is in other fields. Of the jobs I know this year in reputable institutions, the variation has run for non-Ph.D.'s or incipient Ph.D.'s from about $2500 to $3600—the $3600 being in the opulent Southwest. There seems to be no particular correlation between the salary scale and the quality of the institution. The two places I have in mind that are seeking bargains at $2500 are excellent institutions; one of them is among our better universities. There is a little closer correlation between the quality of the institution and the teaching load that you will be expected to carry, but here again there is the widest kind of variation depending in part, of course, on the number of different courses that you are expected to teach. I know of institutions with nine-hour schedules, and I know of institutions with fifteen-hour schedules. I should say that those are about the extremes, although there are a great many which expect fifteen hours. Usually, in that case, there will be perhaps three sections of one course and two other courses—three preparations in all, a life of utopian indolence.

That is about all I have to say, I think, about the business of getting a job. As you can see, I don't know how it is done. It seems to be a regrettably hit-and-miss affair. But having put you on the track of a job, or having professed to have put you on the track of a job, or possibly even having settled you in one, I would like to shift the emphasis and raise some rather different issues—such questions, for example, as, "What is your potential employer looking for? What qualities ought you to be able to offer an institution?" This is perhaps a little late in the game for some of you, and what I shall say is as much a criticism, I think, of graduate instruction as it is of the students.

Some years ago I had occasion to make a study of the placement situation for the history department. It was in 1940-41, I think, when the shortage of jobs was about as acute as it had been at any time in the history of graduate education, and one of the things I did was to send out a questionnaire to all of the Harvard and Radcliffe Ph.D.'s in History for the past decade. Some interesting material resulted, I thought, as regards salary and periods of unemployment and what not, but the thing I am particularly concerned with was some of the comments that came back regarding the Harvard graduate product. For one thing, there was pretty general testimony by these men who had been through the mill that the Harvard graduate in history tended to be overspecialized, that he was likely to be a good scholar, but in many cases had his weaknesses as a teacher. I suspect that the same views might well have come from the alumni of most of our major graduate schools.

For graduate students I think you might state the problem in somewhat this way: some of you are first-rate scholars with interests that are going to carry you into a rather limited field of specialization. You are going to be primarily scholars. Perhaps, to use Miss Stedman's analogy, you are going to be that caviar for which the market isn't wide but is rather distinctive, and if you think that you are outstanding enough to land a job as a specialist in an institution that has use for specialists, then that is a perfectly reasonable procedure. But make sure it is not tainted caviar. If teaching is your primary interest—I'm not trying to set up a false dichotomy here, this is simply a realistic approach, I think—*but if you are primarily interested in teaching* then you ought to expect to land in a liberal arts college. Here the only sensible course is to get just as broad a training as you can, even at the cost of stepping over departmental lines. I don't know enough about the prospects for or the demand in the field of general education, but my impression is that in the next five to ten years it is likely to develop considerably. In other words, there is the caviar of the specialist and there is the tomato soup of the good teacher, the broadly trained fellow. I thought that perhaps Miss Stedman was going to proceed to the next category of academic groceries, shall we call it spoiled vegetable?, which just remains on the shelf, but I'm afraid her tact was a little greater than mine.

Stated in these terms, of course, the point is that the qualities necessary to get a Harvard or a Radcliffe Ph.D. and the qualities that appeal to a college administrator are not necessarily identical. The graduate school is traditionally dedicated to the premise that scholarship is the only thing that matters. I say traditionally dedicated, officially dedicated, but I know that a good many of us have doubts as to whether we ought to hold that fort indefinitely. The president of a liberal arts college who is after an instructor may make his bow before the image of scholarship but then, having paid his respects, he is likely to hurry on where he thinks he can get an effective teacher who will interest students and who will understand the particular type of student who is attending his institution. Most college presidents—and it is perhaps as much a criticism of them as it is of the graduate school—most presidents of arts colleges are not particularly interested in scholarship in the graduate-school sense. Some years ago the members of one of the regional associations of colleges was asked to list the qualities desirable in an under-graduate teacher. I am sorry to tell you that scholarship placed sixth, and last. Again, that is quite as much a criticism of that association as it is of the graduate school. But there is no question that some men whose record in the graduate school is less than first-rate make a greater appeal than the straight-A man. I repeat, I am not venturing here any value judgments between teaching and scholarship. I am merely looking at it from the vulgar point of view of getting a job, and here I repeat that the college, as opposed to the university employer, is probably more interested in getting a man of broad intellectual interests and a flexible mind, with a civilized, attractive personality, than it is in getting a giant of scholarship. I suspect that this difficulty is going to be more and more obvious and is going to put the issue up pretty flatly to our graduate school curriculum.

Another quality that the prospective employer is looking for is adaptability. He wants a teacher who will fit into his particular situation, somebody who will understand an environment that is a good many hundred miles removed from Harvard Square. And there, I'm afraid, you run into the familiar complaint that Harvard men—and if you wish you can read for that, "Radcliffe women"—are not adaptable; they do not fit into the give-and-take of academic life in institutions that are quite different from Harvard and Radcliffe. Now it is only a small number of Harvard men who behave tactlessly when they leave Cambridge and they are usually the ones who behaved tactlessly in Cambridge. And, if they were homegrown products, their performance might be little noticed. But since they come from an eastern graduate school—does one dare say, especially since they come from Harvard—they tend to confirm all the worst apprehensions of their new colleagues.

Let's be honest about it. As one of my alumni correspondents pointed out, on certain campuses a green baize bag is not the most popular symbol imaginable. No doubt, some of this suspicion is pure provincialism, but some of it is a normal reaction to the provincialism of Harvard men in the past. Young Ph.D.'s —especially, I fear, those from the eastern seaboard—have been justly criticized for their patronizing attitude, for their lack of understanding of local ways and local situations, and for talking too much about their own graduate schools. Lest you think that I am merely drawing on rumor, let me read a short passage from a letter which I happened to see some years ago:

> The question of a position brings up your friend Blank who passed the term here. On the whole he seemed a fairly decent sort, with a tendency to talk too much and absence of tact that was colossal. He is, I am afraid, going to have some tough sledding unless he can rid himself of his ability to offend people. Part of his difficulty comes from an unfortunate attitude by which he gives the impression of knowing everything. That, combined with his insistence upon the fact that he received his education at an eastern university and Oxford [practically compounding the felony] offends the local pride . . . As you know, he is really, when you talk with him, different and not a bad sort.

Incidentally, that flower of the New England tradition came from the Rocky Mountain states! It often happens.

It is possible that three or four years in a major graduate school may actually unfit certain students for teaching posts in some institutions—or at least, condemn them to a difficult period of readjustment. President Benjamin Ide Wheeler of the University of California has been quoted as saying that the products of one graduate school—let's break down and admit it, it was Harvard—made excellent faculty members, once they got through the first two years. I am not sure that the instinct of the small college president is entirely at fault when he tends to prefer local understanding and adaptability to scholarly distinction.

Let's assume that you get a post in a smallish liberal arts college. It is a college that is rather different from anything you have experienced as a graduate student or as an undergraduate. There are some things that you are going to have to keep in mind. Remember that you will be scrutinized and criticized rather more severely than if you were one of the local boys. Some of your colleagues may suspect that you are going to patronize them. In other words, you will have to watch your step socially as well as academically. Not only that, but this college is likely to be connected, more or less intimately, with one of the Protestant denominations. This affiliation will raise another set of questions which may or may not be familiar to you. You will probably be expected to appear at daily chapel and perhaps at church on Sunday. You may be invited to teach a Sunday School class—and, other things aside, it's not bad teaching experience. Smoking on the campus may be frowned upon. In short, your private life may seem a bit over-supervised. (I mention these matters with no implication of praise or blame—simply as statements of fact.)

On the academic side, you may find your first post less than ideal. The library will perhaps be inadequate. A good deal of your teaching will have to be pretty straight textbook stuff, with some supplementary reading. Academic standards may not be what you think they ought to be, and your students will doubtless disappoint you. (I never yet saw a young Ph.D. whose students measured up to his expectations.) You may discover that your colleagues don't give you precisely the kind of intellectual association that you had hoped for.

On all these points I can only counsel tact, common sense, and patience. Even if you are correct in your judgment that academic standards are too low, don't try to revolutionize them overnight. It's all right to be known as a "tough marker," measured by the standards that the students are used to. Beyond that you simply defeat your own purpose. I don't praise conformity as the supreme academic virtue, but there is something to be said for a reasonable degree of conformity when the question of holding a job is involved. Again, don't feel that you have gone to a cultural jumping-off place. There are civilized people in every academic community, and it ought not to be too hard to discover them. At the same time, it is dangerous to discover them too quickly. I should be in no great haste to make friends in a new college. For it is a poor institution indeed that does not have a few good rousing faculty feuds in progress, and no new member in his senses is going to get caught up in that sort of thing—not, at least, until he knows what the issues are and what the score is! Above all, don't let yourselves become pedantic and pompous. It's appalling how stuffy some young men get a few years out of graduate school. Perhaps in some colleges there isn't enough rubbing of intellectual elbows; perhaps these chaps are the kind who would become pedants in any environment. But I urge you to remain human, even after you are doctors of philosophy.

As a final injunction, I suggest that, when you take your first post, you identify yourself with the local situation to as great a degree as you can. Begin by finding out all you can about the institution before you get there, so that you can fit in with as little fuss as possible. Learn about its history and traditions, its strong points and its weaknesses. Young Ph.D.'s have been criticized for being so ambitious that all they can think of, while teaching in a particular college, are their chances of moving on. Some tend to regard every appointment as a springboard to higher and better and more profitable things. This is natural enough, in its way, but if you are going to do your job really well, you will have to go native, at least in moderation.

SIGNIFICANT ASPECTS OF HIGHER EDUCATION IN THE UNITED STATES

HOWARD MUMFORD JONES

Chapter XVI

THE ROLE OF HIGHER EDUCATION IN AMERICA

An analysis of the many and varied types of institutions which make up the American educational system. Some of the reasons and accidents which explain their form or location. What do we mean by "college"? What do we mean by "university"? Junior colleges, vocational colleges, and the "liberal arts." Examination of the many sources, public, private, and denominational, from which our educational institutions derive. The appeal of the American college rests for some on a type of living, for others on a conservation of the mores or on a desire for professional training or, ideally, on the attainment of a working philosophy of life.

A single chapter is so obviously inadequate to outline, much less exhaust, the role of higher education in the United States, that I may seem to compound confusion if I spend a good deal of time discussing the ambiguities of fact and terminology that darken counsel when one discusses the subject. I shall, however, divide the discussion into three unequal parts: first, some analysis of the complexity of higher education in this country; second, an examination of certain unusual features of our higher education; and third, an inquiry as to why people go to college.

1

Our system of higher education, if it can be called a system, is probably the most complicated in the world. The Frenchman who said that the United States is a land of 367 religions and only one sauce had not considered the possibilities of our present topic. We are, of course, a continental country and entitled to more colleges and universities than is France or Italy, but the number is nevertheless appallingly large. There are about 850 universities and colleges in the United States. There are about 435 junior colleges. There are some 220 teachers' colleges and normal schools. It is a mark of our uncertainties that it is difficult to secure exact statistical information about higher education. I have not counted in this total of about 1500 institutions, an unknown number of temporary colleges created for veterans. Still, 1500 institutions make a very large number.

The range in size and structure among these 1500 institutions is something to bewilder a foreign critic. The annual report of the Chancellor of New York University concerning the academic year 1947-48 indicates that 56,000 students of all kinds enrolled in that institution—so far as I can discover, the largest enrollment in the country. At the other end of the spectrum there are institutions like Kletzing College, University Park, Iowa, which has 76 students; the Webb Institute of Naval Architecture at Glen Cove, New York, which has 49 students; and Dropsie College in Philadelphia, which has 51. I draw my figures from the *World Almanac.*

Obviously there are profound differences in approaching the educational problem when you are dealing with 56,000 students and when you are dealing with fifty. For example, it might be assumed either that the size of the faculty will be a function of the size of the student body or that the size of the student body will be a function of the size of the faculty. In a general sense, this is true. But it is true only in a general sense. The University of Pittsburgh, for example, enrolls a little more than 22,000 students, for whom 2200 teachers are provided. But Harvard

University, which enrolls about 11,000 students, provides individual instruction for many of its students, so that the proportion of professors to students is no very sure indication of the amount of attention the undergraduate is likely to have from any faculty.

One might also infer that there is some connection between the financial endowment and physical plant of these institutions and the size of the student body. Of 850 colleges and universities, 175 have endowments of two million dollars or more. In 1947 Harvard with its enrollment of 11,000 stood at the top of the list with a capital investment of $160,000,000, whereas New York University, with its enormous student population, does not even appear in the two-million-dollar club and must depend to a large extent upon fees for its existence—the mode of subsistence of medieval universities. Fordham University, in New York, one of the leading Catholic universities, is not in the two-million-dollar club, though it enrolls 8,000 students, whereas Milwaukee Downer College, a small college in Wisconsin, has an endowment of $2,370,000. Clearly, then, there is no necessary connection between the size of the student body and the financial resources of an institution.

We usually think of an educational institution as a unit located in one place, a fact which gives both unity of management and unity of feeling to its personnel. Yet New York University is both at the bottom and at the top of New York City, and the two halves of it are not alike. The University of California, one of the largest institutions in the country, maintains three separate campuses at Berkeley, at Santa Barbara, and at Los Angeles. The University of Idaho is distributed between Moscow and Pocatello, Pocatello being the "branch," albeit the tail now wags the dog. Harvard University exists in Cambridge, in Boston, in Washington, in Climax, Colorado, in Cuba, and in South Africa. How does this geographical scatter come about? Because of the needs of an area? Sometimes. In the case of Harvard, of Boston University, of Western Reserve University in Cleveland, you can see social demand, real-estate problems, historical accidents, and other causes at work; many institutions thus scattered in various places are now torn between a centripetal desire to concentrate their campus and a centrifugal force that tears them apart, with interesting results upon educational policy.

Need sometimes explains university partition, but it does not necessarily create it. Consider two queerly shaped commonwealths—Idaho and Michigan. The central portion of Idaho is a high plateau having very little population. Most of the population is, as it were, on the rim. Moscow is in the north of the state. So long as the university was confined to Moscow, students from southern Idaho had to take a train out of Idaho into Montana and back again into Idaho to reach the state university. When population increased in the southern part of Idaho, the legislature wisely created at Pocatello a branch of the university. But the state of Michigan, populous and wealthy, is divided into the Upper and Lower peninsulas, separated by the Straits of Mackinac, so that, if you do not wish to cross the straits in winter, to get from the Upper Peninsula to the Lower, you have to go through Wisconsin, Illinois, and Indiana. On the other hand, most of the population of that commonwealth is concentrated in the lower tiers of counties of the Lower Peninsula. The people of the Upper Peninsula have had to content themselves with a School of Mines and a teachers' college, whereas the great University of Michigan is at Ann Arbor, the enormous State College is at East Lansing, about forty miles from Ann Arbor, and in Detroit, less than forty miles east of the state university, is Wayne University, part of the public school system of Detroit. Inasmuch as Michigan State College has, in the last decade, developed a liberal arts curriculum and nourishes also a School of Music, you find in Michigan an illogical concentration of what are in fact three enormous universities supported by tax money, all in a small triangle in the southeast portion of the state.

We usually think of academic institutions as exhibiting some unity of function. Vocational schools, however, whether suffering from an inferiority complex or not, are forever tending to take on liberal arts courses. This has been true at Michigan State College; it used to be true at the North Carolina State College of Agriculture and Engineering; and it is true of other institutions. This doubtless enriches the curriculum, but it also confuses the aim of the school.

How many students are there in these institutions? By "college" we usually mean a four-year course of study, and it is relatively easy to count persons in these schools. But what about the University of Chicago, where students progress to a degree as fast as they can? To be sure, we can always count heads and say that such-and-such a number is enrolled, but clearly a young man securing a bachelor's degree in two crowded years is not quite in the category with a student at a standard four-year institution like Colgate. And shall we count the students in 435 junior colleges as part of our academic population? Junior Colleges seem to have arisen in three ways. They may be, as in the case of some state universities, fostered by a parent institution desiring to decrease pressure on the freshman and sophomore years; and in that case students enter their doors as bona fide college students in the usual meaning of the word. But in the Middle West and the Far West, the junior college, instead of coming down from the top, has arisen from below; that is, it is an outgrowth of the local school system. Or, finally, the junior college may be a private venture, sometimes preparing students for the junior year in a four-year college, sometimes offering vocational training, sometimes doing both. An example is a junior college at Hartford, Connecticut, which prepares girls for advanced standing in college, but which has also instituted excellent courses in nursing and in retail salesmanship because Hartford felt the need for this sort of training. How many of its students are properly college students?

Figures for 1947 indicate that we have about three and one-half million college students, an increase of about a million and a quarter over 1938. Of course, an important fraction of this increase, particularly in the last part of the decade, represents the enrollment of veterans. The number of freshmen entering our institutions in 1948-49 was less by about 120,000 than it had been previously. It is estimated, however, that the student population of 1950 will be about three million. The uncertainty accompanying these figures again illustrates how difficult it is to know what you mean by "college," "university," and "student." As one runs the gamut from New York University to Dropsie College, from Harvard to Hartford, from Colgate to Wayne University, common aims tend to disappear amid a diversity of numbers, a diversity of resources, and a diversity of size.

Further to confuse the discussion we have no fixed meaning for commonly used terms. What *is* a college? A college was originally a *collegium,* that is, a collection of persons existing for a single purpose. This meaning of the term appears in such phrases as the college of the apostles, meaning the twelve apostles; the college of cardinals; or the electoral college. These variants offer no difficulties. By "college" we normally have in view an educational institution licensed to grant bachelor's degrees as a reward of four years of study. But trouble immediately begins. Many colleges do not content themselves with granting bachelor's degrees and many institutions not colleges are allowed to grant them. For example, you can earn an excellent bachelor's degree at the Rhode Island School of Design, whereas Radcliffe College, not content with an A.B., also grants the master's degree and the doctor's degree. To award these last two "higher degrees" is, however, usually thought to be a function of a university. Since many "colleges" have graduate "schools"—for example, Radcliffe and Bryn Mawr—confusion in nomenclature increases. Moreover, a "college" may be a two-year junior college, and this, as I have indicated, need not mainly do college work of the usual sort. At the University of Minnesota there exists a "general college" intended for those unfitted for the work of the liberal arts college, doing work which is rewarded by certificates. Are all these "colleges"?

Many colleges are independent institutions; as, Bowdoin, Smith, Mills, Centenary. Others are "coördinated" colleges. Radcliffe is an interesting case in point. It is legally an independent corporation, but as an educational institution all its academic affairs are in the hands of an alien Harvard faculty. Parallel situations are to be found in Pembroke College (Brown University) and Flora Stone Mather College (Western Reserve), except that this last-named institution has its own faculty for undergraduate work. There are also systems of colleges. For example, in the state of New York there are the Colleges of the Seneca, a union for legal and education purposes of Hobart College for men and William Smith College for women. Another interesting case is the Claremont College plan in California. This is a system of three colleges:

Pomona, Scripps, and Claremont College. Each has its own president. Is fusion of aims or independence of administration the more important factor?

Since "college" is neither a copyrighted nor a patentable term, anybody can use it; the result being that there are hundreds of "colleges" in the country that do not grant degrees and do not give academic work. Thus we have barbers' colleges, morticians' colleges, and business colleges—really secretarial and bookkeeping "schools," whereas the Harvard Business School is essentially a "graduate college." An amusing variant of the term in this sense is the College of Cosmetology, an institution which, among other matters, trains "beauticians" to rouge the faces of the dead. But let us return to the academic world.

A college may be a college, but not be called so. The "school" of engineering is in fact a college of engineering, the "school" of law is in fact a college of law, and so on. The term "school" was applied to these institutions for historical reasons, but inasmuch as each of them grants a bachelor's degree, if that be the test, each is in fact a college. Or, if a college is not called a school, it may be called an institute. Thus the Case School of Applied Science in Cleveland has existed happily under that name, but it has now become the Case Institute of Applied Science. It still grants bachelor's degrees.

A final variant appears when, going back to the practice of the Middle Ages, we discover that Yale University, which has a system of undergraduate houses parallel to the Harvard system, prefers to call these, not houses, but colleges, on the ground of a vague parallel of function to the colleges which make up a university like Oxford or Cambridge. But I have said enough to indicate our lack of agreement as to the meaning of "college" in the academic world.

Let us now try "university." A university was originally the *universitas magistrorum et scholarum;* that is, the entire collection (*universitas*) of teachers and scholars (*magistrorum et scholarum*). Within the framework of medieval learning, anything in the way of organized knowledge could be taught and studied by this body of men, and the *studium generale* was the curriculum of the *universitas*. By and by, as frequently happens in the history of languages, one idea was substituted for another, and *universitas* came to take on the overtones of the *studium generale* or total curriculum. Many well-intentioned persons will now tell you that a university is a place which will teach universally; that is, a place in which anything can be studied. The error, if it is one, has been influential in American education, for when Ezra Cornell created the university which bears his name, he said he wanted to found an institution in which anybody could study anything. Cornell still bears the imprint of this idea.

In the usual sense of the term, however, a university is an institution of higher learning, usually composed of several colleges, and possessing sufficient material, financial, and intellectual resources to justify the granting of advanced degrees, particularly the doctorate. In the British Isles the emphasis has been upon the collection of colleges; in the United States the present tendency seems to be on the granting of advanced degrees. You may, of course, have a university composed of a single college, as in the case of Trinity College, Dublin; and long before Harvard had created a graduate school, people referred to the "university in Cambridge." But generally in this country the word "university" implies the power to grant advanced degrees.

This is not universally true, however. The University of the State of New York does not exist in this sense, for there is no school, you can't take courses, and the only degrees it offers are honorary ones. The University of the State of New York, vaguely on the analogue of the University of France, is a legal body corresponding to the state board of education in other commonwealths and charged with the regulation of colleges and universities in the Empire State. On the other hand, Norwich University in Vermont, which is no longer at Norwich, is virtually a military school, the university part of the name being the result of that pioneer optimism which created a good many universities—on paper. Norwich does excellent work, but it is not a university and does not pretend to be one.

Many institutions not called universities perform university functions. An example is the Institute for Advanced Study in

Princeton, New Jersey, which grants no degrees and has, in the usual sense of the word, no faculty, but which is a powerful influence upon research work in our graduate schools.

Let us pass from problems of institutional terminology to other aspects of academic nomenclature. A holder of a bachelor's degree is a *baccalaureus,* whether of arts or of something else. This term appears to come from dairy farming, though how the cow (*bacca*) got involved in academic life, if she did, is a mystery to philology. The baccalaureate degree is usually a degree "in the arts," albeit few of us have any professional knowledge of the arts as we normally use that term. "Arts" here refers to the liberal arts which made up the seven parts of the medieval curriculum—the trivium and the quadrivium. The trivium was grammar, rhetoric, logic. The quadrivium was geometry, astronomy, arithmetic, and music. Medieval music was not an art in our sense, but a mélange of metaphysics, mathematics, and theology.

By the eighteenth and nineteenth centuries this notion of the "liberal" arts had been transformed into a gentlemanly curriculum consisting of Latin and Greek, sometimes Hebrew, natural philosophy, and philosophy itself, not forgetting mathematics. This was the parent of our present confused undergraduate curriculum, which dropped Hebrew, mostly dropped Greek, kept Latin for the diploma (if for that), turned natural philosophy into specialism, teaches no universal philosophy, and confers what is frequently a vocational degree in fact, if not in name. As we do not know whether this curriculum is primarily useful or useless, vocational or liberal, we confuse the A.B. or S.B. degree still further by granting bachelor's degrees in music, in the fine arts, in business administration, in journalism, in domestic science, and in a variety of other subjects. Our one original attempt to keep order failed. This was the creation of the bachelor of science degree, grimly described by President Lowell when he said that the degree guaranteed no knowledge of science but only an ignorance of Latin.

In the Middle Ages the master of arts and the doctor of philosophy, originally licenses to teach in the *studium generale,* were more or less equal. The master's degree fell from this high estate. In British universities, by the eighteenth century, it could be acquired by lapse of time and the payment of a fee. There were decades in the history of Harvard when any bright A.B. could get a master's degree by paying a small fee and staying out of jail —that is, he had to present evidence of good moral character. The A.M. is now, of course, a hobbledehoy degree, neither graduate nor undergraduate, which ought in my judgment to be returned to the faculty of the undergraduate college and awarded by them as a mark of a fifth year of collegiate studies. It is seldom a mark of genuine research.

The doctor of philosophy is seldom a master of metaphysics, and if he is, he will be awarded a Ph.D. in philosophy, which looks like tautology. "Philosophia" is now simply organized knowledge in a field; the degree is chiefly a license to teach in higher institutions of learning. It retains traditional traces of medievalism—a thesis, an oral examination. But the thesis is no longer necessarily a contribution to knowledge; it is rather a demonstration of professional skill, an important modification of the germanic notion of the degree.

2

It would be amusing to comment on the confused notions we have in this country about the office of a dean, a president, or a chancellor, all of them indices of our confused notions of the purpose of higher education, but it is time to turn to another important aspect of the general topic—the peculiar system, or lack of system, found in the United States in contrast to most other countries. We are the only great nation in which the national government does not directly support and administer education. The word "education" does not appear in the federal constitution, and the only federal agency directly and solely concerned with education is the Office of Education, which collects information but directs nothing. The government influences education indirectly by offering grants of money to the states, provided the states will meet the terms laid down by Congress, but this is not the same thing as direct licensing and control which exist in France or Russia.

The principal legal bodies controlling higher education with us are the state legislatures, and part of the confusion in our system arises from the eccentricities of these bodies. They have the power to charter degree-granting institutions either directly or by delegation. In early years state legislatures were highly uncritical of the colleges, so that almost anybody could get a charter for a degree-granting institution, and sometimes degrees were sold by mail. This situation has improved, but there is still no national agreement as to minimum requirements for a charter.

If the federal government has only indirect control, and if the state legislatures vary among themselves, what makes for the general uniformity of American college life? The peculiar invention of the Americans has been the creation of great professional associations such as the American Association for the Advancement of Science, the American Historical Association, the American Mathematical Society, the American Association of University Professors, and the Association of American Colleges. Bodies like these tend both directly and indirectly to set professional academic standards, and their work is paralleled in law, medicine, engineering, and other professions. Out of this activity arise the various accrediting agencies which keep schools, colleges, and universities up to concert pitch. This development is, I think, unique in educational history, an element so unusual we ought to be proud of it instead of taking it for granted, as we do.

Other governing elements in the American "system" of higher education can be best approached historically. In the seventeenth century and later, colleges in this country were instituted as an aid to religion. This religion was uniformly the Protestant religion; and the colleges were often governed by ministers, a significant fraction of their students were ministers in training, and even though a majority of the undergraduates were not to be clerics, the curriculum was colored by Christian ethics and Protestant theology. If the concept of the Christian college was mildly threatened by deism at the end of the eighteenth century, the conservative reaction against the French Revolution restored and even increased academic moralism. As the frontier rolled westward, Protestantism created institutions of higher learning just behind it. The intent was to prevent atheism, deism, or (in certain areas) Roman Catholicism from altering American values. Evangelical zeal dotted most of the country with its products; and, moreover, the Protestant denominations were often indirectly, though not less firmly, in control of many state universities. In the early decades of its existence the University of Georgia was, for example, strongly influenced by the Methodist Church and the University of North Carolina was strongly influenced by the Presbyterians. Church domination, direct or indirect, has left its traces to this day. College officials, particularly presidents, were thought to be better if they had clerical training or, at least, a strong church coloration; and the college professor could not be eccentric except in the framework of Christian ethical principles. When the great University of Chicago was founded in 1893, the regulations provided that the president should be a Baptist, a provision not altered until well into the twentieth century. If the University of the South at Sewanee is still a part of the system of the Episcopalian Church, it is unusual in this respect. An increasing number of colleges and universities originally bound by legal ties to one or another denomination have ceased to be so bound.

This change has meant an increasing tolerance for divergent religious views. In the seventeenth century it would have been difficult for a Baptist to be comfortable at Harvard College, and as for a Catholic, he would have had no chance at all. Nowadays, however, few colleges insist that their students must be communicants of a particular church. The ecclesiastical past of these institutions, however, still colors many formalities. We retain voluntary chapel services, we retain a baccalaureate address, we have prayers at public ceremonies, we feel in general that the college should be sympathetic with the purposes of the Y.M.C.A., the Newman Club, the Menorah Society. The courts, moreover, take the position that the college stands *in loco parentis* to its students and is, in greater or less degree, responsible for their moral welfare. All this rather astonishes European observers accustomed to the notion of the university as a purely intellectual enterprise.

If such is the inheritance of higher education in this country from the seventeenth century, the eighteenth century brought in the spirit of secularism, exemplified in the North by Benjamin Franklin and in the South by Thomas Jefferson. In creating the institution which became the University of Pennsylvania, Franklin sought to increase useful knowledge. He was not interested in training clergymen, and he did not think that Latin, Greek, and Hebrew were essential to higher education. It is amusing to realize that the spirit which he and his generation helped to engender also created Girard College in Philadelphia, the charter of which provides that no clergyman of any sort shall ever set foot within its walls. In his scheme for the University of Virginia, Jefferson deliberately omitted a school of theology and, by and large, was not enthusiastic about clerical interference.[*]

Eighteenth-century secularism has left important marks upon American higher education. Collegiate training was not thought of as merely cultural, merely gentlemanly, merely aristocratic and for the few, but was intended to be "useful"—that is, in the long run, vocational. And in the next place, colleges and universities were supposed to assume a certain responsibility for society. They "extended" knowledge. Nowadays this takes the form of extension courses, night schools, correspondence work, popular lectures, and adult education. It also takes form as an interest in contemporary problems as a formal part of the curriculum, an interest unthinkable in seventeenth-century Harvard.

Our inheritance from the nineteenth century falls into two general divisions. In the first part of that epoch I think the significant thing is the adoption of a philosophy of statism in education. Following the example of Napoleon's reorganization of education in France and inspired also by the example of the German states, states in the Middle West and the South argued that they would in the long run benefit by supporting higher education. New state constitutions, unlike the federal constitution, stipulated that the state is responsible for the support of universities and of university learning. Such support was of course the quickest way by which, in new commonwealths, colleges and universities could be organized and made available at small expense to young residents. This new spirit created (in some cases re-created) the American state university in its most characteristic form. State universities in Michigan, in Illinois, in Iowa, in Wisconsin, and other commonwealths were organized around two governing concepts. One was the doctrine of freedom of teaching and learning, originally stemming from Germany. The other was the theory, partly foreign, partly domestic, of the university in the service of the state.

Today, for example, any farmer in Wisconsin as a matter of course receives, for the asking, any amount of valuable information from the state university, notably from the College of Agriculture. The state university is thought of as the crown of a state educational system extending from the public kindergarten to the Ph.D., supported by public money and deliberately kept as inexpensive as possible.

The second great contribution of the nineteenth century, one coming after the Civil War, was specialism. Industrial advance required technological training; and the consequence was a surge forward in technical schools. Colleges of engineering, for instance, increased in number from six to 125. The federal government enriched and indirectly supported technological schools through federal aid. But as schools of engineering and technology multiplied, so, too, specialism increased in scholarship and pure science. An eighteenth-century professor of natural philosophy at King's College (Columbia) was a man who showed how science thinks God's thoughts after Him, inasmuch as the philosophic point in teaching chemistry or mathematics or geology was to clarify a teleological universe. But the specialist has not had time for these general views. He has made the Ph.D. the union label of specialization, he has more or less created the graduate school which gives it, he operates on government grants, on industrial grants, on research grants for particular and limited purposes, and he demands annual renewal in the shape of young specialists from the graduate schools. It is not too cynical to observe that industry and finance, by supporting universities, secure at small cost to themselves excellently trained technologists. The extent to which the Ph.D. has become a technical degree rather than a degree in philosophic thought is obvious to all observers.

Such, then, are our inheritances from the three centuries during which we have had colleges—moralism from the seventeenth century, usefulness from the eighteenth, statism and specialism from the nineteenth. But in this hasty survey I have omitted reference to the Roman Catholic colleges, which have their special history and which stand a little aside from the main line of American development. In general there are three types of such institutions. The great Catholic University of America is a pontifical university—that is, it is directly responsible to the Vatican. The other Catholic colleges and universities fall into two groups, not always easily to be distinguished: diocesan colleges directly under the supervision of the bishop of the diocese and colleges under the control of the various teaching orders. Possibly the Catholic colleges are more consistent than others in molding all education around a core of what they believe to be religious truth, unshaken and unalterable. Their development has been rapid in the last quarter of the nineteenth century and in the twentieth century. Their standards steadily improve, but Catholic educators themselves say that they are handicapped by lack of funds and by lack of a trained personnel in sufficient numbers.

To my way of thinking the most pressing problem in higher education of the twentieth century is the problem of freedom. More and more of the research work done in the universities has its connection with the military, and a shocking degree of secrecy prevails. The most encouraging development in undergraduate education in the same period may be the return upon a concept of general education, provided this concept be directed towards the shaping of good citizens.

3

Why do the Americans support these hundreds and hundreds of schools? Why do colleges exist? Why do young people attend them? I think there are four notable reasons why millions of young people come to us.

In the first place, the American college offers to all comers, for a period usually of four years, a unique way of life, a way of life to which the student can never return. There is nothing quite like this way of life anywhere else in the world. I refer, of course, to "campus" life, to the life of student activity. We have unwittingly revived the medieval notion of the self-contained college community. For these years the young American can step out of the fiercely competitive life of our economic and social order and lead a life at once competitive and idealized. This campus life—the life of dormitories and fraternities, clubs and teams, dances and picnics, professional societies, college journalism, and all the rest of it—is at once like and unlike life "outside." It is sufficiently a part of America to prepare students for a competitive existence; it is sufficiently guarded and controlled, so that, if the student makes a mistake, the results will not usually be disastrous. Of course, city colleges and universities do not separate themselves so neatly from the nation as do institutions in smaller towns, but by and large campus life is everywhere *sui generis*. In the autobiography of Henry S. Canby, you can trace the parallels between this life and the life of society at large.

In the second place the colleges offer, though they do not commonly say so, vocational or professional training, usually for the middle class. The ivy colleges pretend that this is not so, but many parents send their children to Williams or Dartmouth, Smith or Sweetbriar, to meet the right people, make the right connections, achieve the right values, and learn the ropes of our industrial, financial, or social order. In addition, many colleges offer direct training in all sorts of things from domestic science to meteorology, and so in fact prepare directly for jobs. However "liberal" the liberal college is, it is still a place which, whatever its brave pretensions to philosophy, offers directly or indirectly a considerable degree of professional and vocational education.

In the third place, despite the House Committee on Un-American Activities, despite the sorrowful attacks on universities and university people for being "reds," our colleges and universities are conservative institutions. They mostly follow trends, they seldom institute them. They are not in the least radical. They confirm their students in a way of life. Students go to college in order to understand current society in terms of existing values—a not unimportant procedure in a society constantly under attack.

Finally, an important minority of young people go to college (and some of them into the graduate school) to satisfy that intellectual curiosity without which a culture like ours cannot be dynamic. From the point of view of scholarship this is the true aim of the college. Some of these students will merely increase our technological complexities by inventing new ones, but a smaller portion will reflect upon life and arrive at a philosophy of it. The role of higher education in America is thus what it has been in all societies which have had colleges or their equivalent: to aim at higher learning. What I have tried to do is to show how this elementary aim is overlaid and made tortuous by the extraordinary story of higher learning in America, and to suggest that an understanding of the nature and process of higher education is, in social and historical terms, a far richer and more stimulating study than most of us realize.

WALLACE B. DONHAM

Chapter XVII

EDUCATION FOR DEMOCRACY DEVELOPING RESPONSIBLE STUDENT INITIATIVE

How shall the human race bring up its young? How can they be taught to think freely and act both freely and wisely? Necessity of a vision of unity to make up for weakening of family ties and the lack of other binding forces. What colleges can do to help. The value of the concrete situation or "case method" in teaching students to think responsibly. The carry-over of problems thus studied in college to problems to be solved in community living.

Teaching rightly considered is experimental research. There is great need of teachers who are thoughtfully studying methods of training youth for our democracy. If we do not train youth to meet the needs of a democracy—and particularly the leaders who are largely graduates of our colleges—if we do not train them better, the future of our country is very doubtful. This

NOTE: This chapter is based partly on the author's address given in 1947–48 and partly on a fuller treatment of the subject in his article, "Why Experiment? The Case System in College Teaching of Social Science," in *Journal of General Education,* January 1949.

does not mean subjecting youth to propaganda. In our constant effort to teach subject matter in which we believe, we are apt to forget that successful teaching is getting students to learn. And curiously enough this process is often more emotional than it is intellectual. I am emphasizing teaching because in our specialized graduate training it is so often treated as the least of little things, instead of as the key to that most fascinating of human problems: how shall the human race bring up its young?

What characteristics of our democracy ought we to consider in working out our teaching programs? In the first place, we pride ourselves on freedom of thought, on liberal freedom of speech; we take pride in an organization of society that stimulates independence and self-initiative. In our profession particularly, we value academic freedom of thought and speech. Unfortunately we often value it more for ourselves than for our students. We value many kinds of freedom; perhaps we undervalue the corelative responsibility. These characteristics of our democracy make a free democracy harder to operate successfully for long periods of time than any other type of organized society. Freedom of fleeting majorities easily turns into oppression by militant minorities. Freedom tends to lead away from and often to destroy cooperative and collaborative efforts. Freedom and individual initiative may easily weaken our ability to get along with people, to preserve the unity of the country. We see many illustrations of this. In recent years tensions are growing all around us, tensions between groups, loss of tolerance among individuals and groups, unwillingness to listen and make an effort to understand the point of view of other people both at home and abroad. The sense of responsibility weakens dangerously.

We are losing the ability to work together and at the same time to differ in many ways and opinions. We are losing the ability to understand the point of view of labor, if we are manufacturers, and if we are labor, of employers. Family ties are weakening. Racial and religious tensions increase. These are dangerous symptoms. They do not help us solve international tensions.

Why are we losing progressively the capacity to collaborate? Up to recent years such factors as the strength of custom and tradition, our close-knit neighborhoods, our strong family life, our solid foundation in farm and country, the fact that for most of us our ways of making a living were closely integrated with our whole way of life—all such things enabled us to hold firm our basis of living together.

This situation has changed radically with the advance of science, technology, and industry. Wherever we look, we see gadgets of all sorts, from railroads and automobiles to frozen foods and can openers, which have followed this advance of technology and industry. The sociological consequences are even more far-reaching than the economic. We must learn to cope with all types of changes consequent on these gadgets. Immigration from all over Europe contributed to the disorganization. The rural population diminished as the percentage of our population living in cities grew, sometimes beyond all bounds. By such processes the capacity to collaborate lessened in the family, in the neighborhood, in the factory, in the state, and in the nation. For a long time we did not realize the significance of the established society we were losing as a foundation for collaboration.

To a large extent we have lost the compelling force of religion. That is a major loss. We tend to fight even about religious subjects, instead of being tolerant of differences of opinion within one subject where basically we all make the same claim—the right of each to worship his own God in his own way. While we demand this right for ourselves, we often fail to recognize fully the same right for others. Men have fought long over religious matters, but always under a sense of responsibility to a militant God—not to a loving God. We no longer live in this country as we did three or four generations ago. One of my associates once said, "My grandfather lived all his life under a sense of responsibility to God." We have lost that sense of responsibility and we have not found an effective substitute.

The colleges, instead of doing what they might to counteract this confusion, are doing without thinking many things which make it worse. We have no design of education to counteract the dangers that face us. We have no generally used method of training people to collaborate even while they differ, to tolerate each other's points of view and make a serious effort toward mutual understanding. We knew how to live together in an established society where change was slow during the active life of each individual; we must now learn how to live together effectively in an adaptive society where changes are constantly accelerating, where now all mature men leave a world very different from the world they entered.

This business of learning how to collaborate starts as a small problem in the home, neighborhood, and farm or factory. It expands to the limits of international relations. But for each of us it starts as a small thing. We fail from the beginning to develop the necessary capacity. Students come to college without, on the average, the same capacity to collaborate in a small way that they used to have. Can we as a people collaborate on the major aspects of things if we lack the capacity to do it on the smaller aspect of things? There is a big educational job at all levels from primary school through adult education. It is a long, slow job; there may not be time for it. It is, however, the hope I see for the future. My present emphasis is the college, for there we must train leaders. Germany and Russia saw a vision in the period between the two World Wars. Did we? Sir Richard Livingstone, President of Corpus Christi College, Oxford, suggests that England and America no longer have a clear vision of greatness to stir our uneasy sleep. We at least are not seeing a vision. Yet Germany and Russia saw visions, "perhaps through smoky glass, but still a vision." Livingstone suggests that we in both countries lack that vision of greatness which Whitehead speaks of as the key to a liberal education, and that we have no effective substitute. We must find such a vision. Yet the colleges, instead of hunting for an answer to such needs, have so built up their curricula and their methods as to help destroy any unity and obscure any possible vision. Many of us have little pride in citizenship and lack an intense love of country.

One thing is sure. This vision, this love of country, this unity, presents much more than intellectual problems. Livingstone, in his *Education for a World Adrift* (page 150), has stated the point well:

Citizenship, as I have urged, is practical not speculative, active not passive, an art not a theory—the art and virtue of living in a community. The good citizen, like the good soldier, has learnt to feel and act as a member of a body, to play his part in it, and, if need be, to sacrifice to it his interests and even his life, to do his duty to the State without compulsion and of his own free will. It is a difficult art, commoner perhaps in this country than in others, but not perfected, and needing to be learnt in every generation; a harmony of clashing forces—independence and respect for authority, individualism and teamwork, self-assertion, self-discipline and self-sacrifice, initiative and subordination. Knowledge of "Civics" will help men to practise it, ideals will inspire and show the goal. But Whitehead's saying that moral education is impossible without the habitual vision of greatness needs to be completed by the remark of Aristotle that men acquire virtues, not by knowing what they are nor by talking about them nor by admiring and praising them but by practising them. We become punctual by continually being punctual, we acquire the habit of telling the truth by telling it; and we become good citizens by doing what good citizens do. Social virtue is learnt by social life. So its infant school is the family, where the members, living together, learn how to live together as members of a tiny community. The smaller the family, the worse the school.

Citizenship is not information or intellectual interest, though these are part of it; it is conduct not theory, action not knowledge, and a man may be familiar with the contents of every book on the social sciences without being a good citizen.

Yet a vision is not enough. We must educate affirmatively for collaboration and for responsible living. Today there is no unity in college curricula, no common body of information, attitudes, skills, or interests shared by educated men as a result of their education. Education in college fails in too many cases to bridge the gap between the home, a job, and life after college. The customary college methods do not put sufficient responsibility and initiative on the student. The educational system is oriented not toward the student to answer his needs, not toward democracy and its needs, but toward many different teachers and their specialized subjects. It is not sufficiently related to life as the student must face life's problems.

In our democracy it is important to retain the freedom to think and act individually within reasonable responsible limits. At the same time, it is important to regain, or keep where we have not lost it, the power to collaborate among ourselves as citizens in spite of differences. Tolerance, coöperation, and responsibility—those are things that we must have. Yet these depend on attitudes rather than on intellectual theories. There is a job of training for responsible living to be done, and colleges must do something about it.

We know less about new students when they come to us—this generation of college entrants—than has been true at any time in the past. We know something about the backgrounds from which they spring. They come from every segment of our population. We know that the population is heterogeneous, that its interests and surroundings are very diversified. We know that as a result of two wars and of the progress of pure and applied science and technology, ours is a very disorganized society. We know very little about individual students, and we are slow to get acquainted with them.

There is general agreement that we and Western civilization face a major crisis. The crisis is made more serious because we have difficulty collaborating among ourselves and have not found out how to collaborate with foreign nations. We do not know how to think in a friendly, or rather, in an understanding, way about Russia today. We automatically behave in a manner dictated by our prejudices with relatively little effort to understand that great empire.

New students come therefore from a discordant, disorganized, disturbed, powerful country. Most of us are fond of the country, and yet we lack the kinds of skills needed to keep this nation an effective free democracy. The alternative to free responsible democracy is autocracy. I hate to think what this country, with all its technological skills and powers and all its discordant fears and hates, would be as an autocracy.

The flood of G.I.'s will soon be over. Normally students come to us, roughly, at the age of eighteen. What do we know about them? We know that they can read—badly—and write—very badly. We know that they can do elementary arithmetic and use a few other mathematical tools—with very little skill, as you find if you try to rely on their skills. We know that they have been brought up in good, bad, and indifferent homes with all varieties of social experience. Perhaps the ones that get the largest amount of social experience are those who come from indifferent homes.

Good homes tend to control the youngster too far and bad homes subject him to too many questionable influences.

We have not learned how to take these children in infancy and childhood and carry them through the period when they must have a large amount of family supervision and care, and then how to lessen gradually the amount of family control and introduce them effectively to wider and wider social experience. This wider experience is of first importance for social living. Some families do this, but it is not accomplished for the group as a whole. This magnifies the job of the college.

Our admission requirements in general give us little help in understanding youth who come to us, though real thought is being given to the problem. Many requirements are based on scholastic aptitude tests. I have never been quite sure about such tests. I have seen so many cases of youngsters who wake up suddenly and surprise everybody by their scholastic aptitude after they have been rated as almost sure failures. Perhaps affirmative predictions of success by these tests are more reliable, but they still fail to test all-around human quality. On the other hand, many of you will find yourselves in colleges where you will lack the aid of scholastic aptitude tests. In many state-supported institutions any graduate of a high school in that state is eligible for entrance. High school standards vary from the best to the worst in the states where this is the law. Many students have important aptitudes not covered by our tests. There is much in each student that we could rely on if we only knew what it is.

Contrary to the usual assumption that childhood is a time of little experience on which education can be built, I submit that the first eighteen years of life are filled with immensely diversified and long-lasting activities and experiences. Indeed, I question whether there is any other period in life when so much activity and so much experience is crowded into so few years as between the ages of two and eighteen. There is no other period in which experience has so much effect in molding whole lives.

Unfortunately when the youth goes to college, although he has this immense background of experience, he has almost no training in interpreting it. Interpretation up to this time has been by parents or other close relatives of an earlier generation, by religious leaders, or by teachers. The reasons for the interpretation have rarely been disclosed to the child in ways which place on him responsibility for the interpretation or for action which follows the interpretation. This is another way of saying that he has had little practice in the *conscious process* of abstracting generalizations from the facts of his experience. Yet in his immediate surroundings he makes abstractions at a very early age; for example, in his accurate use of the word "chair" in spite of multifarious differences in shape, form, and material which differentiate chairs. While he continuously abstracts from facts, he never seems to formulate his generalizations consciously. Moreover, he learns readily from the experience of others in his own age group, who like him reach abstractions without conscious effort. He quickly picks up abstractions from them even though he often seems to resist learning from his teachers and his parents. Perhaps this is because his contemporaries are less didactic, usually less authoritarian; although he often learns in this period to follow leaders in or near his own age group. His group experience is frequently large. The widely diversified backgrounds of college students plus this habit of learning easily from contemporaries make the varied experiences represented in a typical college classroom great potential assets to the teacher. We rarely build on them.

When the student leaves home and secondary school for the university, he enters what should be a great new adventure both socially and intellectually. For the first time, in most cases, he is really on his own as a human being. His social activities, being in a wholly new environment, have all the freshness that comes with novelty. Unfortunately, especially in his freshman year, his organized educational activities, unlike his social activities, too often lack emotional appeal. They come to him as a mere continuance of high school. Consequently he too often lacks intellectual stimulus and a sense of adventure. He spends his time in college mainly being told by his teachers or by textbooks, as he was in school, "what he ought to think about what he ought to think about." Under traditional college methods he rarely has an opportunity to take the initiative or to behave responsibly in academic situations involving discretion until he is well along in his college course. Yet his life up to this time has presented many such opportunities and his social life does now. His classroom activities or responsibilities are rarely if ever related to his life, and little is done to expand his responsibilities beyond meeting academic requirements whose significance as training for life he often fails to understand. Indeed, too often they are of doubtful value for this purpose. When this happens, he is apt to look on academic requirements as necessary evils and acquire a gentleman's "C" complex which often lasts through college. Some students may even decide that under these conditions ordinary ethical standards of the community need not be maintained—a degree of irresponsibility most dangerous for their future.

These statements do not apply to extracurricular activities, including a student's whole social life, where the educational results are often greatest. Note, however, that in these social activities he is judged on his actions by his contemporaries, not graded on examinations which are generally designed not so much to test his power and his skills in action as to find whether he has learned what he was told to learn. Moreover, stimulating social experiences start on the opening day of the freshman year, and in many colleges the period extending nearly to the end of the football season coincides with a period preceding the first scholastic checkup—late October or November hour examinations. This is a period when it is easy to unlearn even good study habits established in high school.

The introduction to college is very effective for the normally adjusted boy on the social and athletic sides where men try to get the respect and esteem of their fellows. It is not so successful on the intellectual side where there is little corresponding stimulus. Discipline and enforced minimum standards are poor substitutes for interest. On the other hand, the boy who comes to college with an inadequate background in getting on with his fellows often retreats into isolated intellectual work as a way of avoiding the social contacts and decisions which appear necessary to a well-adjusted life. An intellectual life which excludes or unduly minimizes social contacts and experience is dangerous. It often leads to an inability to cope with the everyday problems of life and to great unhappiness. Most colleges pay far too little attention to this problem. Yet as our college student bodies become more heterogeneous, it becomes more and more serious.

In this country we pride ourselves that college training is primarily intellectual. Yet the lives we lead are primarily emotional. Indeed, in an evolutionary sense the intellectual side of life, which we all value, is a recent gloss on an age-long evolution in which emotions dominated behavior and man in self-defense learned to be a social animal. Emotions still dominate behavior, yet we continuously decry their importance. Too little effort is made to tie the logical and intellectual subject matter taught the student by those responsible for his education into the active life and active new adventure of independence which he is living in his new social and intellectual environment, and by this tying in of subject matter and active life to arouse his emotional interest in education. In our customary methods no adequate mechanism is used for putting the burden of responsibility on the student and for transferring the initiative from the teacher to the student in ways that make his intellectual work become part of his total life experience.

A heavy percentage of the work of the college is passing on information or ideas from the teacher to the student. This kind of education is a one-way street. Perhaps this is one of the most serious difficulties with our education. As Professor Whitehead says, our education is overladen with inert ideas—ideas not used and therefore not useful. As Livingstone puts it, "It is overladen with information which lies on the surface of the brain and rapidly passes away because it is not used, because it is not backed up by experience."

So, our typical education stresses content not used, coverage where coverage is impossible, principles where they will not stand the test of time and constant change. There is little training in independent thinking. We pay almost no attention until the student nears the end of his college training—and then only within the limited area of some specialty miscalled a discipline—to making the student think of things independently and responsibly for himself.

There is no specialty that can stand alone. The social science specialties are on an illogical, unsound, and inadequate basis unless the student of the social science specialty realizes that he is not getting answers to life's problems. He is getting someone's specialized selection of parts of problems, and theory which inevitably ignores the great importance of other parts. In the one field where we have what appears as certainty, in the sciences and in technology, the recent advances of science are all in the direction of proving there is no certainty. There often is strong probability—in the experimental natural sciences, a heavy probability—which enables us to predict results in controlled areas with much assurance, gained by repeated controlled experiments. By this process over a long period of time our scientists have slowly built up a structure which is magnificent in its results. Yet these results are mainly within a narrow range of activities, those dealing with material things and nearly always founded on the average behavior of a multitude of infinitesimal units. Langmuir says, "When scientists reach an area in natural phenomena where things don't behave according to a high statistical probability, they pass on to other things." This comes from a notable scientist. Yet we in social science cannot do this.

The specialized social science can rarely give the answer to complex social problems. To quote a distinguished economist, "The record of prophecy of the economists of the world since 1900 has been grotesquely less than half true." Why shouldn't it be? Economics makes certain indefinite assumptions about men and their behavior and reasons from them. It is valuable reasoning, but because of the areas it excludes from its premises, it cannot settle general social problems, and it should not serve as a guide to action. It serves as a partial guide to policy determination when other areas are also considered, but, alone, it is never a guide to action.

Natural science, the one area in which we think we have a sure foundation, when converted into technology, accelerates the change and the uncertainty of all other areas of human knowledge. The one thing we can be sure of, as science through its own quasi-certainties affects everything else, is that through its collateral consequence it builds up uncertainties.

So, students come to us as apparently blank sheets of paper

on which we are to write out of our greater knowledge. But the paper is already covered with invisible writing. When we fill these blank sheets with visible writing, we obscure but do not obliterate the invisible writing. We forget that our own visible writing deals with subject matter which will change constantly because society changes constantly. To illustrate how rapidly it will change, I took more political economy at Harvard than all but a few undergraduates of my day. It was the day of Dunbar, Taussig, Ashley, and several others—all able men. I learned my banking theory under Dunbar, a remarkable political economist. A few years later I went into banking. The banking theory I learned in college was useful for a period of years; then that theory became obsolete because of social change and largely disappeared. Little of the banking theory I was taught in this university about 1900 had any significance in 1920. I recently made that remark to a friend who commented, "That was a long time for it to be useful. I took my Doctorate in Economics in the middle twenties and little or nothing that I studied remains in emphasis either in the curriculum of Harvard University or in fact. The emphasis is entirely changed."

What can we do for students when change on the intellectual level is so rapid? Is this a counsel of despair? We know that when men leave us at the end of four years they will enter a world about which we can be certain of only one thing: that it is a world of constantly accelerating change. Change is the one constant that we can rely on in the social structure.

My life goes back to the days when youth felt a high degree of assurance about the future. None of us feel that today. We do not know what the future is to be. We didn't then, but we thought we did. It was comfortable to feel such certainty, but it is no longer possible. From our standpoint as teachers, here is a group of young people preparing to enter an unpredictable world. Any content we teach them today will be untrue in the changed tomorrow. I am not talking about sheer facts. But even history will require reinterpretation in the light of changes in the contemporary scene. We see constant reinterpretations of the history of Western civilization. Our task looks hopeless, and is, if we continue to approach it the way we do.

Suppose we start with what we have. True, the youth that come to us have no experience except in small groups, but there is a great variety of these groups, and a great variety of table talk in the homes from which they come. This great variety of social experience and background is valuable experience on which we can build. It is an adequate foundation on which to start teaching not only human relations but many other subjects. Citizenship is not specialized and is not a matter of special theories. It is a matter of the ability of a community to live with itself continuously and of the various people in it to live as responsible members of the community.

We will have these youngsters for four years in college. During that four year period we must try to solve a problem of great social significance—the problem of getting them to the point where they know how to live responsibly in a democratic community. Implicit in this is an intellectual problem. It is not the intellectual problem of building great theories, or of building systems of elaborate logics. It is the intellectual problem of learning how to guide—to lead soundly and sanely groups of people who are primarily emotional and not intellectual. This applies to every one of us. We are primarily emotional rather than intellectual.

Why shouldn't we be? We have millions of years of emotional evolution behind us. The whole evolution of organic life has developed emotions which are adapted to deal with dangers, to adjust to the unexpected. Planning and foresight are very new; for a few thousand years only, men have been using their intellects. Naturally the behavior of us all is dominated primarily by our emotions. The intellectual job of most importance in this world is to find out how people can be trained to work together and to live together happily. How can we learn to control our emotions? When we have learned this, we can do more with our intellects.

The most deep-seated need that we as human beings have is, perhaps, to live socially with other people. Social living with our peers is much more important than the material things that are so highly rated in our particular democracy—far more important, and far more difficult to attain. It is an intellectual task of the utmost difficulty to help others to satisfying social living, but one that is within the capacity of many people. But, if you as teachers adopt this approach, your objective changes from content, theories, principles, and universals to useful ways of looking at things, to minor generalizations that will be useful in life as we lead it, to relegating the initiative to the student and thus expanding his experience.

We must reorient our teaching. Instead of orienting it to the teacher and to the teacher's viewpoint, we should orient it to the student and to the student's needs and interests. It is the student we are trying to turn into a responsible member of society, not ourselves. We do not have the job of filling him up with a particular religion or a particular subject. He must do the filling. When there is a controversial subject, it is not our job to make him feel that our opinion about it is right. We are not propagandists. It is our job to induce him to take the initiative, to help him to make solid, substantial judgments for himself and still be tolerant of the other points of view.

A large part of our classroom teaching, so long as it continues to be teacher-oriented, will be an effort on the part of the teacher to get his own point of view accepted. That is the wrong approach. I know it is hard for a teacher to get away from the idea that teacher knows best. I am watching now a teacher that has been a successful lecturer and even a successful leader of discussions, who is engaged in turning the initiative over to his students as much as possible. He is seriously disturbed about it, even though he knows it is the thing to do, because he has emotionally the usual teacher's complex that it is his job as teacher to make things clear and to save his students the errors they make in fumbling toward their goals. It is not! It is the job of the teacher to help the student come through a state of confusion to the point where the student has thought things out for himself. This is education and when it has happened, clarity where possible is highly desirable. Here the teacher can help. At the beginning, difficult subjects ought not to be clear.

When college teaching is dominated, as most of it is, by the desire of the teacher to make his subject clear to the class, to tell the students what they ought to know and think, it is easy to forget the students and their needs and limitations. In fact, the teacher usually never learns them because students are in the habit of expecting the teacher to keep the initiative. They are trained to expect answers. Yet the real problem is what the student can take, not how much the teacher can give by some form of forced feeding. This presents a difficult teaching job, but it is possible.

We have been experimenting on this particular subject at the Harvard Business School for over a quarter of a century. The Law School's history of experimenting on a similar appraoch is twice as long. The Medical School's experimenting on a similar approach goes back to about the time when Dr. Walter B. Cannon was a student there. At that time he wrote an article in one of the medical journals urging the adoption of a teaching method which would put the initiative on the student instead of on the teacher.

I would describe such a student-oriented system either as the case system or the clinical method. Generally I call it the case system, because it is necessary to get away from the usual implications of the problem method. Problems stated by the teacher are easily stage-managed and teacher-oriented. The problem method in the progressive schools has often lacked system and discipline. So I prefer to call it the case system. Medical schools describe it as the clinical method. Under ideal conditions it reaches its height there.

When the clinical physician comes in to see a new patient on the cot, he does not know what is the matter. He knows a lot about medicine but often little about the patient. He is looking for facts and data. Always he has or can get some scientifically demonstrable facts. He can observe many facts. In addition, he has much that the patient or others say are facts. Here he must recognize that he is dealing not with facts but with what the patient says are facts. The patient may not be able to express himself, and certainly will mix many feelings and opinions with fact. Unless the physician is a general practitioner well acquainted with his patient and his surroundings, there are many things in the social background of the patient that he does not know, such as the patient's family, his responsibility for his children, his job, all sorts of things not taught as medicine. These are not made explicit by the patient and are not obvious on the cot. Yet they are often of first importance in treating the case.

The physician doesn't take the patient's word for what has happened. He must give careful thought to the difference between what the patient says and the reality behind what the patient says. Often, he finds it is impossible to get at the reality. Yet, the skilled physician, particularly if he has been a general practitioner, acquires great capacity in doing this. The competent physician does not go to the patient with his mind made up. He uses his miscellaneous clinical and life experience to the best of his ability.

We have experimented on a considerable scale with methods of tying theory into life experience by cases in social science, for business administration is a social science involving many other social sciences. The "cases" we have developed are concrete situations, segments of actual life, reported as closely as we can reproduce them. We cannot obtain them as readily as law teachers can obtain cases in courts of appeal, but they are far more effectively related to concrete situations as they actually happen. Our cases are not as good as the patient on the cot in a medical clinic because we cannot bring a social situation into our clinic. Where the medical student can see, hear, and feel the patient, we must rely wholly on reports of facts. On the other hand, our cases are better than the medical case in that the very concreteness of the medical case on the cot easily leads the doctor to ignore the fact that patients have families, that they have economic problems, human responsibilities, jobs, and a whole complex of social surroundings. As a result in some respects we have made more progress in getting together effective material because our cases cannot be as easily obtained as law cases nor can our descriptive reports be as realistic as the patient on the cot is in the medical clinic. We have learned to bring in many more of the surrounding circumstances than law schools or the medical profession have yet learned to bring in effectively.

The case system limits the size of teaching sections. I do not know the present limit in the Law School. We at the Business School started in with as many as two hundred students. We cut down to one hundred, in spite of the fact that nearly all the courses are using the method and each one reinforced the other. The student gets experience in handling problems and in approaching problems in several of his courses in a similar way. The faculty would prefer eighty students as a maximum.

At the present time we are teaching, so far as I know, the only course for Harvard and Radcliffe undergraduates taught by the case system. The first year we limited it to thirty-five in a section because we did not know what the effects of a new method in one course only would be. We increased last year to forty and this year to fifty. I would not be inclined to increase beyond fifty in a section until we have more experience. I prefer fifty to twenty because of the greater varieties of experience and ability in the class.

The method is not limited to particular age groups. A type of case method is being carried back to secondary schools with excellent results, though it lends itself badly to the short cut of grading of papers by machines. The emphasis in the case system is on thought and the use of knowledge rather than on memory. It is hard to test this by machine.

For a long time there was a question whether the system should be restricted to graduate schools. I met constantly the statement, "This method works with you, but because you are a graduate school. It won't work with younger groups." Yet many scattered college courses are now being taught this way with good results, and the system is widely used in undergraduate professional schools. Experiments in adult education give a right to believe that by an extension of the method this important field might be kept out of the morass into which it so often sinks.

Once I tried an experiment on my seven-year-old son. I gave him as skillful a lecture adapted to his vocabulary as I could concoct for about ten minutes—a length I was sure was within his attention span. I chose the subject because I thought it ought to be of great interest to him—you see, "teacher-oriented!" "I know something that ought to be of great interest to you. I'm going to tell you about it!" At the end of the ten-minute lecture, he said, "Daddy, can I go out to play now?" I said, "Yes, but before you go out I want to ask you a question." So, I outlined the same situation giving him the facts in the form of a case and asked his opinion—with no expression of my own opinion. That led to an interested half-hour discussion with a lot of level-headed initiative on his part. He forgot all about going out to play.

The survey course which is run by lectures, even when the lecture is supplemented by cases, is rarely successful. It cannot be student-oriented. It is teacher-oriented. Lectures can, however, be used in a different way. They can be given out in advance in mimeographed form or even given systematically in one of several weekly meetings, when the other sessions are devoted to discussions of cases, not to quizzes on the lecture or a textbook. Mimeographed material discussed with the teacher is often more effective than a lecture. However, if you give students cases on which your mimeographed lectures have some bearing or for which your lectures are background, you will find that they get as much out of reading such material as they find useful in considering the case. Because the lecture is useful for what the student wants, the material will stick. Inert facts, inert ideas, do not stick. Used facts and used ideas do.

Today is one of the great turning points of human history. We do not know what the future holds. We do know that our students must live with other people. To this end they need self-education. We do know that the world is safer if, while they live, they behave responsibly.

Things do not come to us in life in the form that they come to us as specialists. Every experience that we face comes as a unity. We must act with reference to all the facts. This unity has human aspects. It may have technological aspects. It has economic aspects. It has a great variety of aspects, but the varied aspects must not be separated in our thinking into water-tight compartments. A total situation comes to us and we must act. There is something we must do or refrain from doing. To refrain consciously and intentionally from doing things is sometimes the most difficult and important form of action. Of course, sheer neglect of action because we are frustrated by a problem is quite a different thing. Most action is a decision not to act at this moment—the time isn't ripe. We have to wait for more information. We have to wait until some associate sees the necessity of acting. Often this involves subtle persuasion instead of orders. We have to wait for the strategic moment. Teaching by the case system gives the training that people need in making such decisions. They need this experience as part of the process of using or building generalizations which are useful.

I know that by using the case system we are succeeding with a large percentage of students in building the habit of consciously interpreting experience to the point where they carry it over into life, and I know we do much to start the lifetime job of developing skilled judgments related to novel facts and developing skills in action. Recently I talked with several groups of men who studied at the Business School twenty to twenty-five years ago, at a time when I was doing no teaching. Without suggesting the response I wanted even by the terminology I used, I found that to them the most important thing they got out of the school, phrased in one way or another, was the ability to look at new problems as they met them in life in the light of the work done in the school and with the skills acquired there. Yet the factual content met in their careers was always different from what they studied in school and the judgments reached always varied with the facts. They picked this out as the thing accomplished in the school which had not previously been done by their undergraduate work.

As one man who graduated ten years ago phrased it to me, "You didn't teach us anything in the Business School." I said, "I will accept that, but in what sense do you mean it?" "Well," he said, "I studied a great number of cases with care, sought my own interpretations of them, discussed them with other members of the class, went into class where we discussed them with the instructor, modified my conclusions, and reached what I thought were good working conclusions not only on the cases but on the subject matter we were discussing. In ten years of experience I have never met a problem on all fours with any case I studied or reached any conclusion that was controlled by the class discussion." I said I would accept that but, "What did the school do for you?" "That," he said, "is simple. It gave me a sense of assurance that I could tackle any problem either because I had the requisite experience or because I knew in what direction to turn when my experience was inadequate."

This type of thing can be done as well in college as in a graduate school of business administration. In fact, in some ways it is an easier problem in the college than in the business school because you can do it without the close attention to technical details and specialized essentials that you have in a professional school. But you cannot do it so long as you as a teacher are primarily interested in presenting some subject matter in a clear and systematic way to your students, instead of inducing your students to think for themselves and think responsibly.

You cannot do it so long as you are seeking universal principles, which you can teach as universals, in some specialty. At that point you are almost surely presenting something that will be untrue as applied to concrete situations which arise in life. The specialized theory fails to cover all the facts. Specialized instruction as it comes to most undergraduates is often objectionable on ethical grounds because it frequently leads the students astray. The discovery that what they learned from specialized instruction does not fit the problems met in life makes them unduly contemptuous of what they studied in college. You can minimize or solve these ethical questions by making clear to students the limitations of your specialty and of its values in the changing world ahead. When we start with factual material not limited to the specialty but in all its complexity as it appears in life, students gain a type of experience close to the reality they must face in life. This training gives them a long start on the responsible handling of the unknown problems they will meet. Such education is as useful in any career in life as it is in community living.

ROBERT ULICH

Chapter XVIII

SIGNIFICANT PHASES IN THE HISTORY OF HIGHER EDUCATION

The history of higher education is a record of man's effort to arrive at new insights into reality through comprehending facts and their interrelationships. In the first great period of Western academic tradition—the period of Scholasticism—the search was based on divine revelation combined with Aristotelian logic. The thinkers of the Renaissance were concerned with the contradictions discovered in Scholasticism and emphasized reasoning based on the supposed nature of Man. "Faith became absorbed into human reason itself." With the rapid expansion of scientific knowledge in the nineteenth century, the basis again shifted through further criticism and rested on experiment, description, and induction with vast implications in all aspects of our thinking. The task of higher learning today is, by drawing on all that has gone before, to arrive at a clearer meaning and purpose for the life of our society.

If we try to understand historically such a complicated phenomenon as higher learning, we have first to look for its inherent principles and goals. Certainly, higher learning should not be a mere process of memorization, nor is it merely a form of research that finds its satisfaction in the investigation of isolated problems. Rather it pushes beyond the level of single facts and relations toward comprehension of a whole. Memorizing represents the first and most primitive dimension of learning, specific research the second, the third dimension being that which should be called "comprehensive understanding."

Therefore, higher learning is never content with itself. It moves toward constantly fleeing horizons and never ceases to ask the question: "To what degree are we able to envisage the whole within the part and the part within the whole; or, to what degree can the part be rendered transparent so that it gives us a vision, however dim, of a deeper reality within and behind the fugitive appearances of life?"

If, according to these principles, we are going to organize the story of higher learning, or higher education—we may be allowed here to use the two terms synonymously—we will find that its success or failure in various historical periods is determined by the passion that motivates men to arrive at new insights into the character of reality. The success of this enthusiasm is, of course, determined by the methods of research and the ways of thinking which the human mind has available at particular periods, for all human thinking is finite.

The first great period in our Western academic tradition was the so-called period of Scholasticism. It has nothing to do with scholastic aptitude tests and other modern inventions of that nature. We could also call it the "theological" period of Western learning. It begins about 1100 when Abelard, in his *Sic et Non,* put side by side contradictory doctrinal statements of the ecclesiastical authorities. There he stopped, without attempting to resolve the conflict on a higher level of thought. Yet, his primitive method was one of the great incentives toward critical or "dialectical" thinking in that it forced the theologian-philosophers of the early universities to accept tradition and authority not merely on face value, but to recognize contrasts and to attempt solutions. In the course of a relatively brief period of one hundred and fifty years this endeavor led from the crude beginnings of *Sic et Non* toward one of the greatest masterpieces of logical architecture, the *Summa Theologica* by Thomas Aquinas. It should be needless to say that the historical evaluation of great systems of thought must always pay a certain reverence to the fundamental premises on which the thought of a period is founded, even if we may no longer agree with them. The central presupposition in Scholasticism consisted of the notion that, by the grace of God, man has received both the divine revelation and the power of rationality, and that, by combining the *ratio divina,* expressed in the Bible, with the *ratio humana,* expressed in Aristotle, we might be able to intuit not only the permanent qualities of the Real, but even those of the *Ens Realissimum,* or God himself.

Scholasticism lost its dominating influence during the fifteenth century. Yet, it would be wrong to suppose that thereafter it disappeared completely as an actor in the intellectual theater. There always were revivals, especially in the Latin countries. Today we have a neo-Scholastic movement even in certain Protestant, not to speak of Catholic circles, in Europe and in America.

Apparently, in every great period of thought there emerge feelings and ideas that have already long tried to rise above the level of consciousness. Therefore each wave of excitement does not begin at a strictly determinable date, nor does it suddenly end with the arrival of new ideas. The something that it added to the understanding of reality will persist as one of the ways by which man tries to understand himself, his environment, his universe, and his relationship to the Divine. The profound essence, so to speak, of a great movement of thought survives the social and political conditions of the society to which, to a large degree, it was subject during its period of prime. This is the reason why even today the Vedas, the writings of Confucius and Lao-tse, the Bible, or the philosophies of Spinoza and Hegel are sources of inspiration to those who have learned the grand art of interpretative reading. Nevertheless, one cannot understand the rise of a spiritual or intellectual development without some recognition of its social setting. The medieval Scholastic philosophers were convinced that there was a hierarchy of ideas, just as medieval society, though not at all without certain democratic features, believed in a hierarchical structure of human relations, with the Emperor of the Holy Roman Empire as the secular and the Pope as the ecclesiastical head of Christian humankind.

But what happens if a special kind of thought ceases to dominate and a new one emerges? The decline of an old pattern of ideas always comes about when it no longer fulfills its original purpose of interpreting reality to the searching mind. People then begin to doubt. In the Middle Ages the first doubt appeared within the Scholastic theologians themselves when they were no longer able to reconcile their secular source of inspiration, the philosophy of Aristotle, with the contents of the Bible. During the thirteenth and fourteenth centuries the Scholastic philosophers, by using Aristotle's works, especially his logical writings, believed they were giving a formal and rational expression to the mysteries of the Gospel. But by allowing logic to become more and more independent from faith, by making logic even the arbiter of the premises of their faith, they introduced a rebellious element. The *ratio humana* began to contradict the authority of the *ratio divina.* Thus a conflict arose concerning the qualities of thinking, or a feeling of insecurity in man's relation to reality, which became of utmost importance for the development of our modern civilization.

What were the consequences of this development for the spirit of higher learning? It gradually abandoned deductive thinking in favor of what we may call Rational Humanism. This term is somewhat vague and confusing because both concepts, that of "humanism" and "rationalism," are often used to characterize various phases of culture. However, after the fourteenth century there emerges with increasing clarity a new attitude of man with respect to the problems of life. No longer was living on earth considered primarily a preparation for the life beyond. The thinkers of the Renaissance and later periods became increasingly confident that for the understanding of reality they did not need a supernatural revelation and belief in authorities, but that the success of human search depended upon the development of better and better methods of critical thinking, concrete observation, and individual courage. Thus theology became increasingly divorced from the work of the philosopher and scientist. During the rise of the great galaxy of scholars from Copernicus to Descartes and Spinoza and to Kant and Hegel, faith became absorbed into human reason itself. As Thomas Aquinas' *Summa Theologica* represents the consummation of the theological period of higher education, so Hegel's *Phenomenology of Mind* (1807) represents the consummation of Rational Humanism. Whereas the *Summa Theologica* was built on the idea that without faith in the Gospel man cannot understand himself, or history, or the universe, for Hegel all life and history is the result of the self-evolution of Reason.

What was the political equivalent of this rationalist period? It was first Absolutism, which, though authoritarian from the modern point of view and appealing to religious traditions ("King by the grace of God"), was nevertheless the assertion of a rational-organizational principle over the medieval principle of organic social structure in which not man's but God's will revealed itself. But soon there developed a concept of society which considered human and political relations subject to the influence and corrections of the human mind as a part of the Universal Mind. Please note that there is still a large metaphysical element in this mode of thought, but it has become more of a secular than of a supernatural quality. The social results of this attitude were the American Declaration of Independence, based on the idea of the inalienable rights of rational man, the French Revolution, and the various liberal movements of the other countries of Europe and of South America.

Why—we may now ask—did also this period decline?

At the beginning of the nineteenth century more and more people discovered that the great idealistic-rational-humanist systems of philosophy could not stand the test of empirical science, which since the seventeenth century had developed under the auspices of the new Rationalism itself. Much of what the great philosophers had said was—though not at all anti-empirical in tendency and assumedly based on experience—nevertheless primarily of intuitive nature and, in that respect, still more an expression of faith than a product of critical scholarship. Beautiful systems of thought had been erected, but the parts of reality which the scientists in their laboratories put under the microscope refused to behave as the philosophers had expected them to do.

Thus, a new wave of criticism arose.

Also on the social and political side there was much change and disappointment. Neither political absolutism with its many hangovers from medieval feudalism nor the French Revolution with its ideals of liberty, equality, and fraternity brought with them the solution of social problems. Absolutism received its decisive blows in the English revolution of 1649 and the French revolution of 1789, and the French revolution itself ended in dictatorship.

Cultural periods overlap, as we cannot sufficiently emphasize in such a bold and general summary of history as this. So we cannot wonder that the signs of a new attitude, critical of the almost religious faith in the universal power of human reason as expressed in the great philosophies from Descartes to Hegel, had come to light before Hegel wrote his main works—in the writings of Locke, Hume, and most radically in Kant's *Critique of Pure Reason* (1781). Kant subjected reason to the critical analysis of reason itself and stated that man's intellectual powers were not of such validity as to explain fully the essence of reality, or the Ding an Sich (reality in itself). Human reason, he declared, is limited, and consequently provides no guarantee for the discovery of universal truth. But even more than by Kant's highly abstract theories, thought and higher learning of the nineteenth century were affected by the rapid development of scientific empiricism.

In spite of all the admiration that modern man is accustomed to devote to the "scientific period," it was not only a period of hope but also a period of resignation. Theology and philosophy, assumedly, had failed. "Rather than indulge in magnificent intuitions," so the scientifically minded scholars of the nineteenth century thought, "let us proceed step by step and build brick on brick. Whether we will ever reach the summit, or ever build a cathedral whose spire reaches into heaven—Heaven knows, if there is a heaven." To be sure, there were always some optimists who believed that "science" would give *the* answer, but they never achieved even the semblance of a comprehensive philosophical system and soon were discarded by their own fellow researchers.

Even the humanists were affected by the new attitude. Ranke, one of the leading scholars of the nineteenth century, recommended that the historian stop writing the kind of history that interprets the whole course of mankind according to general and preconceived ideas. Let us find out "how it really happened." By decent interpretation and evaluation of the sources we have available let us describe concretely and humbly how human beings behaved in the political arena.

The result of this attitude has been an enormous expansion of the descriptive parts of humanities, of anthropology, sociology, psychology, and all kinds of comparative thought. In the field of science there was an unheard of development of theory and of its application to industry which changed man's social, economic, and political environment more intensely than any previous event. It is probably no exaggeration to state that despite all similarity of language and intention between our period and that of Thomas Jefferson, the latter, in many respects of practical life and production, was closer to the age of Pericles than it is to ours.

Great changes took place also in the relation of the university departments to each other. Just as during the period of Rational Humanism, theology had to yield to philosophy, so in the scientific period, philosophy, and to a degree all the old *Artes Liberales,* had to make room for science, engineering, statistics, and many other fields of knowledge. Even in philosophy proper one was afraid of great and comprehensive systems and preferred the specialized, scientific approach with respect to more detailed problems.

The economic and political equivalent to the Era of Science was modern capitalism and the gradual shifting from rational-individualist liberalism toward forms of nationalism and collectivism which partly preserved the liberal pattern, but partly considered human society merely an object for "engineering" without any respect for the old "natural rights of rational man."

But during recent decades science itself has made several discoveries which, though perhaps not so revolutionary as the Copernican theory, have nevertheless shaken the belief in the older concepts of determinism and mechanistic laws of nature which prevailed in the Newtonian pattern. Furthermore, in the general realm of thought more and more people discovered that, by means of experiment and description, man may expand his knowledge enormously, but cannot find the integrating and purpose-giving ideas which he needs for a meaningful life. With respect to moral conduct, we have practically experienced what may happen if such "scientifically vague" and "metaphysical" concepts as "transcendence," "dignity," and "liberty" are willfully dispensed with.

So again, we are in a period of transition. Pessimists believe that we are at the end of our Western civilization, in a situation comparable to that of late antiquity. Others consider our present conflicts the birth pangs of a completely new civilization in which mankind will have learned from its errors and sufferings and finally arrive at peace and maturity.

In such a period of transition the university teacher has a particularly responsible mission—a mission that must combine a great deal of resignation with a similarly great measure of courage. His first responsibility is to know that thinking man cannot jump back to periods of thought which have already fulfilled their historical task, however much we can and should learn from their depth and penetration. In spite of all yearning and by no will and strength can we immediately restore even the relative unity of thought that existed in the Scholastic period and, to a degree, also in the period of Rationalist Humanism.

On the other hand, we ought to learn eventually that the various approaches to reality, as we have described them, do not necessarily exclude each other, though in the historical process they often acted as enemies. If purified from accident, one-sidedness, and superstition, man still needs religion, just as he needs a profound faith in reason and in the advantages of scientific research. None of these approaches can be completely done away with, for each of them represents not only one step toward but also an essential quality of intellectual maturity. Each of us should try to arrive, somehow, at his own *Weltanschauung*, but that will largely be a matter of personal experience and decision. But none of us should try to impose his point of view on his neighbor; nor can we, regarding our total responsibilities to the intellectual scene of the present and the future, still be mere Platonists, Aristotelians, Thomists, Hegelians, or Marxists.

The task before us is neither exclusiveness nor syncretism, but a new synthesis to be prepared by members of a community in spirit, in spite of the plurality of individual opinions. If we have this communality of endeavor and convey its ethics to our students, then they will not leave the university with the feeling that they have been looking at a battle area where some regiments still fight desperately, while others already lie exhausted in the rear. And they will not leave the university with the frustrating sentiment that it does not matter what one thinks and what one believes, if only one knows enough professionally to succeed in his special career.

Unless it is resigned to die an inglorious death, our period, however critical its state, must have before itself the vision of new and better solutions of the conflicts of men. This vision cannot be one of conformity, arrived at by the victory of one intellectual army over all the others. It depends upon the gradual emergence of a faithful realism on the level of which the accomplishments and failures of the intellect, all together, will contribute to that mature attitude of the mind which we call "wisdom," or "comprehensive understanding." This alone can help us to find better answers to the problems of man.

A SHORT BIBLIOGRAPHY

A SHORT BIBLIOGRAPHY

(Most of the books mentioned in the foregoing chapters are listed here.)

Allport, Gordon W. *Personality—A Psychological Interpretation.* New York: Henry Holt, 1937.

Barzun, Jacques. *Teacher in America.* Boston: Little Brown, 1945.

Cantor, Nathaniel. *The Dynamics of Learning.* Buffalo: Foster and Stewart, 1946.

Conant, James Bryant. *Education in a Divided World.* Cambridge: Harvard University Press, 1948.

Denifle, Heinrich. *Die Universitäten des Mittelalters bis 1400.* Berlin: Weidmann, 1885.

Donham, Wallace B. "Why Experiment? The Case System in College Teaching of Social Science." *Journal of General Education,* Vol. III, No. 2 (January 1949.) Part of this article has been substituted in Chapter 17 of this book for the earlier treatment when Chapter 17 was originally formulated in 1947–48.

Fuess, Claude M., and Basford, Emory S., editors. *Unseen Harvests.* New York: Macmillan, 1947.

General Education in a Free Society. Report of the Harvard Committee. Cambridge: Harvard University Press, 1945.

Gowers, Sir Ernest. *Plain Words.* London: His Majesty's Stationery Office, 1948.

Haskins, Charles Homer. *The Rise of Universities.* New York: Henry Holt, 1923.

Havighurst, Robert J., and Taba, Hilda. *Adolescent Character and Personality.* New York: John Wiley, 1949.

Hayakawa, Samuel Ichiyé. *Language in Action.* New York: Harcourt, Brace, 1941.

Higher Education for American Democracy. Report of the President's Commission on Higher Education. 6 vols. Washington: Government Printing Office, 1947.

Hutchins, Robert M. *The Higher Learning in America.* New Haven: Yale University Press, 1936.

Huxley, Thomas Henry. *On a Piece of Chalk: Essays.* New York: Macmillan, 1929.

Irsay, Stephen d'. *Histoire des universités françaises et étrangères, des origines à nos jours.* Paris: Picard, 1936.

Kaufmann, Georg. *Die Geschichte der deutschen Universitäten.* Stuttgart, 1888–1896.

Livingstone, Sir Richard. *Education for a World Adrift.* Cambridge, England: University Press, 1943.

——— *The Future in Education.* Cambridge, England: University Press, 1941.

——— *Some Thoughts on University Education.* Cambridge, England: University Press, 1948.

Lynd, Helen. *Field Work in College Education.* New York: Columbia University Press, 1945.

Mayo, Elton. *The Social Problems of an Industrial Civilization.* Cambridge: Harvard Graduate School of Business Administration, 1945.

McGrath, Earl J. *Science in General Education.* Dubuque, Iowa: W. C. Brown, 1948.

Mencken, Henry L. *The American Language.* New York: Knopf, 1919.

Morison, Samuel Eliot. *Three Centuries of Harvard.* Cambridge: Harvard University Press, 1936.

Nash, Arnold S. *The University and the Modern World.* New York: Macmillan, 1943.

Ortega y Gasset, José. *Mission of the University.* Princeton: Princeton University Press, 1944.

Powers, Edwin, and Witmer, Helen L. *Can Delinquency Be Prevented?* (To be published.)

Quiller-Couch, Sir Arthur. *A Lecture on Lectures.* London: Hogarth Press, 1927.

Rashdall, Hastings. *The Universities of Europe in the Middle Ages.* Edited by E. M. Powicke and A. B. Emden. 3 vols. New York: Oxford University Press, 1936.

Rider, Fremont. *The Scholar and the Future of the Research Library.* New York: Hadham Press, 1944.

Rowse, A. L. *The Use of History.* London: Hodder and Stoughton, 1946.

Seeley, Reginald S. K. *The Function of the University.* Toronto: Oxford University Press, 1948.

Sorokin, Pitirim A. *The Reconstruction of Humanity.* Boston: Beacon Press, 1948.

Stouffer, Samuel A., *et al. The American Soldier: Adjustment during Army Life.* Princeton: Princeton University Press, 1949.

Tead, Ordway. *College Teaching and College Learning, a Plea for Improvement.* New Haven: Yale University Press, 1949.

Ulich, Robert. *History of Educational Thought.* New York: American Book Co., 1945.

——— *Three Thousand Years of Educational Wisdom.* Cambridge: Harvard University Press, 1947.

United Nations Educational, Scientific and Cultural Organization. *Study Abroad—International Handbook of Fellowships, Scholarships and Educational Exchange.* Vol. II. Paris: UNESCO, 1949.

Unwin, Sir Stanley. *The Truth about Publishing.* London: Allen and Unwin, 1946.

Whitehead, Alfred North. *Adventures of Ideas.* New York: Macmillan, 1933.

——— *Aims of Education and Other Essays.* New York: Macmillan, 1929.

——— *Science and the Modern World.* New York: Macmillan, 1925.

Wills, Elbert V. *The Growth of American Higher Education—Liberal, Professional and Technical.* Philadelphia: Dorrance, 1936.

Yeomans, Henry A. *Abbott Lawrence Lowell, 1856–1943.* Cambridge: Harvard University Press, 1948.

Znaniecki, Florjan. *The Social Role of the Man of Knowledge.* New York: Columbia University Press, 1940.

INDEX

INDEX

DATE DUE

Jan 5 '83 RETURNED			
Apr 13 '82 RETURNED			
Apr 26 '83 RETURNED			

GAYLORD PRINTED IN U.S.A.